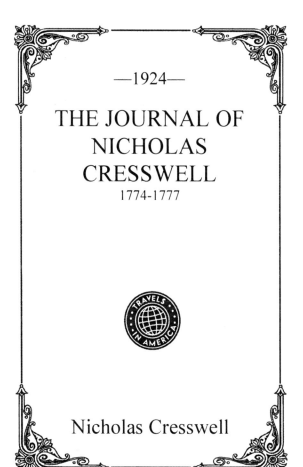

—1924—

# THE JOURNAL OF NICHOLAS CRESSWELL
### 1774-1777

## Nicholas Cresswell

Volume 251

APPLEWOOD BOOKS
Carlisle, Massachusetts

Thank you for purchasing an Applewood book. Applewood reprints America's lively classics—books from the past that are still of interest to modern readers. This facsimile was printed from digital files prepared by the Library of Congress. Applewood's facsimile edition of this work may include library stamps, scribbles, and margin notes as they exist in the original book at the Library of Congress. These interesting historical artifacts celebrate the place of the book in the library's collection. In addition to these artifacts, the work may have additional errors that were either in the original, in the scans prepared by the Library of Congress, or introduced as we prepared the books for printing. If you believe the work has such errors, please let us know by writing to us at the address below.

First Edition

ISBN: 1-4290-0587-4 (Paperback)

For a free copy of our current print catalog, write to:
Applewood Books
PO Box 365
Bedford, MA 01730

For more complete listings,
visit us on the web at:
awb.com

# THE JOURNAL OF
# NICHOLAS CRESSWELL

*At the Sign of*

# THE CUPID AND LION

———

THE JOURNAL OF NICHOLAS CRESSWELL

HERNANDO DE SOTO
*by R. B. Cunninghame Graham*

THE MEMOIRS OF STEPHEN BURROUGHS

TALKS WITH GERHART HAUPTMANN
*by Joseph Chapiro*

GEORGE MACDONALD AND HIS WIFE
*by Greville Macdonald*
*with an introduction by G. K. Chesterton*

———

**1924**

*The Journal of*

# Nicholas Cresswell

## 1774-1777

LINCOLN MACVEAGH

## THE DIAL PRESS

NEW YORK · MCMXXIV

PORTRAIT OF NICHOLAS CRESSWELL

# FOREWORD

NICHOLAS CRESSWELL, the Diarist, was the eldest son of Thomas Cresswell of Edale, a parish in the Peak of Derbyshire, which was formerly part of the Forest of High Peak, Derbyshire, one of the largest forests in England. Nicholas was born at Crowden-le-Booth, Edale, in December, 1750. He was, therefore, twenty-four years old when he went to America in 1774. His mother was Elizabeth, wife of Thomas Cresswell, and a daughter and heiress of Richard Oliver of Smalldale in Bradwell, near to Castleton in Derbyshire. His father was a local land-owner, who owned and farmed his estate in Edale and was a large sheep farmer. No doubt he was a very hard ruler, but he was a man very much respected in the Peak district, and he established a school for the education of the children about his own home. I believe that Nicholas was educated in this school and in the Wakefield Grammar School.

The Cresswell family originally came from Cresswell in Northumberland, where they held land under the English Kings in consideration of their keeping up Castle Cresswell and assisting, whenever required, in repelling the Scotch when they invaded England. A younger member of the Northumberland Cresswell family settled near Chapel-en-le-Frith in the Peak of Derbyshire and founded a family there, which held lands under the Crown in and about Chapel-en-le-Frith from about 1350 down to 1631. Ralph Cresswell, of Malcoff in Chapel-en-le-Frith, sold his property there about 1631 to the Ford family and took a grant

[ v ]

of land with Giles Barber in Edale when it was disafforested. The original grant was from the Trustees of the Corporation of London. The Corporation had lent Charles I a large sum of money in return for a grant of Crown lands and these Trustees sold land in Edale to Ralph Cresswell. His share was known as Crowden-le-Booth, now called Upper Booth and situated at the north end of the Edale Valley. The Edale branch of the Cresswell family used the same coat of arms as the Cresswells of Northumberland, and Mr. Justice Cresswell, President of the Probate and Admiralty Court, who was at one time the head of the Northumberland family, acknowledged the Derbyshire branch as being descended from the Northumberland family of the same name.

This Ralph Cresswell was one of the twenty-one founders of the Chapel of Ease at Edale under the mother church at Castleton. The stipend of the Vicar of Edale was provided by each of the original founders charging his estate with an annual sum. Crowden-le-Booth possessed very large grazing rights for sheep and cattle on the hilly district of the Peak, and here it was that the Cresswell family settled and built their home. A local photograph shows the original house and the cluster of buildings around it. In the old building is a large barn which was turned into a schoolhouse and a residence for the schoolmaster, and this was provided by Thomas Cresswell for the children of the immediate neighbourhood.

Nicholas Cresswell was helping his father on his Edale estate when he decided to go to America in 1774. He went to Virginia, sailing from Liverpool in 1774, and returned to Edale in 1777. He kept a diary from the time he left Edale until his return. On April 21st, 1781, he married, at Wirksworth Parish Church, Derbyshire, about fourteen miles north of Derby, Mary, the youngest daughter, a co-heiress, of Samuel Mellor of Southsitch, Idridgehay, in the Parish of Wirksworth, in the County of Derby. He died when fifty-three years of age on July 14th, 1804, at Idridgehay, and was buried at Wirksworth Parish Church.

His son, Robert Cresswell, owned the Edale and other estates in the Peak and also the Idridgehay property. He succeeded to the Edale property on the death of his grandfather, Thomas Cresswell, in 1808.

The "Kirk" referred to in the Diary as a storekeeper was evidently a son of the blacksmith of Edale, who had settled in Virginia and who befriended Nicholas because he knew his people.

The Diary came into my possession on the death of my father, Frederick Thornely of Helsby, Cheshire. Joseph Cresswell was the youngest brother of Nicholas Cresswell and his daughter Ann married my grandfather, Samuel Thornely of Liverpool. My father, Frederick Thornely, eventually came into part of the Edale property and also Southsitch, Idridgehay, which had formerly belonged to Nicholas Cresswell. My father also came into the Nicholas Cresswell diary and on my father's death in 1918 it came to me.

The portrait of Nicholas Cresswell also came to me with the diary. I also have the original sea-chest, which Nicholas Cresswell had made by John Braddock of Chapel-en-le-Frith and took with him to America and brought back again. I also have a bison horn, silver mounted, which Nicholas brought home with him. One of my sisters has an Indian headdress which was presented to Nicholas by the North American Indians when he traded amongst them, and we also have at home the snowshoes and tomahawk which he possessed.

Crowden-le-Booth passed to Nicholas Cresswell's eldest son, Robert, and on his death in 1862 it went to George Cresswell, who about 1889 sold it to Mr. William Champion of Edale and Riddlesworth Hall, Thetford, Norfolk, who is the present owner. In Crowden-le-Booth was some very old oak furniture, which formerly belonged to the Cresswell family. This is now owned by Mr. George Cresswell, who lives in Herefordshire.

Samuel Thornely

Drayton House
Nr. Chichester
West Sussex
March, 1924

# CONTENTS

CHAPTER                                                        PAGE

I. PREPARATIONS . . . . . . . . . . . . . . . . . .    1

II. THE VOYAGE — FIRST GLIMPSES. . . . . . . . .    10

III. VIRGINIA — ILLNESS — BARBADOS . . . . . . .    16

IV. VIRGINIA AGAIN — PROPOSED TRIP TO ILLINOIS .    43

V. OVER HILL AND STREAM — THE KENTUCKY RIVER    62

VI. THE OHIO RIVER — THE INDIAN COUNTRY . . .    87

VII. BACK IN VIRGINIA — NEWS OF THE REVOLUTION .    125

VIII. ATTEMPT TO LEAVE — SUSPECTED AS A SPY . . .    152

IX. A WINTER OF DISCONTENT . . . . . . . . . . .    172

X. HAMPTON — WILLIAMSBURG — VOYAGE TO NEW
YORK . . . . . . . . . . . . . . . . . . . . .    203

XI. TWO MONTHS IN NEW YORK HARBOUR . . . . .    218

XII. GENERAL WASHINGTON — THE COLONIES . . .    251

XIII. RETURN VOYAGE — EDALE ONCE MORE . . . . .    273

APPENDIX — COMPARATIVE TABLE OF DATES . . .    286

# THE JOURNAL OF
# NICHOLAS CRESSWELL

# *The* JOURNAL *of*
# NICHOLAS CRESSWELL
## 1774 — 1777

## I

### PREPARATIONS

*E**DALE* — *Tuesday, March 1st, 1774.* I have been studying and deliberating for a long time how to shape my course in the world, and am this day come to a determined resolution to go into America, be the consequence what it will. I am certain to meet with every possible obstruction from my Parents and Friends, but I am resolved to brave them all and follow my own inclination for once. From the best accounts I have been able to get, and from my own Idea of the country, I am sensible a person with a small fortune may live much better and make greater improvements in America than he can possibly do in England. Especially in the Farming way, as that is the business I have been brought up to. I have made it my study to enquire more particulars about it. The land I am told is good and the price is very low. Consequently Agriculture must be in its infant state. The Climate must be good on some part of the Continent, for it is all climates in extent.

I have almost from my infancy entertained some thought of going to America at some period of my life, and none is more suitable than the present. Supposing I had no inclination to go to America, I have a number of Cogent and Substantial though private reasons, that rather oblige me to leave home, not altogether on my own account, but in hopes it will be for the future peace and quietness of those for whom I shall always have the greatest esteem. Therefore I am determined to make a Voyage to Virginia, as I like the situation of that Colony the best; if I like the Country to return immediately and endeavour to prevail upon my Friends to give me something to begin the world with. I shall by this Voyage be better able to judge what will suit the Country or whether the Country will please me well enough to fix my future residence in it or not. Admit I do not approve of it, it will be a means of settling me on this side the Atlantic; not only that, but I am in hopes it will have its good tendencies in other respects to those I leave behind. If this last purpose is effected I shall be happy — if neither, Miserable.

Intend to get Mr. James Carrington to speak to my Father about it, and break the way a little. I am sorry I dare not do it myself; I believe he may have some influence with my Father, if any one has. Determined to keep a daily and impartial Journal from this day, by which I hope to square my future conduct.

*Wednesday, March 2nd, 1774.* Went to Mr. Carrington to get him to intercede with my Father in my behalf. He with some reluctance promises to come to-morrow. I confess I have no great opinion of his oratorical abilities, but believe he will be honest and do me every service in his power, as he finds I am resolutely bent upon it. *Thursday, March 3rd, 1774.* This evening Mr. Carrington came and by his aid and assistance got the consent of my Father to go into America. I believe it is with very great reluctance he grants it. I am sorry he will not converse with me on the subject, but am determined to persevere. *Friday, March 4th, 1774.* Employed at home. I have found a great deal of difficulty to get the consent of my Mother. In short all my Friends think me mad for attempting to go abroad. But they are utterly unacquainted with my true reasons for taking this surprizing whim, as they call it. *Monday, March 7th, 1774.* My Father, contrary to my expectations, went to Mr. Hall to get a letter of introduction to Mr. Latham of Liverpool. Intend to set out for Liverpool to-morrow.

*Warrington — Tuesday, March 8th, 1774.* Set out for Liverpool. Dined at Manchester. Lodged at Warrington, the sign of the *Nag's Head.*

*Liverpool — Wednesday, March 9th, 1774.* Got to Liverpool. Dined at the *Golden Fleece.* After Dinner waited on Mr. Latham, who went with me to look at several Ships that are bound for Virginia. None pleases me so well as the Ship *Molly* which is bound for the Rappahannock River in Virginia in a fortnight. The Captain, whose name is Parry, is not in town but expected to-morrow. Spent the evening at the *Fleece* with Mr. Latham. *Thursday, March 10th, 1774.* Drank Tea at Mr. Latham's. After Tea met with Tom Middleton who went with me to Captain Parry's. Agreed with him for my passage for 10 Guineas, and am to be in Liverpool by the last of the Month. Spent the evening at Tom Middleton's.

*Manchester — Friday, March 11th, 1774.* Left Liverpool. Dined at Warrington. From Warrington in Company with Mr. Whitaker to Manchester. Supped and spent the evening at Mr. Greatrix's with Sam Jackson. Lodged at *The Swan.*

*Edale — Saturday, March 12th, 1774.* Left Manchester. Dined at Stockport. At Chapel-en-le-Frith ordered Edward Ford to make me some Clothes. Got home in the evening. Found my Brothers Tom, Ralph and Joe, ill of the Measles. *Sunday, March 13th, 1774.* In the forenoon went to Chapel. I believe the Parson made a Sermon on purpose for me. His text was taken from the parable of the Prodigal Son. It is very strange that these Sons of the Clergy cannot forbear meddling in other people's affairs. After Dinner went to Castleton to return Mr. Hall thanks for the trouble he has taken in my behalf. *Monday, March 14th, 1774.* At Home, employed in preparing things ready for my Voyage. My Father has scarcely spoken to me since I came from Liverpool. This is very disagreeable, but I must submit to it, tho' it is of great disadvantage to me, as I do not know what he will give me and cannot tell how to act with any degree of propriety. *Friday, March 18th, 1774.* Went to the new smithy for direction to James Kirk in Virginia. It will be absolutely necessary to have some acquaintance on the other side the Atlantic, or I cannot possibly get so good a knowledge of the Country as I could wish.

*Wakefield — Saturday, March 19th, 1774.* This morning my Father gave me 12 Guineas and desired me to set out for Wakefield, which I did immediately. Dined at Mottram with my Aunt. Drank Coffee at Peniston. Got to Wakefield late in the evening.

*Ughill — Monday, March 21st, 1774.* After breakfast Mr. Ellis gave me this advice: Always to put my trust and confidence in God; to do justice to every one; to act with Honor and Honesty in all my dealings; and that these rules strictly adhered to will support me in any troubles or adversities that may happen to me. This Sincere and Friendly advice I will endeavour to follow as far as the Frailty of human Nature will admit. Dined at Sheffield with Mr. Furnis. Bought some Hardware of Messrs. Broomheads and a small quantity of Mr. Furnis. Very merry with Mr. Furnis and Mr. Magnel at the *Rose and Crown.* Got to Ughill late in the evening; all the Family in bed.

*Edale— Tuesday, March 22nd, 1774.* Breakfasted at Ughill. Got home to dinner. In the evening John Briddock brought my Chest home. The sight of it affected my Father the most of any thing I have yet seen. I believe he is most heartily vexed and very uneasy at my proceedings. Am sorry for it. What I do proceeds from good motives, and I will persevere. *Wednesday, March 23rd, 1774.* In the forenoon employed in packing up my Clothes. This has cost my Mother many tears. After dinner went to Chapel-en-le-Frith to put up my other Clothes and see my Chest in the waggon for Liverpool. Spent the evening with Doctor Green. From him I understand that people in general think that I am *Non Compos Mentis.* Some attribute the reason of my going to one thing, some to another, but they are most of them far wide of the real Cause. Got home late in the evening. *Thursday, March 24th, 1774.* At home settling my affairs ready for my departure. A disagreeable business. I wish I was gone.

*Milnthorp — Friday, March 25th, 1774.* Set out for Milnthorp. At Hope my horse fell sick. Borrowed one of Jacob Hall and proceeded, got to Milnthorp late in the evening.

*Edale, Saturday, March 26th, 1774.* Dined with Mr. Perkin at the *Rose and Crown* in Sheffield. Paid Messrs. Broomheads for the goods I had bought of them. Miss

Perkin gave me a Letter to her Cousin in Barbadoes. Got home very late in the evening. *Sunday, March 27th, 1774.* Went to the Chapel in the forenoon. Mr. Bray, John Bore, John Hadfield, and Michael Bradbury came to bid me farewell. John Hadfield wants to send his son along with me, but I will not be connected with any person whatever. *Monday, March 28th, 1774.* Went to Castleton to bid Mr. Hall Adieu. Widow Hall made me a compliment of a pair of stockings. Am at a Loss to know what is her motive for it. Spent the evening with Mr. Bray, Jacob Hall, John Hadfield and Michael Bradbury at the Castle. Find Bradbury to be an Insinuating, Lying, Backbiting Scoundrel; am sorry I ever had any connections with him, but will avoid such acquaintance for the future. *Tuesday, March 29th, 1774.* Received a Letter from Tom Middleton which informs me the Ship sails on Friday next. Employed in settling my private affairs and preparing everything ready for my Voyage. Intend to set out for Liverpool on Thursday.

*Wednesday, March 30th, 1774.* This day I have been taking leave of my Friends. Very disagreeable employment indeed. They all are, or pretend to be, very uneasy at my going away. Some of them that I had least expected shed tears plentifully; but whether they are real or affected they are the best judges. Drank Tea with my Grandmother. The good Old Lady is very uneasy. She tells me it is the last time she expects to see me in this life. Went and bid farewell to my worthy Friend, Mr. Champion, who gave me every good advice that lay in his power in a very sincere and affecting manner. I am very sorry to part with this most valuable Friend. My Mother and all the Family very uneasy. This has been a disagreeable evening.

*Warrington — Thursday, March 31st, 1774.* Early this morning my Father gave me what he thought proper and I set out for Liverpool. The parting with my Friends has been one of the most affecting scenes I have ever yet experienced. Plenty of Tears on all sides, but this is nothing more than what is usual on such occasions. My Brother Richard overtook me at Chapel-en-le-Frith and insists on going with me to Liverpool. Called at Stockport to see Nat. Pickford, but he has got a Girl with Child and will not be seen. Dined at Mrs. Dixon's in Manchester. From there to Warrington in company with Sam Jackson, Charles Greatrix and my Brother. After supper went to see the Waxworks and spent the evening very merrily.

*Liverpool — Friday, April 1st, 1774.* Reached Liverpool before Dinner. Found my Chest and goods at Mr. Latham's, Captn. Parry informs me that the Ship will not sail this week. *Monday, April 4th, 1774.* This morning my Brother set out for home with Mr. Baker. Supped and spent the evening at Mr. Sykes's with Sam Jackson, Greatrix, and a Captain May. All of us very merry. Intend to go to Mr. Sykes to get acquainted with Navigation if the Ship does not sail next week. It will be much better than idling about in the manner I do at present. *Tuesday, April 5th, 1774.* This morning Sam Jackson and Greatrix set out for Manchester, and I entered at Mr. Sykes's school. In the evening the *Burrows*, Captain Bostock, from Guinea, came into the Dock. Went on Board to see Bob Middleton who is Steward of her, but he was so disguised with dirt and sickness I did not know him; indeed I never saw such a. Scene of Sickness and Confusion before. The Captain could scarcely stand, and several of the men not able to get out of their Hammocks. As a remarkable instance of the

Guinea Sailor's being accustomed to Mortality — a Gentleman came on board to enquire for a passenger from Jamaica: "D — m my Blood," says one of the Sailors, "he's dead three weeks ago, but we have pulled his guts out and stowed him away on the Ballast below," with a great deal of indifference. *Wednesday, April 6th, 1774.* I am pursuing a desperate design — at least it appears so in the eyes of all my Friends. In short, I have not one friend in the world, to my knowledge, that approves of my proceedings, Mr. Champion excepted. Therefore I ought to act with the greatest caution and prudence. I have a number of difficulties to encounter: brought up to no business and almost ignorant of the ways of the world, the deceits and knavery of mankind in general, more particularly the part of the world to which I am bound; my education very slender; in a Distant Country, no friend that I dare trust to advise with, and little money to support me; a certainty of losing a considerable part of my Independence at home. All these things added together are not sufficient to counterbalance a natural impulse, and the uneasiness of mind I have laboured under at certain periods when at home. What I have undertaken is with a good design, not to wrong or defraud anyone, but with this in view, to be a benefit to myself and service to my friends. What will be the consequence is in the hands of the Disposer of all things and the womb of time to bring forth. As I engage in it voluntarily, from honest and generous motives, I am reconciled to my Fate, be it what it will. If I am fortunate, I make no doubt but my friends will say that I have acted prudently and wisely to persevere. If I am unsuccessful, not only my friends but every Rattleskull will condemn me, put on a wise countenance and say they knew my plan would never answer, that I was too well at home, of a restless, rambling disposition, and possibly in the height of their profound penetration will tax me with extravagance and dissipation, without making the least allowance for the common vicissitudes of life. To avoid these imputations it is necessary to lay down short rules, to govern and direct my proceedings: First, To act Honestly and pay my debts as far as I am able, as an effectual means of procuring credit when I may want it. (Mem. Never to contract any debts that I can possibly avoid.) Secondly, Not to be over hasty in making any purchase, or engaging with anyone for any length of time till I have considered the Temper and disposition of the people, the Climate, their trade and Commerce, the fertility of the soil, with the nature, quality, and quantity of the produce, their form of Government and Colonial or Provincial Polity. Thirdly, If I like the Country, to return as soon as I have made what observations I think necessary and endeavour to go out on a better footing and live as frugally as I can with decency. These general rules observed may be of great use to me. Spent the evening with Mr. James Longsdon at the *Fleece. Thursday, April 7th, 1774.* Find navigation is not so hard to learn as I at first imagined. Spent the evening with Mr. Longsdon, who gave me a pattern Book and desires me to do some business for him, but will avoid all connections in the Foreign trade. *Friday, April 8th, 1774.* Orders to be on Board to-morrow morning by Seven o'clock. Bought a Sea Bed; paid Captn. Parry my passage. Got my chest and things on Board. Understand we are to have three other passengers, but do not know who they are. Spent the afternoon on Mount Pleasant with Mr. Oaks of Sheffield. Wrote to Gustavus Bradford. Got everything ready for going so soon as the wind serves.

## II

## THE VOYAGE—FIRST GLIMPSES

*S*HIP "*Molly*" *towards America — Saturday, April 9th, 1774.* This morning got up very early and wrote to my Father. Got on Board about Nine o'clock. Set sail with a fair wind and tide in our favour; in the afternoon calm and pleasant; came to an Anchor off Ormshead. We are Four passengers, but don't as yet know the others. All of us very merry at supper, tho' I believe most of us Young Sailors are rather squeamish. At Eight in the evening, a Breeze sprung up; hove up the Anchor; about Ten saw the Skerry Lighthouse. *Sunday, April 10th, 1774.* Last night in attempting to get into my Hammock the hook at the foot gave way and I had like to have broke my bones with the fall, to the no small diversion of my fellow passengers. The Hammock is a hard piece of canvas suspended up to the roof of the Cabin at each end with cords. *Monday, April 11th, 1774.* Fine pleasant weather. In the afternoon saw Bardsey Island on the Welsh Coast and Carmarthen Bay. Yesterday it blew fresh and I was very sick, but to-day I am something better. Sleeping in a Hammock is very agreeable, though very different from a bed on shore. *Tuesday, April 12th, 1774.* Slept pretty well last night. This morning made St. David's Head, the N.E. promontory of Wales. Fine pleasant breezes. Much better of my sickness; at least I am as well as the rest of the passengers. Saw the rocks called Bishop and Clarks at Night. *Wednesday, April 13th, 1774.* Saw Ireland about 12 leagues Distance. Fine pleasant weather. Believe I have got over my sickness. *Thursday, April 14th, 1774.* Fresh Gales and a large rolling sea. Broke our Fore Top Gallant Yard. Took our Departure from Holyhead in lat$^d$. 53°°– 23″ North, Long$^d$. 4°°–40″ West. Got clear of the Channel with the wind at N.E. Find I am much deceived — very sick all day. *Friday, April 15th, 1774.* A fair wind and pleasant. Drank a Quart of sea water which operated both ways very plentifully and did me great service. Spoke a Brig from Leghorn bound to Bristol. *Saturday, April 16th, 1774.* Fair wind and pleasant weather. Our passengers are the Rev. John Baldwin and his Brother, Thomas Baldwin, from Chester, bound to Bermudas as they say for the benefit of their health. But it seems a little strange that they should come aboard under fictitious names. The other is a certain Captain Alexander Knox, a Scotchman, bound to Maryland. This evening drank our Sweethearts in a large Can of Grog. It is a custom at Sea on Saturday nights. Very sick indeed.

*Sunday, April 17th, 1774.* Sunday and we, having a Parson on Board, expected prayers. But instead of praying he amused himself by reading a Treatise on the Scurvy, while most of the Sailors were reading in their Common Prayer Books. I find these men not such an unprincipalled set of beings as they are represented to be. It is true they swear most horridly in general, but when they pray, which I believe is very seldom, they do it heartily. Pleasant weather and good wind. Pretty free from sickness. *Monday, April 18th, 1774.* A fine N.E. Breeze and pleasant weather. Begin to be hungry, which they tell me is a sign that the sickness is going off. This is certainly one of the most disagreeable sicknesses in Nature, continually sick at the Stomach, Dizziness in the Head and list-lessness, with a loathing to all sorts of food. *Wednesday, April 20th, 1774.* Pleasant and a fine wind. Paid forfeit one Bottle of Rum for going aloft. *Thursday, April 21st, 1774.* Fine weather and light breeze. Saw a large Fleet of Porpoises playing about the Vessel. Some of them appeared to be 10 ft. long, but we caught none of them. *Friday, April 22nd, 1774.* Pleasant weather. Spoke a Brig from Lisbon. Dined on Stock Fish and Potatoes. This Fish is cured in the Frost without salt. Before it is boiled, they beat it with Iron hammers against the Anchor Stock to soften it. A general dish on Fridays and is reckoned a great delicacy, but to me it is none, for I hate the smell of it. Saw Corve one of the Western Islands bearing S.S.E.½ E. Distance about 14 Leagues. Pretty well over my sickness. The Sea begins to be agreeable. *Saturday, April 23rd, 1774.* Fine pleasant breeze this morning. But this evening blows hard and I am sick. *Sunday, April 24th, 1774.* Hard Gales from the Eastward. The Ship rolls and pitches the worst I have yet experienced. Very often the waves break over the Long boat. Broke our Mizzen Yard. Very sick. Messrs. Baldwin in the same condition. *Monday, April 25th, 1774.* More moderate to-day. But still blows hard. *Tuesday, April 26th, 1774.* Strong Gales and a high Sea. The first thing that I saw after I got upon Deck was the Carpenter tumbling from one side of the Deck to the other in a great Sea we had Shipped, in which he lost his Hat and Wig. Saw him soon after and asked him what he had done with them. " D — m my eyes," says he, " they are gone to Davy Jones's Locker." This is a common saying when anything goes over board. Very sick. *Wednesday, April 27th, 1774,* Strong Gales all day. My sickness continues so bad that I could almost wish myself ashore again.

*Thursday, April 28th, 1774.* Fine pleasant breeze and smooth water. Took a drink of Sea water, which operated very well, and gave me a good appetite. Mr. Baldwin caught a Fish called a Portugeeze Man of War. It is about 9 inches long and appears like a bladder upon the water, always swimming upon the top. I believe it never goes under water. Of a transparent blue colour. The part that appears like a bladder serves as a sail. The body is like a bunch of red worsted with a long tail. The one that Mr. Baldwin caught was 16 Foot long and no thicker than a straw. If you touch the tail or body it causes a sensation the same as if you had touched a Nettle. *Friday, April 29th, 1774.* Fresh Breezes with Rain. *Saturday, April, 30th, 1774.* Fresh Gales from the Eastward and cloudy weather. *Sunday, May 1st, 1774.* Light breeze and clear weather. Evening calm. No prayers to-day. *Monday, May 2nd, 1774.* Pleasant weather with light showers of rain. *Tuesday, May 3rd, 1774.* First part of the day strong gales with rain. Saw a Ship to windward. Evening very heavy Rain with Thunder and Lightning. *Wednesday, May 4th, 1774.* Light airs with clear hot weather. The Thermometer to 73 Degrees. Expect to make the Land in a week. Evening calm. *Thursday, May 5th, 1774.* Pleasant weather but Foul wind. *Friday, May 6th, 1774.* Fresh Gales, but contrary, with cloudy, hazy, rainy weather. Saw a Ship to windward. *Saturday, May 7th, 1774.* Foul wind with cloudy weather. Lightning and Rain. *Sunday, May 8th, 1774.* Pleasant weather but a foul wind. Spoke a Brig from Georgia bound to Lisbon. No prayers to-day. *Monday, May 9th, 1774.* Sultry hazy weather. Saw several Grampuses. They appear to be very large and throw the water a great height into the air, it is said through their nostrils. At six this evening the wind came to the Eastward. *Tuesday, May 10th, 1774.* Light winds but a great swell from the North. Sultry, hazy weather. *Wednesday, May 11th, 1774.* Pleasant weather and a fair wind. *Thursday, May 12th, 1774.* Cloudy, hazy weather, but fair wind. *Friday, May 13th, 1774.* A fair wind with hazy, cloudy weather at six in the evening. Hove the Lead and struck Ground in 25 Fathom of water. Sandy bottom, but see no Land.

*Ship " Molly " Chesapeake Bay — Saturday, May 14th, 1774.* At 10 o'clock this morning made the Land from the Masthead. At 2 afternoon abreast of Cape Henry, from which we see Cape Charles E.N.E. about 18 Miles distant. Got a Pilot on Board. The Land appears low and sandy, covered in Pines. Wrote to my Father by a Ship bound to London. At 7 this evening came on a gust of Thunder, Lightning, and rain from the N.W. Obliged to let go our Anchor in 6 Fathom water at the tail of the Horse Shoe. It is a custom with all passengers to pay a bottle of rum to the Sailors as soon as they make the Land. We, agreeable to that custom, have paid ours and I believe every man aboard (the Captn., Passengers, and first Mate excepted) are drunk, swearing and fighting like madmen. Blowing very hard. Thundering very loud and Lightning so strong and quick that I can see to write without Candle.

*Sunday, May 15th, 1774.* At 5 this morning weighed Anchor with a fresh breeze and cloudy weather. At Noon Clear and pleasant. The land appears from the Masthead to be level and covered with lofty Pines. A great number of Rivers empty themselves into the Bay. Can count Nineteen Sail of Vessels and see the Land on every side. This is one of the finest prospects I have ever seen. What makes it more agreeable, not seeing land before these 27 days. At 7 in the evening, calm. Let go our Anchor off Windmill point. *Monday, May 16th, 1774.* A Head wind and, as we have got an indifferent Pilot, the Captn. does not think it prudent to move. Still at Anchor. Captn. Received a Letter from Liverpool that informs him the two Baldwins are in debt at home and obliged to go abroad.

## III

## VIRGINIA — ILLNESS — BARBADOS

*Urbanna, Rappahannock River, Virginia — Tuesday, May 17th, 1774.* Contrary wind. Our Ship at Anchor. Captn. Parry, Captn. Knox, Messrs. Baldwin, and I went ashore in the Pilot Boat. Landed at this place after a passage of thirty-eight days from Liverpool. This is a small Village pleasantly situated on a Creek of the same name; the Custom House for the Rappahannock River, and Tobacco warehouses for the County are kept here. Messrs. Baldwin went to the house of a Merchant whom they had Letters of introduction to, Knox and I stayed at the Inn. *Wednesday, May 18th, 1774.* At Urbanna, waiting for the Ship; took a walk into the Country. Find the Land sandy and barren to all appearance, but it produces excellent Garden stuff. Green Peas are in plenty. Intend to keep a Diary for the future. *Thursday, May 19th, 1774.* This day the Ship came up. Captn. Knox and I hired a Boat to carry us us to Nanjemoy on Potowmeck River, about 60 Miles from Alexandria, which place I intend to go to as soon as possible. Went up to Deep Creek and got our Baggage on Board the Boat. Parted with Messrs. Baldwin, who are bound to Norfolk in Virginia. Got down to Urbanna, but so late at Night obliged to sleep in the Boat all night. *Friday, May 20th, 1774.* Left Urbanna about 8 in the morning. Our Boat manned with three Negroes. At 2 in the afternoon got into the mouth of Potowmeck River, which is about 12 Miles wide. A great number of

[ 16 ]

pleasant seats on the Banks of the River. At 10 in the evening came to an Anchor in Majotack Creek.

*Nanjemoy, Maryland — Saturday, May 21st, 1774.* Early this morning weighed and stood over to Ladlor's Ferry in Maryland, where we got breakfast at the Ferry house. After Breakfast got under way again, but run the Boat aground on a sand bank in the River where we stuck two hours, but by lashing the Canoe to the Masthead and filling her with stones, Heeld the Vessel on one side and got her off. Arrived at Nanjemoy in the afternoon. Captn. Knox's Brother has a House here, but he is not at home. He introduced me to his Brother's partner, Mr. Bayley, who behaves very civilly to me and insists that I shall stay a week with him. Don't intend staying any longer than I can get a passage to Alexandria. *Sunday, May 22nd, 1774.* This is a small Village of about five houses. All Planters except Knox and Bayley, who keep a store. (What they call stores in this country are Shops in England.) In the afternoon drank Tea with Captn. Knox and Mr. Wallace (Knox and Bayley's Clerk) at Colonel Harrison's. Captn. Knox introduced me to every house in the Village. The people are remarkably civil and obliging, appear to live very well, and exceedingly happy. *Monday, May 23rd, 1774.* Captn. Knox and I went to Mrs. Marsden, a widow lady in the neighbourhood. Got some very indifferent Strawberries and Cherries. *Tuesday, May 24th, 1774.* Dined on Board a Scotch Ship called the *Jenny*, Captn. Mc-Leash, Master.

*Wednesday, May 25th, 1774.* Saw them plant Tobacco. The Land is first hoed into small round hills about the size of Molehills and about 4000 of them in an acre. The plants are something like small Cabbage plants; they only make a hole with their fingers or a small stick and put them in, one in each hill. Two Negroes will plant three acres in one day. Small Blisters are broke out all over my body, attended with an intolerable itching. They call it the Prickly heat and say it is very wholesome. It may be so, for everything I can tell, but it is very troublesome. *Thursday, May 26th, 1774.* Waiting for an opportunity to go to Alexandria by water, but I believe Captn. Knox does everything in his power to disappoint me, for fear I should go away. Drank Tea at Mrs. Leftwich's. *Friday, May 27th, 1774.* Dined on Board the *Jenny*, McLeash. It is true we had excellent Porter and Wine, but had our stomachs been of a squeamish nature, they would have been disobliged at their Scotch cleanliness.

*Saturday, May 28th, 1774.* The Land here is level, sandy and barren in general, except where it is mixed with Oyster shells which renders it very fertile. Agriculture is in a very poor state. In short, they know very little about farming. Tobacco and Indian corn is all they make and some little wheat. All done by Negroes. The Tobacco is all worked with Hoes, the Indian corn with Ploughs, but of a bad sort and without a Colter. The furrow they make is not more than two inches deep and does little more than kill the weeds. Land sells upon an average here, at about three Dollars pr. acre. (Thirteen shillings and Sixpence Sterling.)

*Sunday, May 29th, 1774.* Captn. Knox went to Bulo in Virginia to see his brother. Here is no Church within 14 or 15 miles of the place. Mr. Bayley and I went to see a Negro Ball. Sundays being the only days these poor creatures have to themselves, they generally meet together and amuse themselves with Dancing to the Banjo. This musical instrument (if it may be so called) is made of a Gourd something in the imitation of a Guitar, with only four strings and played with the fingers in the same manner. Some of them sing to it, which is very droll music indeed. In their songs they generally relate the usage they have received from their Masters or Mistresses in a very satirical stile and manner. Their poetry is like the Music — Rude and uncultivated. Their Dancing is most violent exercise, but so irregular and grotesque. I am not able to describe it. They all appear to be exceedingly happy at these merry-makings and seem as if they had forgot or were not sensible of their miserable condition.

*Monday, May 30th, 1774.* Dined at Colonel Harrison's. Nothing talked of but the Blockade of Boston Harbour. The people seem much exasperated at the proceedings of the Ministry and talk as if they were determined to dispute the matter with the sword. *Tuesday, May 31st, 1774.* Waiting for a Passage to Alexandria, but can't meet with an opportunity. This is doing nothing. *Wednesday, June 1st, 1774.* Waiting with a great deal of impatience for a passage to Alexandria. I am informed that the Land is much better the higher you go up the River. If it is not, I will not settle in this part of the Country. *Thursday, June 2nd, 1774.* Spent the afternoon at Colonel Harrison's. Find him a very intelligent man and seems to take a pleasure in communicating the customs and manners of his countrymen. Captn. Knox returned to Nanjemoy this evening and gave me an invitation to go with him to Annapolis, which I intend to accept.

*Port Tobacco, Maryland — Friday, June 3rd, 1774.* Hired a horse and crossed Nanjemoy Creek. Got to Port Tobacco in the evening. This is a small town situated at the head of a Creek of the same name. The County Courts are held here and a Warehouse for the inspection of Tobacco. Several Scotch Factors are settled here.

*Marlbro, Maryland — Saturday, June 4th, 1774.* Left Port Tobacco in company with Mr. John Creig, a Scotch Merchant, Doctor Gustavus Richard Brown, and Captn. Knox. Dined at Piscataway, a small town 16 miles from Port Tobacco. Our victuals badly drest, and sour. Madeira Wine at 7/6 per Bottle. From Piscataway to Marlbro 16 miles. Saw the quarter of a Negro man chained to a Tree for murdering his overseer. Land in general appears barren and thinly inhabited, some places sandy and others a sort of stiff clay, but plenty of fine Orchards, and I observe they generally plant a Peach Orchard on the worst land. They had a frost on the 9th. of May, which has killed a great number of Trees, the woods for a mile together seem dead and withered.

*Annapolis, Maryland — Sunday, June 5th, 1774.* Left Marlbro early this morning. Crossed Potuxen River at Mount Pleasant Ferry. Some good Land after this River. Breakfasted at Rollin's, a Public House, but in this Country called Ordinaries, and indeed they have not their name for nothing, for they are ordinary enough. Have had either Bacon or Chickens every meal since I came into the Country. If I still continue in this way shall be grown over with Bristles or Feathers. From Rollin's to London town on South River. This is a small, pleasant place at the head of the Bay, but no great trade. Crossed the South River and on to Annapolis to Dinner, 22 Miles from Marlbro. Land very indifferent from London town to Annapolis.

*Monday, June 6th, 1774.* This is the Capital town or rather City in the Province and the seat of the Governor, situated at the Head of Chesapeake Bay. It is not very large or populous, but regularly built and some of them good buildings. They are now building an elegant State House of Brick, which is to be covered with Copper. A place of very little trade, chiefly supported by the meeting of the Provincial Assembly. There is a great number of people collected together to get Bills of Credit out to the Provincial Loan Office. A considerable sum in Four, Three, Two, One, Two-thirds, One-third and One-Ninth of a Dollar Bills, is struck in these Bills of Credit by an Act of the Provincial Assembly. An office is opened and the money divided into Lots of 1000 Dollars each. Any person a resident in the Province may take up a Thousand Dollars, if he has an Estate in the Province of twice the Value and clear of Entail or Mortgage, which Estate he Mortgages into the Office as security for the money, which he has at 4 per cent for Ten years, and then the Bills are called into the office again. It is Death to Sell or Mortgage an Estate that is Mortgaged to this Office till the expiration of the time, and in default of paying the interest the Treasurer of the Loan Office has a right to sell the whole estate and appropriate the whole of the money to the Province's use. These Bills are a lawful tender and the greatest part of the business is done with this sort of money. Not only this Province, but every Province, and Colony on the Continent has large sums of this kind of money issued by their different Houses of Assembly. I suppose the Credit of these Bills must be indisputable, if one may be allowed to judge from the number of people that apply for them. It appears to me that there is a scarcity of Cash amongst the people of all ranks here. They Game high, Spend freely, and Dress exceedingly gay, but I observe they seldom show any money, it is all Tobacco Notes. Great number of Scotch tradesmen here, but very few English. Provisions are as dear here as in England. Mutton and Beef at 6d. per lb. A Violent pain in my Head this evening.

*Piscataway, Maryland — Tuesday, June 7th, 1774.* This morning Captn. Knox and I left Annapolis. Dined at Marlbro, Lodged at Piscataway. A most violent pain in my Head attended with a high Fever, obliged to stop and rest myself at several houses on the road. Captn. Knox behaves exceedingly kind to me. *Wednesday, June 8th, 1774.* Got to Port Tobacco with great difficulty. Captn. Knox insists on me applying to Doctor Brown. I have taken his advice and he told me it is a Fever with some cussed physical name. He has given me some slops and I am now going to bed very ill.

*Nanjemoy, Maryland — Thursday, June 9th, 1774.* Find myself no better, However, the Doctor has given me more physic. Got to Nanjemoy. Almost dead with pain and fatigue, added to the excessive heat, which caused me to faint twice. *Wednesday, June 15th, 1774.* Very ill, confined to my room. This is the first day I have been able to stir out of it. I am much reduced and very weak, but my spirits are good and I hope in God I shall get better. Captn. Knox, Mr. Bayley, and the whole neighbourhood behaves with the greatest kindness to me, some of them has attended me constantly all the time. *Friday, June 17th, 1774.* Much better. The Doctor tells me I am out of all danger, but advises me to take some physic to clear my body and to drink a little more Rum than I did before I was sick. In short, I believe it was being too abstemious that brought this sickness upon me at first, by drinking water.

*Saturday, June 18th, 1774.* Able to walk about the house. It is such excessive hot weather or I should mend faster. *Sunday, June 19th, 1774.* Dined at a certain Mr. Hambleton's. Supped and spent the evening at Mrs. Leftwiches with some young ladies from Virginia. After supper the company amused themselves with several diverting plays. This seems very strange to me, but I believe it is common in this Country. Find myself much better to-day. Hope I shall be able to go to Alexandria next week. *Monday, June 20th, 1774.* Gathering strength very fast, the Doctor sent me a Box of Pills with directions to take two at night and two in the Morning. These are the last I intend to take. Dined at Mrs. Leftwiches. After went over to Virginia with some young ladies, but returned in the evening. *Wednesday, June 22nd, 1774.* Taking the Pills the Doctor gave me, but these don't seem to work, only cause a bad taste in my mouth. Will take three this evening. *Thursday, June 23rd, 1774.* This morning took 4 Pills which has caused a violent pain in my bowels all day, attended with a constant thirst and a very bad taste in my mouth. But affects me no other way. Coln¹. Harrison sent me a Humming Bird. This is supposed to be one of the smallest Birds that is known. It is Green on the back, its neck and breast of a beautiful azure, the belly and thighs are of a whitish colour. It has a long beak about the thickness of a needle which it darts into the flowers and extracts the Honey upon which it lives. They are only seen in the Summer time, their nests are very rarely found, and are looked upon as a great curiosity. *Friday, June 24th, 1774.* Much worse, my throat and tongue much swollen. Have sent for the Doctor. Confined to my bed. Am afraid that I am poisoned with his confounded Pills. A continual thirst, but these people will not let me drink. *Saturday, June 25th, 1774.* Captn. Knox sent an express for the Doctor, who came about eight this morning. After he had examined the Pills, he came with a truly physical face to the bedside and felt my pulse. Began to beg pardon for the mistake he said his Prentice had inadvertently committed by sending me strong Mercurial Pills, in the room of cooling ones. I immediately gave him as hard a blow as I could with my fist over the face, and would have given him a good trimming had I been able. This discomposed his physical muscles a good deal, and made him contract them into a most formidable frown. He did not attempt to resent it. Begged I would moderate my passion, follow his directions, and in a short time I should be well again. I believed myself poisoned and grew desperate, abused him most unmercifully. However, he left me some Brimstone and Salts which I took immediately after he was gone, which worked very well and has given me a great deal of ease. Tho' I am still full of pain and much swelled, spitting and slavering like a mad dog, my teeth loose and mouth very sore. I believe I have little to trust to but the strength of my constitution for my life. Much difficulty to write, but if I happen to die I hope this will appear against the rascal. *Sunday, June 26th, 1774.* This morning took a dose of Brimstone, laid in bed all day and sweat abundantly. This has made me very weak and faint. Doctor came to enquire after me, but did not come into the room. Much easier. *Monday, June 27th, 1774.* A great deal better but much relaxed and very weak, able to sit up most part of the day. *Wednesday, June 29th, 1774.* Mending very fast, able to walk about the room. The swelling gone away, my throat got well, but my mouth is very sore, which I wash every two hours with Vinegar. I understand the Doctor sends every day to enquire how I do. Had it not been for the extraordinary care of Captn. Knox, I must certainly have died. *Thursday, June 30th, 1774.* Took a dose of Salts, able to walk into the Yard. *Saturday, July 2nd, 1774.* Continue mending, but very slowly. *Sunday, July 3rd, 1774.* Rode out with Mr. Wallace to Colonel Tayor's Plantation. It is only two miles, but I find it has fatigued me too much.

*Monday, July 4th, 1774.* Went to see them reap Wheat. The greatest slovens I ever saw, believe that one fourth part is left on the Field uncut. Some of them mow it with sticks fixed on the scythe in parallel lines to lay the grain straight. This makes worse havoc than the reapers. The grain is but indifferent and their crop very light, seldom that they get seven bushels from an acre, but they put it into the ground in such a slovenly manner without any manure, it is a wonder that they get any. *Tuesday, July 5th, 1774.* Took another dose of Salts, which I hope will be the last I shall have occasion to take at this time. Find myself pretty well. Free from pain, but very weak and much reduced. My clothes hang about me like a skeleton. The Doctor has never come in my sight since I struck him. Intend to go and pay the rascal to-morrow. *Wednesday, July 6th, 1774.* Went to see the Doctor, who (contrary to my expectation) treated me with the greatest kindness and acknowledged that he had given me just cause of complaint, though inadvertantly, and absolutely refused being paid till I am quite recovered. I understand their Doctors' Bills in this country are very extravagant. Returned to Nanjemoy much fatigued. *Thursday, July 7th, 1774.* Took my passage on board a small schooner bound to Alexandria. Captn. Knox and Mr. Bayley pressed me to stay a week longer and get a little stronger before I attempt to move. I think I am able to go to Alexandria as it is only 100 Miles by water. I am under infinite obligations to these worthy people, every possible care has been taken of me in my late illness, had I been their Brother more tenderness could not have been used for my recovery. They absolutely refused taking anything for my board so that I must remain under obligations to them which I am afraid it will never be in my power to repay. Calm in the evening, the Captn. and I went ashore, to what they call a reaping frolic. This is a Harvest Feast. The people very merry, Dancing without either Shoes or Stockings and the Girls without stays, but I cannot partake of the diversion.

*Potowmeck River — Friday, July 8th, 1774.* Contrary wind, came to an anchor off Maryland Point. Went ashore and dined at Capt. Harrison's. Had a very genteel dinner, but the Captn. is a violent opposer of the Government. Got on board in the evening. Fair wind, got up to Colonel George Washington's, came to an Anchor in the Creek. Here is a small Insect which appears in the Night like sparks of Fire. Every time it extends its wings there is something of a luminous nature on the body, just under the wings, which is seen only when it extends them, only discernible in the night, and is called the Fire Fly. A great number of pleasant Houses along the River, both on the Virginia and Maryland side. All Tobacco Planters, some of them people of considerable property. This River parts the Province of Maryland and Colony of Virginia. *Saturday, July 9th, 1774.* Waiting for a load of Flour from Col. Washington's Mill. I am now got pretty well, but weak and feeble. *Sunday, July 10th, 1774.* Went to see the Mill. It is a very complete one. Dressing and Bolting Mills the same as in England with a pair of Cologne, and a pair of French stones, and make as good flour as I ever saw. Land much better here than it is lower down the River.

*Alexandria, Virginia, Monday, July 11th, 1774.* Got our Cargo on board. Weighed and got up to Alexandria about three o'clock. After dinner waited on Mr. Kirk with my letters. He seems to be very glad to see me, gives me great encouragement and insists on me making his house my home as long as I stay here. Got my baggage ashore.

*Tuesday, July 12th, 1774.* Viewing the Town, which is laid off in squares of an acre each, streets 80 feet wide, several good brick buildings, and when it is completed according to the plan, will be a beautiful and regular town. Their chief trade is Wheat, Flour and Tobacco. Mr. Kirk tells me they exported 100,000 bushels of Wheat and 14,000 barrels of Flour from this Port, the last year. Here is as good Wheat as I ever saw, brought to this market from the back country. I am told the land is very good about eighty miles to the Westward of Thiston. I have told Mr. Kirk of my scheme, he approves of it, and advises me to take a tour into the back country as soon as I am able to travel on horseback. Promises to give me every assistance that lies in his power. In the afternoon introduced me to Capt. William Buddecombe, a Gentleman from Liverpool, and several other gentlemen in town. Am very glad to find him so well esteemed amongst the people. *Wednesday, July 13th, 1774.* I begin to gather strength very fast. Find this an agreeable place.

*Thursday, July 14th, 1774.* An Election for Burgesses in town (their Elections are annual). There were three

Candidates, the Poll was over in about two hours and conducted with great order and regularity. The Members Col. George Washington and Major Bedwater. The Candidates gave the populace a Hogshead of Toddy (what we call Punch in England). In the evening the returned Member gave a Ball to the Freeholders and Gentlemen of the town. This was conducted with great harmony. Coffee and Chocolate, but no Tea. This Herb is in disgrace amongst them at present. I have been seized with a Violent griping of pain in my bowels and obliged to leave the room very early if it still continues. I am afraid of a relapse. *Friday, July 15th, 1774.* I have had a most violent pain in my Bowels all night and a very severe lax — some symptoms of the Flux. If it happens to prove the Flux I am certain to die. Mr. Kirk and the Doctor advise me to take a short Voyage to Sea as the only method to reestablish my health. I have written to my Father, informing him that I have drawn upon him for Thirty Pounds. I am not able to go to Sea without a supply of money. This money I believe will pay my funeral expenses. *Monday, July 18th, 1774.* Confined to my room, sick of the bloody Flux. I am in a most miserable condition, so weak I can scarcely get across the room and afflicted with a most excruciating pain in my bowels. I believe my death is approaching very fast. I am wholly resigned to the will of Heaven and submit to my fate without repining. My conscience does [not] accuse me with any wicked or unpardonable crimes, therefore, I hope to find mercy in the sight of a just and merciful God. I have not yet drawn a Bill upon my Father, and if it pleases God to take me out of the world, I have effects sufficient to bury me decently. If I die, I hope Mr. Kirk will send this Book home. He behaves to me like a parent, and hope he will not refuse the request of a dying Man. *Tuesday, July 19th, 1774.* The virulence of my disorder begins to abate, I find myself surprisingly better to-day. Am singularly obliged to Mr. Kirk for his great care of me. He advises me to go to Sea as soon as possible. I believe I will take his advice and go the first Vessel that goes out of port if I am obliged to be carried aboard. *Wednesday, July 20th, 1774.* Able to walk about the house, but I appear more like a skeleton than a man. Agreed with a certain Captn. Speake to go to Barbados in a small Schooner. Sold my hardware to Mr. Kirk, of whom I bought 33 Br$^{lls}$. Sea Bread which I intend to take as a venture. Got my Bread aboard and if the wind answers we sail to-morrow. A certain Mr. Dundass advises me to drink Port Wine. Am afraid I have drunk too much.

*Schooner " John," Potowmeck River — Thursday, July 21st, 1774.* Slept very well and undisturbed last night. Find myself pretty well, only weak. Early this morning the Captn. sent for my Chest and bed. About 9 o'clock I went on Board the Schooner *John,* Francis Speake, Master, Bound for Barbados. Fell down to the mouth of Broad Creek, where we came to an Anchor. *Friday, July 22nd, 1774.* Slept very well last night. I believe the Flux has entirely left me. Fell down with the tide to Stumpneck Point. The Captn. went ashore and bought us some Stock. Much fatigued with the motion of the Vessel, scarce able to stand. *Saturday, July 23rd, 1774.* Able to walk the Quarter Deck. Fell down to Cedar Point. A severe gust of Thunder, Lightning, and the largest Hailstones I ever saw, and the hardest like pieces of Ice cut some of the people's faces till the blood came. Mr. Richard Brooks, another passenger, came on board. He is an Invalid. *Sun-*

*day, July 24th, 1774.* Fell down to the Maryland Office. Went ashore with the Captn. to clear out his Vessel. Lodged ashore at the Office. The Gentleman refuses to do any business on Sunday.

*Schooner "John," St. Mary's River — Monday, July 25th, 1774.* Fell down to St. Mary's River. Went ashore with the Captn. to the Office. All Vessels are obliged to clear out at both Offices. I am now perfectly well, but very weak. *Tuesday, July 26th, 1774.* At Anchor with a contrary wind. About noon a Pilot Boat came along side to invite the Captn. to a Barbecue. I went with him and have been highly diverted. These Barbecues are Hogs, roasted whole. This was under a large Tree. A great number of young people met together with a Fiddle and Banjo played by two Negroes, with Plenty of Toddy, which both Men and Women seem to be very fond of. I believe they have danced and drunk till there are few sober people amongst them. I am sorry I was not able to join them. Got on Board late. *Wednesday, July 27th, 1774.* Still at Anchor with a contrary wind. After Dinner went ashore and bought some Stock. In attempting to get aboard again, was very near oversetting the Boat. Obliged to lodge ashore at Mrs. Miles-Herberts. People chiefly Roman Catholics. *Thursday, July 28th, 1774.* Got on Board before five o'clock this morning, weighed and got into the Bay. Calm, obliged to come to an Anchor.

*Schooner "John," towards Barbados — Friday, July 29th, 1774.* Early this morning got under way with the wind at N.N.W. and stood down the Bay with an easy breeze. I am now able to walk the Deck for an hour together. *Saturday July 30th, 1774.* At 10 this morning abreast Cape Henry Lat^d. 37°°–oo″ North, Long^d. 75°°–

24" West, from whence we take our Departure. *Sunday, July 31st, 1774.* This morning the Captn. killed a Jew Fish with the gig. It weighed 74 lbs and measured 5 feet long. Something like a Cod. Eats very well. Fair Wind and pleasant. *Monday, August 1st, 1774.* Squally weather, with calms. *Wednesday, August 3rd, 1774.* Squally weather and a heavy rolling Sea. Begin to be Seasick. *Friday, August 5th, 1774.* Yesterday at M. begun to blow very hard from the N.W. Before 2 P.M. it hauled round Easterly to the S.W., when we were obliged to lay her to under her close reefed F. S. At 10 P.M. to furl the F.S. and scud under bare pole. At 12 P.M. broke the Tiller and gave up all for lost. Expecting the Vessel to sink before we could rig another. About 2 A.M. got a new Tiller, the weather begun to moderate, but our Vessel made a great deal of water. At 8 A.M. set the F.S. and Jibb still blowing very hard and a monstrous Sea. At 6. P.M. set the Mainsail more moderate, but a very great Sea. Very sick these two days. *Saturday, August 6th, 1774.* Fine pleasant weather. This is very agreeable after such rough Sea. *Sunday, August 7th, 1774.* Pleasant weather and light winds. Crossed several rippling currents, about 100 yards broad, setting to the S.W. What they are, our Captn. is neither Sailor nor Philosopher sufficient to determine. At 10 P.M. Hove to for fear of the Rocks of Bermudas. *Tuesday, August 9th, 1774.* Cloudy, hazy weather with squalls of rain. We are now in the Horse Latitudes. The Sailors are possessed with a notion that it is impossible to cross them without rain and squally weather. I am now (Thanks to the Almighty) as well as ever I was in my life, only weak, but I have a good stomach and hope I shall recover my strength shortly. *Wednesday, August 10th, 1774.* Squally with rain, contrary wind. *Saturday, August 13th, 1774.* Light breezes and clear hot weather. Calm this evening and heavy rain. *Sunday, August 14th, 1774.* Quite calm and smooth water, the people bathed in the Sea. They had not been on board half an hour before a Shark came alongside. We baited a hook, but he would not take it. Appeared to be about 10 foot long of a Brown colour. There was a Pilot Fish with it. This is a beautiful Fish, about a foot long, variegated with stripes of Black and White, quite round the body. Generally accompany the Sharks. *Monday, August 15th, 1774.* Light winds with clear hot weather. *Tuesday, August 16th, 1774.* Morning light breeze. This evening blows fresh and has carried away our Main Croggik Yard. *Wednesday, August 17th, 1774.* Pleasant weather but hot. We have been in the Trade winds ever since we crossed the Tropic. They always blow from N.E. to S.E. but generally to the North of East. *Thursday, August 18th, 1774.* Saw Three Tropical Birds. They appear to be about the size of Rooks, but Milk white with long Feathers in the Tail, of a very singular appearance. *Friday, August 19th, 1774.* Moderate breezes and pleasant weather. Caught a Dolphin. This is one of the most beautiful Fishes I ever saw. About three Foot long, adorned with every colour of the Rainbow. After it is taken out of the water it changes its colour every instant till it dies, when it is of a light Blue inclining to a purple. The flesh is very white but eats dry. *Saturday, August 20th, 1774.* Pleasant weather but excessively hot. *Monday, August 22nd, 1774.* Strong gales of wind and hazy weather. Paid a bottle of Rum for my footing in the Tropic. I ought to have paid it according to custom when we crossed the Tropic of Cancer, but I believe the people had forgot. *Wednesday,*

*August 24th, 1774.* Fresh Breezes and cloudy weather. *Thursday, August 25th, 1774.* Fresh Breezes with squally hazy weather. Saw five Land Birds about the size of Ducks, of a brown colour. I believe they call them Boobies. By my reckoning Barbados Bears S.S.W. Distance 102 Leagues at Meridian. *Friday, August 26th, 1774.* Fresh Breezes, with showers of rain and hazy weather. At M. saw a Sail standing to Eastward. *Saturday, August 27th, 1774.* Light winds and calms. Saw a great number of Boobies. *Sunday, August 28th, 1774.* Light winds with clear and hot weather. Took a dose of Salts. I have enjoyed as good a state of Health all the time as ever I did in my life. Could eat and sleep very well. But a continual bad taste in my mouth. *Monday, August 29th, 1774.* Fresh Breezes and clear weather. At M. in the Lat$^d$. of Barbados, the Captn. is ashore by his reckoning, I want 10 Leagues. Saw a great number of Land Birds, and something floated alongside which we supposed to be the body of a Man. *Tuesday, August 30th, 1774.* Fine pleasant weather. At M. made the Island from the Masthead, distance about 5 Leagues. At 3 P.M. abreast the N.E. end of the Island and one of the most beautiful prospects I ever saw. High land like one entire Garden interspersed with Gentleman's Houses and Windmills in a delightful manner. At 9 P.M. abreast Bridge Town, laid her to till morning.

*Bridge Town, Barbados — Wednesday, August 31st, 1774.* At 8 this morning run into Carlisle Bay and came to an Anchor in eight Fathoms of water. A passage of 41 days from Alexandria. Moored the ship and went ashore with the Captn. to Bridge Town. Dined with Mr. Charles Willing, the Merchant that the Vessel was consigned to. Slept on Board. *Thursday, September 1st, 1774.* Went ashore and saw my Bread landed. Have attempted to sell it but find I cannot get first cost, such quantities are arrived from Philadelphia. Have stored it with Mr. Willing in hopes the price may rise a little before we sail. Dined at Mr. Willing's who appears to be a genteel man. Gave me a general invitation to his house. Agreed with Captn. Speake to live on board, find it too expensive for me to live ashore. They ask half a Johannes per week for Board. Excessively hot.

*Speights Town, Barbados — Friday, September 2nd, 1774.* By accident met with M. Thos. Blackets, a relation of Mr. Perkins, who invited me to Speights Town where Mr. Perkins is. Dined with Mr. Hazlewood. After dinner went to Speights Town in one of the Market Boats, found Mr. Perkins ill in bed. Lodged at Mr. Blacket's. *Saturday, September 3rd, 1774.* Last night it blew a hurricane. Drove several ships from the moorings, and has continued raining all day. *Sunday, September 4th, 1774.* Early this morning bathed in the Sea, which is very refreshing in this hot climate. After breakfast viewed the town. It is small and dirty. Has a pretty Church but very little frequented, the People amuse themselves with Shooting on Sundays. In the evening went with Mr. Perkins to see Mr. Kid's Plantation. The Sugar works and Rum distilleries are very extensive. The juice of the cane is pressed between two Iron rollers which are turned by the wind and then boiled into Sugar or made into Rum. The Cane is planted in Hills, is ripe about Christmas. Its present appearance is like large Sedge grass. It is all tended by Negro slaves with Hoes, never use ploughs.

*Bridge Town, Barbados — Monday, September 5th, 1774.* Some prospects of selling my Bread to a little profit,.

but the person is not at home. Went to Bridge Town in the Market Boat. Dined ashore with the Captn. in the evening. No prospect of selling or bartering here to any advantage. Must go to Speights Town.

*Speights Town — Tuesday, September 6th, 1774.* After dinner went to Speights Town. Called at Hole Town. This is a small Village with a Church. This evening as Mr. Perkins and I walked along the Shore were attacked with a shower of stones from a Mangeneel Grove by some Negroes, but were not hurt. These Negroes are very rude in the night to people unarmed. Lodged at Mr. Blackets. Gave Mr. Perkin the knives his Uncle had sent him and the letter from Miss R.

*Bridge Town, Barbados — Thursday, September 8th, 1774.* Cannot sell my Bread at Speights Town. Got to Bridge Town to dinner. Most intolerably hot. *Friday, September 9th, 1774.* Sold part of my Bread, but cannot get the first cost. The other part I have exchanged for Cotton. This Article sells well in Virginia, hope to make up my loss by it. *Saturday, September 10th, 1774.* Got my Cotton on board. Wrote home and to Sam Jackson, put the letters on board a Ship for London. *Sunday, September 11th, 1774.* Took a ride with Mr. Iffil, one of Mr. Willing's Clerks, to his Father's about 10 Miles from Bridge Town. The road is very bad and rocky. Where it is level the land appears very rich, a fine black mould, but I am in a new world, I know neither Bush nor Produce. Dined on a roasted kid, and lodged at Mrs. Iffil's. *Monday, September 12th, 1774.* Got to Town to Dinner, very well pleased with my jaunt.

*Tuesday, September 13th, 1774.* Went ashore and saw a Cargo of Slaves land. One of the most shocking sights

I ever saw. About 400 Men, Women, and Children, brought from their native Country, deprived of their liberty, and themselves and posterity become the property of cruel strangers without a probability of ever enjoying the Blessing of Freedom again, or a right of complaining, be their sufferings ever so great. The idea is horrid and the Practice unjust. They were all naked, except a small piece of blue cloth about a foot broad to cover their nakedness, and appear much dejected. Supped and spent the evening at Mr. James Bruce's.

*Wednesday, September 14th, 1774.* Captn. Thos. Bragg and Richard Rouse Dotin Esqre., a Merchant in town, dined on board. In the evening went ashore with them to the Jews' Synagogue, to see one of their grand Festivals called the opening of the Five Books of Moses. The ceremony was begun before we got there, they were just bringing out the Books under Canopies of Green Silk something like Umbrellas adorned with small bells of gold or brass. They carried them into the middle of the Congregation where the Rabbi or Chief Priest made a long and loud talk in Hebrew. He had a long Black Gown like a Surplice and a large Fur Cap with venerable long beard. The Jews worship standing and their Hats on, with a long piece of white silk or fine linen (according to the persons' circumstances), like a Towel with the ends tied together. They put their arms through it and the loose part lies across their backs. They appear to perform their religious ceremonies with great solemnity. The Building is neat and elegantly finished within. Spent the evening at Captn. Bragg's in company with eight young ladies, very merry. *Thursday, September 15th, 1774.* Went ashore and dined at the Five Bits Tavern, what they call a Bit is half a Piatereen or

Sixpence sterling. This is one of the cheapest Taverns in town. I believe, there is only two other houses that you can get dinner or anything to eat. Captn. Bragg, Mr. Dotin and four other Gentlemen supped and spent the evening on board the Schooner.

*Friday, September 16th, 1774.* This Island is one of the most windward and eastward of the West India Islands situated in Lat$^d$. 12°°–58″ North. Long$^d$. 58°°–50″ West, about 20 Miles long and 12 broad, contains about 20,000 White Inhabitants and 90,000 Blacks. Exports about 20,000 Hh$^{ds}$ of Sugar and 6000 Hh$^{ds}$. of Rum annually. They are supplied with the greatest part of their provisions from the Colonies and all their slaves and lumber come from there, with Horses and Livestock of all kinds. In exchange for which they give Rum, Sugar and Cotton, but very little of the last article. It is a high rocky Island and reckoned the most healthy Island in the West Indies. I suppose there is one eighth part of the land too rocky for cultivation. The roads are very bad. It is nothing uncommon to see twelve yoke of oxen to draw one Hh$^d$. of Sugar, but their cattle are very small. Their chief produce is Sugar, Indigo, Pimento and Cotton. The Pimento grows on large Trees like small berries, the Cotton on small bushes which they plant annually. The Indigo is planted in the same manner.

There is a great variety of Fruits — Pine Apples, Bananas, a fruit like a large Bean pod very sweet. Plantains something in the same shape, these when roasted are a good substitute for Bread. Alligator Pear or Vegetable Marrow; this is exactly the shape of a Pear, but has a large stone in it, the flesh has the taste and appearance of real Marrow. These all grow on Trees, except the Pine Apple. Tammarinds grow on very large trees, the bodies of the trees are full of prickles like a briar. Shaddocks are a large fruit, like an Orange, but much larger. Limes in plenty. Oranges and Lemons are very indifferent here. Guavas are a small fruit something like a Lime, but have a sickly taste. They make a fine jelly from them. Mamme Apples are larger than an Orange with a stone in them, the flesh has the appearance of a Carrot and tastes something like it. The Mangeneel Apple has the smell and appearance of an English Apple, but small, grows on large trees, generally along the Seashore. They are rank poison. I am told that one apple is sufficient to kill 20 people. This poison is of such a malignant nature that a single drop of rain or dew that falls from the tree upon your skin will immediately raise a blister. Neither Fruit or Wood is of any use, that I can learn. The Cabbage tree is very beautiful, grows very lofty, the bark of a fine green and remarkably smooth, the Fruit is good pickled as Cabbage, but does not appear like it on the tree. The Coco Tree grows to an amazing height, some of them 80 foot, with only a tuft of leaves at top. The Fruit grows at the root of the leaves, as some are ripe others are blossoming, so that they are never without Fruit. It is surprising with what agility the Negroes climb these trees. There is a number of other fruits I am not acquainted with. Yams are like our potatoes but much larger.

This is the chief Town in the Island and was pretty large, but a great part of it burned down in the Year 1766 and is is not yet rebuilt. Here is a Good Church dedicated to St. Michael, with an Organ. The Church yard is planted round with Coco Trees which makes a pretty appearance. The houses are built of stone, but no fireplaces in them only in the Kitchen. The heat of the climate renders that unnecessary, only for cooking. Indeed it would be insupportable was it not for the Sea breeze which blows all day, and from the Land at Night. All the S.E. Part of the Island is fortified with Batteries, the windward part of the Island is fortified by nature. No Garrison or Soldiers here, only the militia which are well disciplined to keep the Negroes in awe. The Planters are in general rich, but a set of dissipating, abandoned, and cruel people. Few even of the married ones, but keep a Mulatto or Black Girl in the house or at lodgings for certain purposes. The women are not killing beauties or very engaging in their conversation, but some of them have large fortunes, which covers a multitude of imperfections. The British nation famed for humanity suffers it to be tarnished by their Creolian Subjects — the Cruelty exercised upon the Negroes is at once shocking to humanity and a disgrace to human nature. For the most trifling faults, sometimes for mere whims of their Masters, these poor wretches are tied up and whipped most unmercifully. I have seen them tied up and flogged with a twisted piece of Cowskin till there was very little signs of Life, then get a dozen with an Ebony sprout which is like a Briar. This lacerates the skin and flesh, and lets out the bruised blood, or it would mortify and kill them. Some of them die under the severity of these barbarities, others whose spirits are too great to submit to the insults and abuses they receive put an end to their own lives. If a person kills a slave he only pays his value as a fine. It is not a hanging matter. Certainly these poor beings meet with some better place on the other side the Grave, for they have a hell on earth. It appears that they are sensible of this, if one may judge from their behaviour at their funerals. Instead of weeping and wailing, they dance and sing and appear to be the happiest mortals on earth. Went with Mr. and Mrs. Dottin to see the Funeral of Mr. Stephenson, a Capital Merchant in Town. Most part of the Men were drunk. No tears shed but by Mulatto Girls. Spent the evening at Captain Braggs. *Saturday, September 17th, 1774.* Dined at Mr. Willing's, got all our cargo on board. Drank Tea at Mr. Dotin's, who is desirous of keeping a correspondence with me. At 8 in the evening weighed Anchor and stood out of the Bay, with a stout breeze at E.N.E.

*Schooner " John" towards Virginia — Sunday, September 18th, 1774.* Fresh breezes and clear weather. Saw Martinico. It appears high land. At 8 P.M. a rainbow by moonlight. *Monday, September 19th, 1774.* Fresh breezes at 2 P.M. saw Monserrat, 4 P.M. abreast Desseada Lat$^d$. 16°°–20" North Long$^d$. 60°°–10" West from whence we take our departure. Seasick. *Saturday, September 24th, 1774.* Pleasant weather for the past four days, but a great deal of Thunder and Lightning. *Sunday, September 25th, 1774.* Pleasant weather, but a foul wind and more lightning, but no Thunder. *Friday, September 30th, 1774.* Moderate breezes and pleasant weather for several days back. Mr. Brooks, the other passenger, I don't expect to live till morning, the Captn. has treated him most barbarously. The Captn. and I have quarrelled about it. (Mem. To give him a drubbing when I get ashore.) *Saturday, October 1st, 1774.* Fine pleasant weather. Saw the body of a Man float alongside. Calm this evening. *Sunday, October 2nd, 1774.* Pleasant weather. Mr. Brooks begins to mend a little, but is in a most shocking condition. *Monday, October 3rd, 1774.* A remarkable whirlwind this morning which put the Vessel about in a Minute and then fell calm for two hours. At 4 P.M. blew very hard at N.E., obliged to lay the Vessel to under her foresail. *Tuesday, October 4th, 1774.* By our reckoning we are pretty near Cape Hatteras. Still lying to under F. Sail. Blowing very hard at N.E. Shipped several heavy Seas, one of which has carried away our Starboard Quarter Rails with three bags of Cotton. Two of them belong to me. This is all my venture, I am now a beggar. This is a stroke of fortune I can badly bear at present, but must submit. Blows very hard and a great Sea.

*Wednesday, October 5th, 1774.* At 4 P.M. the wind came to the Southward, made sail under Fore Sail and Jibb. Have been obliged to eat raw meat the last two days. Very uneasy, but must submit to the Frown of Fortune. Caught a Dolphin, in his belly found a Fish of a peculiar shape. It was about two inches long something like a Frog, but neither Fins or Feet, of a whitish colour and covered over with small prickles like a Hedgehog. Saw a number of Flying Fish. One of them lighted on board the Vessel, shaped like a Trout and about that size. The shoulder Fins are long and thin, with these it is able to fly as long as the Fins keep wet and then they dip in the Sea. By this method they elude the Dolphin which preys upon them. *Thursday, October, 6th, 1774.* Pleasant breezes and clear weather. *Friday, October 7th, 1774.* Fine weather. At 8 P. M. hove the lead, got ground in 15 Fathom sandy bottom. *Saturday, October 8th, 1774.* At 8 this morning got abreast Cape Henry with a fine breeze. At 7 P.M. came to an anchor off the Tanjier Islands. *Sunday, October 9th, 1774.* Calm, diverted ourselves with catching Crabs. *Monday, October 10th, 1774.* Last night it came to blow and obliged us to bear away for the Rappahannock River. Came to an anchor in Fleets Bay. Went ashore with the Mate to buy stock in the character of a Sailor, and have been highly diverted with the frolic. *Tuesday, October 11th, 1774.* Went ashore to Col. Fleets who gave us very bad account of their proceedings in the Colonies. Nothing but War is talked of. Captn. Botson of the Brig *Two Betsys* dined with us. Fair wind this evening, got out of the River.

*Schooner " John," St. Mary's River — Wednesday, October 12th, 1774.* Came to an Anchor in St. Mary's. Went ashore with the Captn. Pleasant weather. *Thursday, October 13th, 1774.* Got up to Cedar Point. The Captn. gone to Port Tobacco for orders. *Friday, October 14th, 1774.* At Anchor. The Captn. returned this evening. *Saturday, October 15th, 1774.* Got into Port Tobacco Creek. The Vessel is to discharge her cargo here. *Sunday, October 16th, 1774.* Went to Port Tobacco Church. Dined in town. Nothing talked of but War with England. After dinner called at Doctor Brown's who proffers to send a Boy and Horses with me to Alexandria. Obliged to lodge at a little House along ashore, could not get on board this evening. *Monday, October 17th, 1774.* Company on board spent the evening very merrily. *Tuesday, October 18th, 1774.* Sent Mr. Knox some sweetmeats and Cocoanuts by the Captn. who is gone to Nanjemoy. Left the Vessel and went to Doctor Brown's.

# IV

## VIRGINIA AGAIN — PROJECTED TRIP
## TO ILLINOIS

*A* LEXANDRIA, *Virginia* — *Wednesday, October 19th,
*1774.* This morning settled with the Doctor who has
charged me 14 Guineas and has the impudence to tell me
it is very cheap. I was obliged to comply with it, and gave
him an order on Mr. Kirk. Got horses and a Boy from
him. Dined at Piscataway. Arrived at Alexandria in the
evening. Mr. Kirk condoles with me on my mis-fortune,
but seems very glad to see me return in good health. He
tells me that he never expected to see me alive again, and
had deferred writing home till the Vessel arrived, supposing
that it would bring news of my death. *Saturday, October
22nd, 1774.* Settling my accounts, which will not turn out
to my satisfaction. *Sunday, October 23rd, 1774.* Went to
Church and heard a very indifferent Sermon. *Monday,
October 24th, 1774.* This morning balanced my accounts
and find myself in debt to Mr. Kirk £47:10:2 Virginia
Currency without one Sixpence in my Pocket. I am under
the disagreeable necessity of drawing on my Father for £50
Sterling. I have no orders for this, but as I have not
wantonly squandered away what he gave me, think it better
to trust to his paternal regard than be in debt without prospect of paying. This gives me much uneasiness but necessity, absolute necessity, compels me to do it.

Everything here is in the utmost confusion. Committees
are appointed to inspect into the Characters and Conduct

of every tradesman, to prevent them selling Tea or buying British Manufactures. Some of them have been tarred and feathered, others had their property burnt and destroyed by the populace. Independent Companies are raising in every County on the Continent, appointed Adjutants and train their Men as if they were on the Eve of a War. A General Congress of the different Colonies met at Philadelphia on the 5th. of last month are still sitting, but their business is a profound secret. Subscription is raising in every Colony on the Continent for the relief of the people of Boston. The King is openly cursed, and his authority set at defiance. In short, everything is ripe for rebellion. The New Englanders by their canting, whining, insinuating tricks have persuaded the rest of the Colonies that the Government is going to make absolute slaves of them. This I believe never was intended, but the Presbyterian rascals have had address sufficient to make the other Colonies come into their Scheme. By everything that I can understand, in the different company I have been in, Independence is what the Massachusetts people aim at, but am not in the least doubt but the Government will take such salutary and speedy measure, as will entirely frustrate their abominable intentions. I am afraid it will be some time before this hubbub is settled and there is nothing to be done now. All trade is almost at a stand, everyone seems to be at a loss in what manner to proceed. For my own part, did I not think this affair would be over in the spring, I would immediately return home. But I am very unwilling to return in a worse condition than I was when I came out and be laughed at by all my friends. If I return now and matters are settled they will never consent to my leaving England again, and I am very sensible from what I have already seen of the Country, that I can with a small sum make a very pretty fortune here, in a little time if I am any ways fortunate, as a Farmer. Mr. Kirk advises me to stay till Spring and take a Tour in the back Country, gives me every possible encouragement, and offers me every assistance in his power. I will take his advice. Am determined not to return till I can do it with credit, without those rascals do persuade the Colonies into a Rebellion. *Tuesday, October 25th, 1774.* This day agreed with Mrs. Fleming to dine at her house everyday at 1ˢ. per day Vir. Currency. I breakfast and sup at Mr. Kirk's. Must live as cheap as possible. *Thursday, October 27th, 1774.* Exceedingly uneasy in mind. I do not know what to do or in what manner to proceed for the best. *Friday, October 28th, 1774.* Supped and spent the evening with Mr. William Horner, a merchant from Liverpool. *Saturday, October 29th, 1774.* The Schooner arrived, got my Chest ashore and paid £20 Vir. Currency for my passage. *Sunday, October 30th, 1774.* Went to Church, a pretty building and large congregation, but an indifferent Parson. *Monday, October 31st, 1774.* Mr. Kirk tries to make my time agreeable, but find myself very low-spirited. Drank Tea and Coffee at Captn. Sandford's.

*Tuesday, November 1st, 1774.* This evening went to the Tavern to hear the Resolves of the Continental Congress. Read a Petition to the Throne and an address to the people of Great Britain. Both of them full of duplicity and false representation. I look upon them as insults to the understanding and dignity of the British Sovereign and people. Am in hopes their petitions will never be granted. I am sorry to see them so well received by the people and the sentiments so universally adopted. It is a plain proof that the seeds of rebellion are already sown and have taken very deep root, but am in hopes they will be eradicated next summer. I am obliged to act the hypocrite and extol these proceedings as the wisest productions of any assembly on Earth, but in my heart I despise them and look upon them with contempt. *Wednesday, November 2nd, 1774.* Writing to my Friends at home. Obliged to put the best side outwards and appear a little Whigified, as I expect my letters will be opened before they get to England. *Thursday, November 3rd, 1774.* Saw the Independent Company exercise. The Effigy of Lord North was shot at, then carried in great parade into the town and burnt. *Saturday, November 5th, 1774.* Wrote to Mr. Champion. It is very hard I cannot write my real sentiments. *Sunday, November 6th, 1774.* Went to a Presbyterian meeting. These are a set of rebellious scoundrels, nothing but political discourses instead of Religious Lectures.

*Monday, November 7th, 1774.* Drew a Bill upon my Father for £50 in favour of Mr. Kirk, payable at Messrs. Greaves, Lofters & Brightmores to Messrs. Broomheads. Forty days after sight. I hope it will be duly honoured or I am forever ruined. The thought makes me miserable. *Tuesday, November 8th, 1774.* Wrote to my Father, but dare not inform him what my intentions are in staying here. *Saturday, November 12th, 1774.* Exceedingly uneasy and low-spirited. Mr. Kirk gives me some hopes of getting a Commission for purchasing Wheat. *Sunday, November 13th, 1774.* Went to Church, but won't go any more to hear their Political Sermons. Captn. Buddecombe's Brig sailed to-day. By her, I sent my letters and a box with some Sweetmeats and Cocoanuts to my Friends. *Wednesday, November 16th, 1774.* Exceedingly unhappy. *Thurs-*

*day, November 17th, 1774.* Went on some business for
Mr. Kirk to Bladensburg in Maryland about 20 Miles from
Alexandria. This is a little town of considerable trade,
but the land about it is sandy and barren. Returned in
the evening. *Friday, November 18th, 1774.* Drank Coffee
at Col. John Carlile's, a gentleman from Carlisle in England. *Thursday, November 24th, 1774.* Waiting in expectation of getting a Wheat Commission, but am disappointed. Great quantities of this article is brought down
from the the back Country in waggons to this place, as good
Wheat as ever I saw in England and sell from 2/9 to 4/6
sterling, per bushel. It is sent to the Eastern markets.
Great quantities of Flour are likewise brought from there,
but this is generally sent to the West Indies, and sometimes
to Lisbon and up the Streights. I am doing nothing here,
am determined to take a Tour immediately. *Friday,
November 25th, 1774.* Hired a Horse and intend to set
out for Berkeley County to-morrow.

*Mosses Ordinary, Loudoun County, Virginia — Satur-
day, November 26th, 1774.* Left Alexandria in company
with Captn. Buddecombe. Got to this place in the evening
about 20 miles from Alexandria. Land pretty level, but
not very good, either stiff brown clay or sand.

*Leesburg, Loudoun County, Virginia — Sunday, Novem-
ber 27th, 1774.* Got to Leesburg, 40 miles from Alexandria. The Land begins to grow better. A Gravelly soil
and produces good Wheat, but the roads are very bad, cut
to pieces with the waggons, number of them we met to-day.
Their method of mending the roads is with poles about 10
foot long laid across the road close together; they stick fast
in the mud and make an excellent causeway. Very thinly
peopled along the road, almost all Woods. Only one pub-

lic House between this place and Alexandria. *Monday, 28th, 1774*. Viewing the town. It is regularly laid off in squares, but very indifferently built and few inhabitants and little trade, tho' very advantageously situated, for it is at the conjunction of the great Roads from the North part of the Continent to the South and the East and West. Lodged at Mr. Moffit's, Mr. Kirk's partner in a store which he has here. *Tuesday, November 29th, 1774*. Went with Captn. Buddecombe about 10 miles into the Country. Find the land stony intermixed with Spar but brings good Wheat.

*Wednesday, November 30th, 1774*. This being the Anniversary of St. Andrew, the titular Saint of the Scotch, was invited to spend the evening with Captn. William Douglas and a number of other Scotch guests. Have been genteelly treated and am now going to bed drunk. This is the first time. *Thursday, December 1st, 1774*. Sick with my last night's debauch.

*Saturday, December 3rd, 1774*. Went to several places in the neighbourhood of the town. The Land is pretty good, but is monopolised and consequently thinly inhabited. Gravelly soil in general. *Sunday, December 4th, 1774*. Went to a Methodist meeting. This Sect is scattered in every place and have got considerable footing here, owing to the great negligence of the Church Parsons. *Monday, December 5th, 1774*. Set out in company with Captn. Buddecombe and Mr. Moffit. Crossed the Blue Ridge. This is a high barren mountain, producing nothing but Pines. It runs North and South through Virginia and Maryland, Carolinas and Pennsylvania. Crossed the Shanandoe River on the west side of the mountain. Here is some of the finest land I have ever seen. This is called Key's ferry. Got to Whitington's Mill. Lodged at a Poor House. The land is exceedingly fine. From the Shands River to this place 80 miles from Alexandria.

*Frederick County, Virginia — Tuesday, December 6th, 1774.* Went from the Mill to a place called Hopewell, a fine plantation belonging to Mr. Jacob Hite. Here is some of the finest land I ever saw either for the plough or pasture. Got to Mr. Wm. Gibbs's, an acquaintance of Mr. Kirk's. We have travelled over some as fine land to-day for about 25 miles as I would wish to see. Limestone in general, abounds with Shumack, Walnut, and Locust trees which are certain indications that the Lands are rich, pretty level, it is rocky in some places, but affords excellent pasturages and well watered. Produces good Wheat and Barley. The people appear to be more industrious in this part of the Country than they are on the other side of the Blue Ridge.

*Wednesday, December 7th, 1774.* Went to Winchester. It is one of the largest towns I have seen in the Colony, the capital of this Colony. Regularly laid out in squares, the buildings are of limestone. Two Churches, one English and one Dutch, but the Dutch Church is not finished. General Braddock built a stockade Fort here, in the year 1755, but it is now demolished.

Saw four Indian Chiefs of the Shawnee Nation, who have been at War with the Virginians this summer, but have made peace with them, and they are sending these people to Williamsburg as hostages. They are tall, manly, well-shaped men, of a Copper colour with black hair, quick piercing eyes, and good features. They have rings of silver in their nose and bobs to them which hang over their upper lip. Their ears are cut from the tips two thirds of the way round and the piece extended with brass wire till it

[ 49 ]

touches their shoulders, in this part they hang a thin silver plate, wrought in flourishes about three inches diameter, with plates of silver round their arms and in the hair, which is all cut off except a long lock on the top of the head. They are in white men's dress, except breeches which they refuse to wear, instead of which they have a girdle round them with a piece of cloth drawn through their legs and turned over the girdle, and appears like a short apron before and behind. All the hair is pulled from their eyebrows and eyelashes and their faces painted in different parts with Vermilion. They walk remarkably straight and cut a grotesque appearance in this mixed dress. Got to Mr. Gibbs's in the evening. *Thursday, December 8th, 1774.* Confined in the House to-day with rain.

*Friday, December 9th, 1774.* Riding about the neighbourhood with Mr. Gibbs. Find the land good, the country healthy and a good neighbourhood. I am exceedingly pleased with these two Counties, and am determined to settle in one of them, if ever these times are settled. Here is every encouragement. Land is purchased at 30 shillings, this currency per acre, that is 26 shillings sterling. It will produce any sort of grain, the average of wheat is about 12 bushels to the acre, but it is not half ploughed and manure of any sort is never used. Meadows may be made with little trouble. and the range for stock is unlimited. Horses sell amazingly high, and fat cattle of all sorts. When lean are bought very cheap. The Farmers here are little acquainted with breeding cattle, indeed they are too lazy. Public taxes are very trifling. Little Tobacco is made in the Counties of Frederick and Barley.

*Leesburg, Loudoun County, Virginia — Saturday, December 10th, 1774.* This morning left Mr. Gibbs, who has behaved with the greatest civility and gave me a pressing invitation to come and spend part of the winter with him. Crossed the Shanandoe River at the fording place, a little above the Ferry. Dined at Pursley's Ordinary on the east side of the Blue Ridge. Got to Leesburg in the evening. Well pleased with my journey. *Sunday, December 11th, 1774.* but no prayers. *Monday, December 12th, 1774.* Court day. A great number of litigious suits. The people seems to be fond of Law. Nothing uncommon for them to bring a suit against a person for a Book debt and trade with him on an open account at the same time. To be arrested for debt is no scandal here. *Tuesday, December 13th, 1774.* Saw the Independence Company exercise. A ragged crew.

*Alexandria, Virginia.— Wednesday, December 14th, 1774.* Returned to Alexandria in company with Captn. Buddecombe and Mr. Maize. *Thursday, December 15th, 1774.* Nothing but Committees and Politics, which puts everything in confusion. *Tuesday, December 20th, 1774.* Exceedingly cold, frosty, and bad weather, the winter is now set in and more severe than ever I felt it in England. Cannot get any sort of employment to get a living, must be obliged to winter here and live as cheaply as I can in hopes that the differences between the Mother Country and the Colonies will be settled in the Spring. *Saturday, December 24th, 1774.* Great quantities of Hogs killed in town. They salt the Pork and export it to the West Indies. It makes a considerable branch of commerce. Sells at 13/6 per hundred. *Sunday, December 25th, 1774.* Christmas Day. But little regarded here. *Saturday, December 31st, 1774.* Mr. Kirk, Captn. Buddecombe and I have spent the past week as merrily as can be expected considering the times. This year ends with confusion, but am in hopes the ensuing one will put an end to the quarrel.

*Sunday, January 1st, 1775.* The Parson is drunk and can't perform the duties of his office. This is the first day of the New Year, which seems to be big with matters of great consequence. I have spent the last to little purpose, but am in hopes things will answer better this. *Wednesday, January 4th, 1775.* Amused myself with shooting wild Geese and Ducks. Here is incredible numbers in the River likewise Swans. It is said they come from the Lakes. *Thursday, January 5th, 1775.* This being my birthday, Mr. Kirk. Captn. Buddecombe, Mr. Wm. Sydebottom and Mr. Fleming, all of them Englishmen, spent the evening with me. All of us very merry and good company. Mr. Sydebottom comes from Marple Bridge.

*Friday, January 6th, 1775.* Mr. Kirk and Mr. Sydebottom have got shares in a large purchase of land in the Illinois Country and have offered me one third part of it at the first cost if I choose to accept it, or they will give me 5000 acres to go and take a view of it for them and to be left to my choice, to take the third of their share at my return. They tell me their influence is pretty considerable with a great many of the other proprietors and they will endeavour to get me a Surveyor's Warrant. As I am not much acquainted with the situation of this country they have given me their Deeds to peruse, and I am to give them my answer in a week. I have just received an invitation ticket to a Ball this evening.

*Saturday, January 7th, 1775.* Last night I went to the Ball. It seems this is one of their annual Balls supported in the following manner: A large rich cake is provided and cut into small pieces and handed round to the company, who at the same time draws a ticket out of a Hat with something merry wrote on it. He that draws the King has the Honor of treating the company with a Ball the next year, which generally costs him Six or Seven Pounds. The Lady that draws the Queen has the trouble of making the Cake. Here was about 37 ladies dressed and powdered to the life, some of them very handsome and as much vanity as is necessary. All of them fond of dancing, but I do not think they perform it with the greatest elegance. Betwixt the Country dances they have what I call everlasting jigs. A couple gets up and begins to dance a jig (to some Negro tune) others comes and cuts them out, and these dances always last as long as the Fiddler can play. This is sociable, but I think it looks more like a Bacchanalian dance than one in a polite assembly. Old Women, Young wives with young children in the lap, widows, maids and girls come promiscuously to these assemblies which generally continue till morning. A cold supper, Punch, Wines, Coffee and Chocolate, but no Tea. This is a forbidden herb. The Men chiefly Scotch and Irish. I went home about two o'clock, but part of the company stayed, got drunk and had a fight. Spent this evening with Mr. Kirk, Capt. Buddecombe, Capt. Wroe, and Capt. Scott at the Tavern very merry.

*Tuesday, January 10th, 1775.* These three days I have spent in making enquiries about the nature and situation of the Land in the Illinois Country, and have fortunately met with two gentlemen who resided there some time. The lands are exceedingly rich, produces Tobacco, Indigo and Wheat, situated at the conjunction of the Ohio with the Mississippi River about 1000 Miles from New Orleans, and 2000 miles from this place. It likewise abounds with Lead and mines of Copper, but very few inhabitants and those French. I am told by these gentlemen that there will be some risk in going down the Ohio River. The Indians often cut the White people off, in their passage down to the Mississippi. I think I have a prospect of making it worth while and will hazard the passage. I have agreed to go if Messrs. Kirk and Sydebottom will use their interest to procure me Surveyor's Warrant. This they have promised to do and will write to Philadelphia to the Gentlemen who are concerned in the purchase in my behalf. Some of the principal people are in England. If I can by any means make Friends sufficient to get their interest, the place of Surveyor will be worth some hundreds a year, exclusive of the opportunities a Surveyor has of taking up lands for himself. If that fails, 5000 acres of land will amply pay me for my trouble of going there, I can do nothing here till times are settled, and am in hopes that I can get back before September next and go home in the fall. By that time I expect this affair will be settled upon a permenent footing. In short, I have no other prospects of making up my losses but this, and I cannot bear the thought of returning a beggar. *Wednesday, January 11th, 1775.* Intend to go to Capt. Knox at Nanjemoy to get some instructions in surveying from him.

*Brig "Potomeck" — Thursday, January 12th, 1775.* This morning came on board the Brig *Potomeck*, Capt. Wroe. Got around at Rozious Bluff. The sharpest frost I ever knew. The spittle freezes before it falls to the deck. *Friday, January 13th, 1775.* Fell down to Crany Island. *Saturday, January 14th, 1775.* Got to Checamuxen. Went ashore and dined at Mr. Wm. Smallwood's.

*Nanjemoy, Maryland — Sunday, January 15th, 1775.*

Got to Nanjemoy in the night. *Monday, January 16th, 1775.* Captn. Knox seems very glad to see me. Introduced me to his brother, and will give me every instruction that is in his power. *Tuesday, January 17th, 1775.* Went over the River to Mr. John Alexander's. Dined there. Returned in the evening. *Saturday, January 21st, 1775.* Industriously employed these four days with Captn. Knox in surveying a tract of land. *Sunday, January 22nd, 1775.* Dined at Mrs. Marsden's on a roasted Swan. The Flesh appears black, but eats very well. *Monday, January 23rd, 1775.* Went with Captn. Robert Knox to a plantation of his called Thornsgat. On our return dined at a Public House called the *Trap*, after dinner went to Ignatius Ryan's and danced most part of the night with some young ladys. *Tuesday, January 24th, 1775.* Most part of this day at Mr. Ryan's, got to Nanjemoy in the evening. *Wednesday, January 25th, 1775.* This morning saw a Negro Quarter of Mrs. Marsden's burnt down. In the evening went on board a Brig called the *Renfew*. Capt. James Somerville with Capt. Knox. Both got drunk. *Thursday, January 26th, 1775.* Sick with my last night's debauch. *Tuesday, January 31st, 1775.* Employed for several days in drawing plots and practising the different branches of surveying. Find it very easy in the woods from what it is in enclosed lands.

*Stafford County, Virginia — Wednesday, February 1st, 1775.* Left Nanjemoy in company with Captn. Alexander Knox. Lodged at Mr. Richard Fouxe's. *Thursday, February 2nd, 1775.* Travelled over some hilly broken bad land about 14 Miles. Lodged at Pilchard's Ordinary. *Friday, February 3rd, 1775.* Got breakfast at a Plantation of Captn. Knox's in Acquire County. In the evening got to another Plantation of his in Stafford County. *Saturday, February 4th, 1775.* Dined at Captn. Innis's, and spent the afternoon in company with two agreeable ladies. *Sunday, February 5th, 1775.* Dined at Mr. Bailey Washington's *Monday, February 6th, 1775.* Drank Coffee at Capt. Innis's. The Land in this neighbourhood is sandy and poor. Obliged to dung their Tobacco grounds. Sells at 35s. Currency per acre. *Tuesday, February 7th, 1775.* Dined at Mr. John Raules's, an Englishman. *Wednesday, February 8th, 1775.* Left Buloe. Crossed the Rappahannock River. Lodged at Fredericksburg.

*Fredericksburg, Virginia — Thursday, February 9th, 1775.* This is a pretty large town, situated at the falls of the River on the West Bank. The River is navigable for vessels of considerable burden up to the town. Great quantities of Tobacco is shipped from this place. Saw the Independent Companies exercise. They make a poor appearance. Dined with Mr. William Horner. After dinner crossed the River and went to Mr. John Tollever's. *Friday, February 10th, 1775.* The land is pretty good in this neighbourhood and produces a great deal of Wheat. Saw a machine for threshing wheat with horses. After dinner went to Mr. Horatio Dave's in Stafford County. *Saturday, February 11th, 1775.* Got to Mr. John Alexander's. *Sunday, February 12th, 1775.* At Mr. Alexander's, the wind is too fresh. Can't cross the River. This is a most abominable cold house and bad fires.

*Nanjemoy, Maryland — Monday, February 13th, 1775.* Got to Nanjemoy in the evening. This jaunt has only cost me 5s. Vir. Currency. The people are remarkably hospitable — are affronted if you don't call at their house, even if you are a perfect stranger. *Saturday, February 18th,*

*1775.* Very busy with Captn. Knox all this week in running the courses of his plantation and jaunting about in the neighbourhood.

I understand the Committee are going to take me up for a Spy. I will save them the trouble by decamping immediately. The Committees act as Justices. If any person is found to be inimical to the liberties of America, they give them over to the mobility to punish as they think proper, and it is seldom they come off without tarring and feathering. It is as much as a person's life is worth to speak disrespectfully of the Congress. The people are arming and training in every place. They are all liberty mad.

*Monday, February 20th, 1775.* Left Captn. Knox, who has treated me with the greatest kindness and civility. Went to Captn. Fouxe's, spent an agreeable evening with the Misses Fouxes, who sang and played very well upon the Spinet. *Tuesday, February 21st, 1775.* Went to Doctor Brown's at Port Tobacco. *Wednesday, February 22nd, 1775.* Left Doctor Brown's and went to Mr. Frank Marsden's. Found my old fellow-traveller, Mr. Brooks, very well, contrary to expectation. *Friday, February 24th, 1775.* At Mr. Marsden's, shooting wild Geese and Ducks, of which there is incredible numbers. I am told 60 ducks have been killed at one shot. *Saturday, February 25th, 1775.* Mr. Brooks sent his boy and horses with me to Alexandria. He is exceedingly grateful for the assistance I gave him in his passage from Barbados. Mustering in every Village, they will all be soldiers by and by. Confusion to them altogether.

*Alexandria, Virginia — Sunday, February 26th, 1775.* No letters from home. I am afraid none will arrive, while the times are in such confusion. The rascals seize all Foreign letters. *Monday, February 27th, 1775.* Mr. Kirk informs me he has received letters from Philadelphia and assures me of a Surveyor's deputation, admit I can get the consent of the Gentlemen Proprietors at home. I am determined to risk this, and my life. Have confirmed the bargain for to take the 5000 acres for going to view the land at my own expense, and the first refusal of the third of Mr. Kirk and Sydebottom's share. I can carry out some Silver trinkets and barter with the Indians for Furs, and probably do something more than bear my expenses, as I can get what credit I please. *Tuesday, February 28th, 1775.* This is the last day Tea is allowed to be drank on the Continent, by an act of Congress. The ladies seem very sad about it.

*Wednesday, March 1st, 1775.* Mr. Finley, a Gentleman who has been at the Illinois, advises me not to set out till the latter end of April, then to go down the Ohio River with the flood. I believe, there will be some difficulty in persuading any one to go with me in this place. *Thursday, March 9th, 1775.* These eight days have made it my business to find out a person proper to go with me, but can find none that are willing to undertake the journey. I intend to go to Mr. Gibbs, as the likeliest place to get a man for my purpose. *Thursday, March 16th, 1775.* Employed this week in preparing for my journey. Got some Silver trinkets made by a Silversmith in town, by the directions of Mr. Finley, who has been an Indian Trader and has given me some general instructions concerning the trade. *Friday, March 17th, 1775.* Went to a Ball made by the Irish Gentry in commemoration of St. Patrick, the titular Saint of the Irish. Conducted with great decorum. Just going to bed at two o'clock in the morning.

*Saturday, March 18th, 1775.* This day the Gentlemen

and Mechanic Independent Companies reviewed by Colnl. George Washington. All of them in uniform. The Gentlemen, blue and buff. The Mechanics red and blue. In all about 150 men, and make a formidable appearance. *Sunday, March 19th, 1775.* The Parson is too lazy to preach. *Tuesday, March 21st, 1775.* Preparing for my journey. Got my silver ware packed up in as small a compass as possible. Mr. Finley advises me to trade with a party of Delawares that are settled on the Øuabash River for Beaver skins. Mr. Finley gave me a letter of credit to Mr. Richard Winston at Kafkasky Village, Illinois.

*Wednesday, March 22nd, 1775.* This day a certain Richard Taylor from Tideswell came to town with a quantity of Rum. Spent the evening at Mr. Kirk's. Sensible, industrious man. *Thursday, March 23rd, 1775.* Bought me a Gun, Powder, and lead. *Friday, March 24th, 1775.* Mr. Henly, Mr. Caul, and Mr. Richard Harrison spent the evening at Mr. Kirk's. A dispute arose (about politics) between Mr. Kirk and Captn. Buddecombe, they differed in sentiments and abused each other most unmercifully. It is most absurd for individuals to quarrel about state affairs. Both of them remain obstinate. *Saturday, March 25th, 1775.* Wrote to my Father. Intend to set out for Mr. Gibb's to-morrow. Mr. Kirk and the Captn. refuse to be reconciled. (Mem. Never to enter into Political disputes with Mr. Kirk. He has rebellious principles.)

*Leesburg, Loudoun County, Virginia — Sunday, March 26th, 1775.* Left Alexandria in company with Captn. Buddecombe. Dined at Moss's Ordinary. Got to Leesburg in the evening. *Monday, March 27th, 1775.* Went with Captn. Buddecombe to Mr. Canby, who informs me Mr. Edward Snickers is the likeliest person to get me a guide. Gave me a letter of Introduction to Mr. Snickers. *Tuesday, March 28th, 1775.* Captn. Buddecombe set out for Alexandria and intends to go to England, the first opportunity. This Gentleman has always behaved to me with the greatest civility and kindness, but think him rather too much of a Sycophant. *Wednesday, March 29th, 1775.* Went to look at a silver mine. Saw some appearance of metal, but don't know what it is. *Friday, March 31st, 1775.* At Leesburg waiting for my gun and goods coming from Alexandria. The Peach Orchards are in full blossom and make a beautiful appearance. *Saturday, April 1st, 1775.* Wrote to Mr. Kirk and Captn. Buddecombe. *Sunday, April 2nd, 1775.* But no Parson. It is a shame to suffer these people to neglect their duty in the manner they do.

*Winchester, Frederick County, Virginia.* — *Monday, April 3rd, 1775.* Got my things from Alexandria. Hired a Horse for £4 Currency from Mr. Moffit to carry me to Fort Pitt. Left Leesburg. Crossed the Blue Ridge at Snicker's Gap. B.O.B. Dined at Mr. Snickers but he is not at home, but his Son-in-law gave me a letter to a certain George Rice, whom he recommends as a proper person to go with me. Crossed the Shanandoe River. Got to Winchester. Land is very rich from the River to the town. All Limestone, well watered and very level. I am sorry it is not in my power to settle here. Winchester is about 80 miles from Alexandria. *Tuesday, April 4th, 1775.* Met with Mr. Gibbs and George Rice. Mr. Gibbs recommends him as an honest man and a good hunter. Agreed to give him 500 acres of land to go with me. He is going to his brother's near Fort Pitt with two horses and intends to set out to-morrow. This is very lucky. Bought some Blankets, Gunpowder, lead, flints, camp kettle, frying pan and tomahawk, with several other necessaries. Got letters of introduction to several Gentlemen in the neighbourhood of Fort Pitt from Mr. John Neville. Gave my boots and spurs to the care of Mr. Gibbs till my return. Must wear leggings. These are pieces of coarse woollen cloth wrapped round the leg and tied below the knee with a string to prevent the snakes biting you.

*Winchester, Frederick County, Virginia — Wednesday, April 5th, 1775.* After dinner left Winchester and got to Rinker's Tavern 10 Miles from Winchester. Captn. Douglas and Mr. Valentine Crawford came here this evening. They are going to Fort Pitt. Land is good from Winchester to this place. *Thursday, April 6th, 1775.* Left Rinkers in company with Captn. Douglas and Mr. Crawford. Breakfasted at the Dry Tavern, a little Dutch house, nothing to drink but Whiskey. Crossed the Cape Capon Creek and north branch of Potowmeck River. Captn. Douglas and Mr. Crawford left us. We had travelled about 30 miles to-day over barren hills and bad ways, and we are now going to sleep in the open air, no other covering than the Heavens and our Blankets, and it is very cold and freezes. But we have got a good fire.

## V

## OVER HILL AND STREAM — THE
## KENTUCKY RIVER

*APPALACHIAN Mountain—Friday, April 7th, 1775.* Slept very little last night  Mr. Rice tells me it is because I did not take off my clothes.   Water frozen in Kettle about 10 foot from the fire.   Crossed Little Cape Capon Creek and the south mountain, which is one entire rock.   Dined at Runnel's Tavern.   Travelled over barren hills to Ashby's Fort on Patterson's Creek.   Camped about 2 miles to the West of it.   About 30 miles to-day.  *Saturday, April 8th, 1775.*   Slept very well last night, considering the hardness of our bed.   Crossed the Knobby Mountain. Called at Creig's Tavern for a supply of Rum, then over the Devil's Hunting Ground to Tittle's Tavern.   This is the worst road I ever saw, large rocks and bogs.   Crossed the Savage Mountain and through the Shades of Death. This is one of the most dismal places I ever saw.   The lofty Pines obscure the Sun, and the thick Laurels are like a Hedge on each side, the Road is very narrow and full of large stones and bogs.   I measured a Pine that was blown down, 130 ft. long.   Camped about 2 miles west of the Shades. 28m.  *Sunday, April 9th, 1775.*   Crossed the Little Meadow Mountain, supposed to be the highest part of the Appalachian or Allegany Mountain.   The waters begin to fall to the westward.   Crossed the Negro Mountain and the winding ridge.   Crossed the line between Maryland and Pennsylvania.   It is cut through the woods in a west course from some part of Delaware Bay about 20 yards wide. It is on the top of the winding ridge. Crossed the Yaughaganey River at the Begg crossings. Camped 2 miles west of it. Shot some Pheasants, which have made a good supper.

*Monday, April 10th, 1775.* Crossed the Fallen Timbers. Occasioned by a violent gust of wind from the east. The Trees are either torn up by the roots or broke off near the ground. Some Oaks 2 foot diameter are broke off and the tops carried to a considerable distance. Scarcely one tree left standing. I am told it continues 100 Miles in a west course and about a mile broad. Dined at the Great Meadows, a large marshy place clear of trees. Saw the vestiges of Fort Necessity. This was a small picketed Fort built by Colnl. Washington in the year 1754. About a mile to the westward of this Fort, General Braddock is buried at a small Run. They tell me he was buried in the middle of the road to prevent the Indians digging up his body. Crossed the Laurel Mountain. Saw the place where Colonel Dunbar was encamped when he received the news of General Braddock's defeat in 1755. Great quantities of broken Bombshells, cannon, bullets, and other military stores scattered in the woods. This is called the Laurel Mountain from the great quantities of Laurel that grow upon it. A most delightful prospect of the country to the westward of it. Called at Gist's Fort. Crossed the Yaughagany River at the Steward's Crossings. Got to Zachariah Connel's, Brother-in-law to George Rice. Much fatigued this evening. Heavy rain most part of the day.

*West Augusta County, Virginia,—Tuesday, April 11th, 1775.* The Appalachian or Allegany Mountain is not one entire Mountain, but a number piled one on the top of another, with some narrow Valleys between them. The mountains are barren and rocky, but the Valleys tho' very narrow are in general rich, very thinly inhabited. The road is but very indifferent, tho' loaded waggons frequently cross it in the Summer. Here is some excellent land about this place and all the way from the foot of the mountain. Every necessary of life is very dear here, provisions in particular, occasioned by the Indian War last Summer. Grain is not to be got for money. In the evening went to Mr. Valentine Crawford's with Captn. Douglas. With much difficulty have got half a bushel of Rye for my horse.

*Wednesday, April 12th, 1775.* Went with Captn. Douglas to Captn. John Stephenson's. This Gentleman is a great Indian Warrior, but appears to be a good-natured man. *Thursday, April 13th, 1775.* Captn. Stephenson advises me to build our canoe here, provisions are cheaper than at Fort Pitt. Rice professes to be a Carpenter and understands the building of them, is acquainted here and will undertake to have one finished in a fortnight. *Friday, April 14th, 1775.* This morning, Rice and another man begun to cut down a tree to make a Canoe. Have left it entirely to his management. Captn. Douglas and Captn. Stephenson to the Steward's Crossings to Major Crawford's. Returned to V. Crawford's in the evening. Agreed to go with Captn. Douglas to Fort Pitt to-morrow. *Saturday, April 15th, 1775.* Left Mr. Crawford's in company with Captn. Douglas. Crossed Jacob's Creek and Saweekly Creek. Got to Mr. John De Camp's. Land very rich and level.

*Fort Pitt, Virginia — Sunday, April 16th, 1775.* Left Mr. De Camp's. Travelled over small hills, woods, and dirty roads to Bush Creek, called at a Mill where by acting the Irishman, got a feed of Corn for our horses. Crossed Turtle Creek. Dined at Myer's Ordinary. After dinner got a man to conduct us to the place where General Braddock was defeated by the French and Indians the 9th. July 1755. It is on the Banks of the Mon-in-ga-ha-ly River. Found great numbers of bones, both men and horses. The trees are injured, I suppose by the Artillery. It appears to me the front of our Army never extended more than 300 yards and the greatest slaughter seems to have been made within 400 yards of the River, where it is level and full of underwood. Farther from the River it is hilly and some rocks where the enemy would still have the advantage of the ground. We could not find one whole skull, all of them broke to pieces in the upper part, some of them had holes broken in them about an inch diameter, suppose it to be done with a Pipe Tomahawk. I am told the wounded were all massacred by the Indians. Got to Fort Pitt in the evening. Land very good, but thinly inhabited. Our landlord seems to be very uneasy to know where we come from.

*Monday, April 17th, 1775.* After breakfast waited on Major John Connoly, Commandant at the Fort, to whom I had a letter of introduction. Find him a haughty, imperious man. In the afternoon, viewing the town and Fort. It is pleasantly situated at the conjunction of the Moningahaley and Allegany Rivers, the Moningahaley on the S.W. and the Allegany on the North side the town. These two rivers make the Ohio. The town is small, about 30 houses, the people chiefly in Indian trade. The Fort is some distance from the town close in the forks of the Rivers. It was built originally by the French, deserted by them, and the English took possession of it under the Command of

General Forbes, November 24th, 1758. Besieged by the Indians but relieved by Colonel Bouquet in August, 1763. Deserted and demolished by own troops about three years ago, but repaired last summer by the Virginians and has now a small garrison in it. It is a pentagonal form. Three of the Bastions and two of the curtains faced with brick, the rest picketed. Barracks for a considerable number of men, and there is the remains of a genteel house for the Governor, but now in ruins, as well as the Gardens which are beautifully situated on the Banks of the Allegany well planted with Apple and Peach trees. It is a strong place for Musketry, but was cannon to be brought against it, very defenceless, several eminences within Cannon Shot. Spent the evening at Mr. Gambel's, an Indian Trader in town.

*West Augusta County, Virginia — Tuesday, April 18th, 1775.* This morning Mr. Gambel informed me that Adam Grant lived about 12 Miles from town. Left Fort Pitt. Dined at Turtle Creek. Escaped drowning very narrowly in crossing Turtle Creek. Got to Adam Grant's late in the evening. Great scarcity of every necessary of life in this house, but the man is glad to see us and gives us the best he has got with a hearty welcome. He has got a small tub mill and land enough, but it is of little value in this part of the world. Very heavy rain all day. *Wednesday, April 19th, 1775.* Left Adam Grant's. Got to Saweekly Creek, but it is too high to Ford. Returned to Mr. De Camps. We have been lost several times to-day. The by-roads are only small narrow paths through the woods and in some places not the least appearance of a road. *Thursday, April 20th, 1775.* Left Mr. De Camp's. Crossed Jacob Creek and Saweekly Creek. George Rice has joined some other people that are going down the Ohio in assisting them to Build canoe. They go about 600 Miles down the River and will be ready to set out in eight or ten days.

*Friday, April 21st, 1775.* This day made a full agreement with George Rice to go with me to the Illinois Country, on condition that I will wait for him at the Kentucky River Ten days. I have agreed to do this and give him 500 acres of Land for his trouble. This Contract was made before Captn. William Douglas, who wants to take one half of my purchase, paying half my expenses in going to the Illinois and coming back. Am to give him a positive answer in two days. Wrote to Mr. Kirk. *Saturday, April 22nd, 1775.* Employed in getting provisions for the voyage. *Sunday, April 23rd, 1775.* Went to Major Crawford's, who gave me an account of the different Rivers on the Ohio and the distances between them. *Monday, April 24th, 1775.* Employed in getting provisions. Find them very scarce and dear. *Tuesday, April 25th, 1775.* Agreed to let Captn. Douglas have one half of any land I may purchase of Mr. Kirk or Mr. Sydebottom at the Illinois. He is to pay half my expenses there. Have nothing to do with the Land that Messrs. Kirk & Sydebottom give me, or anything to do as a Surveyor. Wrote to Mr. Kirk that will take his share if the times are settled as formerly. Captn. Douglas is to advance all the money and I am to pay no interest for Five years after the money is paid. I have now a prospect of making money without advancing any. This suits my circumstances very well. *Thursday, April 27th, 1775.* Got our Canoes finished and our provisions collected together. Intend to set out to-morrow.

*Yaughagany River, Virginia — Friday, April 28th, 1775.* Left part of my clothes with Mr. Crawford till my return.

Parted with Captn. Douglas by whom I returned the Horse. Launched our Canoes. One of them we called the *Charming Sally*, the other *Charming Polly*. They are 30 foot long and about 20 inches wide, made of Walnut trees, dug out something like a manger. Proceeded down the Yaughagany River. Obliged to get Pilots to carry the Canoes down the Falls, very bad navigation. Full of dangerous rapids. Camped at Washington's Bottom, expect the rest of the company to join us in the morning. I may now bid adieu to sleeping in beds or houses for some months. *Saturday, April 29th, 1775.* This morning we were joined by Mr. James Nourse, an English gentleman going down to the Kentucky River to take up land in right of his Brother who is an Officer in the Navy, Mr. Benjamin Johnston and Captn. Edmund Taylor, who are going to take up land on the Kentucky River. Got all our provisions on board. Mr. Nourse, Captn. Taylor, Mr. Nourse's servant, and me in the *Charming Sally*, Mr. Johnston, his servant, George Rice, Captn. Taylor's Brother and a servant of his in the *Charming Polly*, proceeded down the River to the mouth of Saweekly Creek. The navigation very bad. Obliged to push the Canoes over the shoals for two miles together. A great number of rapids, is a very dangerous navigation. Mr. Nourse insists on me taking one half of his tent; this is very agreeable.

*Sunday, April 30th, 1775.* This day we have been detained by the rain. Settled our accounts concerning Vessels and provisions. The Land from the foot of the Laurel Mountain to Fort Pitt is rich beyond conception. Walnut and Cherry Trees grow to an amazing size. I have seen several three foot diameter and 40 foot before they come to a limb. Great plenty of Wild Plum Trees and a Species of the Pimento, these are small Bushes. The soil in general is Black and of a Fat Loamy nature. Coal and Limestone in the same quarry. I have seen stratums of Coal 14 feet thick equal in quality to the English Coal. Land is at a very low rate, 1000 acres might be purchased for £100 Pennsylvany Currency. Very thinly inhabited. The few there is, are in general great rascals.

*Yaughagany River, Virginia* — *Monday, May 1st, 1775.* After breakfast left Saweekly and stood down the River. Crossed several Fish pots. These fish pots are made by throwing up the small stones and gravel something like a mill weir, beginning at the side of the River and proceeding in a diagonal line, till they meet in the middle of the stream, where they fix a thing like the body of a cart, contracted where the water flows in just to admit the fish, but' so contrived as to prevent their return or escape. Got over the shoals by hauling our canoes. Fell into the Mon-in-ga-ha-ley about noon. Eat our dinner at Magee's Fort. This is a stockade fort, built the last summer.

*Mon-in-ga-ha-ley River* — *Monday, May 1st, 1775.* This River is about 100 yards broad and it confluxes with the Yaughagany, and has continued its breadth. Upon the banks of this river, where they are high and broken, I observed stratums of leaves about a foot thick twenty foot below the surface of the earth. They appeared to be sound and not concreted together, much like those that are driven together by winds in autumn. Fell down a little below Braddock's Field, where we camped in a heavy shower of rain. One of our company shot a wild Turkey, which made us an excellent supper.

*Ohio River* — *Tuesday, May 2nd, 1775.* Proceeded down the River. Our Canoes are so heavily loaded that we

[69]

are in great danger of oversetting, the water is within three inches of the gunnel which adds to the exceeding crankness of our vessel and makes me uneasy. Called at Fort Pitt and bought some necessaries such as lead, flints and some silver trinkets to barter with the Indians. Dined at Mr. John Campbell's. After dinner proceeded down the Ohio River. Passed McKey's Island, it is about a mile long, and belongs to Captn. Alexander McKey, Superintendent of Indian affairs. Camped at the lower end of Monture's Islands, three fine Islands belonging to John Monture, a half Indian. The Land exceedingly rich. *Wednesday, May 3rd, 1775.* This morning Mr. Robert Bell and one Harrison left us to go to their plantations in this neighbourhood. They had come with us from Yaughagany River and have been very serviceable in instructing us how to navigate our little barks. Proceeded down the River, passed Logg's Town (an old Indian town but now deserted). It is on the W. side, then Bigg Beaver Creek on the W., then little Beaver Creek on the W., neither of them so large, but they may be foul in dry weather. A little before dark stopped at a farmer's house to bake bread. Agreed to lash our vessels together and float all night. The River is very high and rapid, suppose we can float two miles in an hour. *Thursday, May 4th, 1775.* In the morning found ourselves opposite Yellow Creek on the W. Very heavy rain for several hours. Very few inhabitants, not a house to be seen in 40 miles, tho' the land is exceedingly rich, in general. The River is exceedingly crooked, full of small Islands and rapid. If there is high land on one side there is always a rich level bottom on the opposite shore. Got to Wheeling Creek, Fort Fincastle on the East side of the River. This is a quadrangular picketed Fort on a little hill beside the River, built last summer by Lord Dunmore, a small garrison in it. Here we took into our company Captn. George Clark. Lashed our canoes together and drifted all night. Stopped at Grave Creek about 2 in the morning.

*Friday, May 5th, 1775.* Got up very early and went to view the Grave. It bears East of the River, about a mile from it and above the mouth of the Creek. The great Grave is a round hill something like a sugar loaf about 300 feet in circumference at bottom, 100 feet high and about 60 feet diameter at top where it forms a sort of irregular basin. It has several large trees upon it, but I could not find any signs of brick or stone on it, seems to have been a trench about it. There is two other hills about 50 yards from this, but not much larger than a Charcoal pit and much in that shape, with other antique vestiges. Some appear to have been works of defence but very irregular. *Friday, May 5th, 1775.* All these Hills appear to have been made by human art, but by whom, in what age, or for what use I leave it for more able antiquarians to determine. The Indians' tradition is that there was a great Battle fought here and many great Warriors killed. These mounds were raised to perpetuate their memory. The truth of this I will not pretend to assert. Proceeded down the River, entertained with a number of delightful prospects in their nature, wild yet truly beautiful. Passed several Creeks and small Islands, few inhabitants but rich land. Got to the head of the long reach where we have a view of the River for 15 miles. Drifted all night. *Saturday, May 6th, 1775.* Found ourselves opposite Muddy Creek. The heavy rain obliged us to take shelter in a lone house and stay all night.

*Sunday, May 7th, 1775.* This morning Captn. Clark (who I find is an intelligent man) showed me a root that the Indians call pocoon, good for the bite of a Rattle Snake. The root is to be mashed and applied to the wound, and a decoction made of the leaves which the patients drink. The roots are exceedingly red, the Indians use it to paint themselves with sometimes. Left Muddy Creek, passed two small Islands to the Big tree Island, so called from the number of large trees upon it. Went ashore on the Big tree Island and measured a large Sycamore tree. It was 51 feet 4 inches in circumference one foot from the ground, and 46 foot circumference five feet from the ground, and I suppose it would have measured that twenty feet high. There are several large trees, but I believe that these exceed the rest. One of the company caught a large Catfish which made a most delicious pot of Soup. Past the Muskingum River on the W. Fine land between that and the little Muskingum. Passed the Little Kanhawa River on the East. Barren land about the mouth of it. Stopped to cook our supper at Fort Gower, a little picketed Fort built last summer, but now deserted at the mouth of Hokkskin on the W. Drifted all night. *Monday, May 8th, 1775.* Heavy rain this morning which obliged us to make a sort of awning with our tent cloths and blankets. Got round the Horseshoe, a large curve of about 4 Miles made by the River in the form of a horseshoe from whence it takes its name. Here is excellent land. Passed a number of small Islands. River continues rapid. Camped about 4 Miles below the Horseshoe, where we met with some people who gave us very bad encouragement, say that the Indians are broke out again and killed four men on the

Kentucky River. My courageous companions' spirits begin
to droop.

*Tuesday, May 9th, 1775.* Proceeded down the River.
Passed four Islands. About noon got to the mouth of the
Great Kanhaway or Conhanway River. Here is a large
picketed fort called Fort Blair, built last summer by Colnl.
Andrew Lewis, who entirely defeated the Shawannee Indians about a mile from it, in August 1774. It is now
garrisoned with 100 Men, under Captn. Russell, who invited us to dine with him, and treated us as well as his
situation would admit. Confirms the account we heard
yesterday. My companions exceedingly fearful and I am
far from being easy, but am determined to proceed as far as
anyone will keep me company. Drifted all night. *Wednesday, May 10th, 1775.* Found ourselves opposite Guian-
dot Creek on the east side the River. Rowed hard and got
to Sandy Creek to breakfast, where we found Captn. Charles
Smith encamped with 22 men. He was taking up land as
we are now out of the inhabitants. I intend to stay here
for Captn. Lee. *Thursday, May 11th, 1775.* Employed
in washing our linen and mending our clothes. *Friday,
May 12th, 1775.* This day held a Council whether we
should proceed or turn back. After much altercation our
company determined to persevere, tho' I believe they are
a set of Dammd cowards. With much persuasion prevailed
upon them to let me endeavour to make our Vessels more
safe and commodious. This has been a most arduous task
to effect, so difficult it is to beat these people out of their
own course when it is for their safety.

*Saturday, May 13th, 1775.* Camped at the mouth of
Sandy Creek. Employed in fixing our Canoes together by
two beams, one athwart the heads, the other at the stern,

setting the Canoes about one foot apart. In the middle of the aftermost piece, I fixed a strong pin, on that hung the rudder, made something like an oar, but bent down towards the water and projected about two feet astern of the Vessel, rigged her out with four oars and called her the *Union*. Some of our company laughs at it and declare she will not answer the helm. But it pleases me well and hope it will deceive them. *Sunday, May 14th, 1775.* Camped at the mouth of Sandy Creek. This morning very wet. After breakfast Mr. Edmund Taylor and I entered into discourse on politics which ended in high words. Taylor threatened to tar and feather me. Obliged to pocket the affront. Find I shall be torified if I hold any further confab with these red-hot liberty men. (Mem. Taylor's usage to be remembered.) *Monday, May 15th, 1775.* Left Sandy Creek. Captn. Lee not arrived. Find our Vessel answers well and gives universal satisfaction to the company. One of the company shot a turtle which made us an excellent supper. Land good and level in general. All of us strangers to the River. Drifted all night, but keep watch, spell and spell about. *Tuesday, May 16th, 1775.* Passed the mouth of the Sioto River in the night. This river is on the N.W. side. Stopped to cook our breakfast on a small gravelly Island where we found plenty of Turtle eggs, with which we made pancakes equal in goodness to those made with hen's eggs. It must be people of a nicer taste than me that can distinguish the difference. These animals come out of the water and lay their eggs in the sand to be hatched by the Sun. They are white, but smaller than those of a hen and perfectly round with a tough skin instead of a shell. The inside has all the appearance of a fowl's egg. Generally find about twenty together, about two inches below

the surface. *Tuesday, May 16th, 1775.* After breakfast
attempted to fix a sail in our Vessel but the wind soon blew
up the River which rendered it useless. Passed several
Creeks and Islands, but unknown to us. This evening Mr.
Rice and I went ashore and each of us killed a wild Turkey,
which made us an excellent supper. Drifted all night.
*Wednesday, May 17th, 1775.* This morning did not know
where we were, or whether we had passed the mouth of any
River in the night. I believe our watch had slept most of
the night. Fell down to a Creek. By the description Mr.
Johnston had from his Brother we take it to be Bracken
Creek.

*Wednesday, May 17th, 1775.* Stopped at Bracken Creek
and went a hunting as they call it here. Mr. Rice, Johnston
and I went together. In a short time Mr. Rice fired at a
Buffalo. Johnston and I went to him and found him standing behind a tree loading his Gun and the beast laid down
about 100 yds. from him. As soon as he was ready we
fired at him again, upon which he got up and run about a
quarter of a mile, where our dogs bayed him till we came
up and shot him. It was a large Bull, from his breast to
the top of his shoulder measuring 3 feet, from his nose
to his tail 9 feet 6 inches, black and short horns, all before
his shoulders long hair, from that to the tail as short as
a mouse. I am certain he would have weighed a thousand.
Camped a little below the Creek. *Thursday, May 18th,
1775.* All hands employed in curing our Buffalo meat,
which is done in a peculiar manner. The meat is first cut
from the bones in thin slices like beefsteaks, then four
forked sticks are stuck in the ground in a square form, and
small sticks laid on these forks in the form of a gridiron
about three feet from the ground. The meat is laid on this

and a slow fire put under it, and turned until it is done. This is called jerking the meat. I believe it is an Indian method of preserving meat. It answers very well, where salt is not to be had, and will keep a long time if it be secured from the wet. The lean parts eat very dry. The Buffalo flesh differs little from beef, only ranker taste. Hot weather.

*Friday, May 19th, 1775.* Proceeded down the River. Passed the mouth of the little Miamme River on the N.W. and Salt River or Licking Creek on the S.E. Saw an Elk and a Bear cross the River, but could not get a shot at them. Got to the mouth of the Great Miamme River on the N.W. It is about 100 Yds. wide at the mouth and appears to be pretty gentle current. Stopped to cook and take a view of the land on the S.E. side of the Ohio River. It is a little hilly but rich beyond conception. Wild Clover, what they here call wild Oats and Wild Rye in such plenty it might be mown and would turn out a good crop. The great quantity of grass makes it disagreeable walking. The land is thin of timber and little underwood. Drifted all night.

*Saturday, May 20th, 1775.* In the morning in doubt whether we had passed Elephant Bonelick or not. Went ashore at a small Creek on the S.W. side in quest of it, but in vain. Believe we are too low down the River according to our Charts. Begun to rain about noon. Floated down the River till night where we moored to a stump in the middle of the stream. Some of our company are in a panic about the Indians again. Shot at a Panther this afternoon, but missed him. Hot weather with Thunder.

*Kentucky River — Sunday, May 21st, 1775.* Proceeded down the River. About noon, got to the mouth of the Kentucky River on the S.E. side. The Ohio is about three quarters of a mile wide here, the Kentucky is about 130 yards wide at the mouth and continued its width about two miles when we camped in a Beechey bottom. Our company in great fear of the Indians. Some of them insisted on sleeping without a fire. After a long contest it was agreed to put the fire out when we went to sleep, but I believe it was not done. Whatever my companions may be, I am not uneasy. I suppose it is because I do not know the danger of our situation. Rainy weather. *Monday, May 22nd, 1775.* Notwithstanding the danger of our situation last night I slept sound and undisturbed, tho' some of the company were kept in perpetual alarm by the barking of the dogs and their own fears. This morning held a council to consult our present safety, when after many pros and cons it was determined to keep two men on each side the River as scouts, the rest to work up the Vessel and relieve each other by turns. It happened to be my turn to walk as a scout, but found it disagreeable clambering over gullies and wading amongst the weeds as high as my head in some places and raining all the forenoon. Saw several Buffalo tracks and a flock of Paroquets. At noon went aboard and rowed all night. Find the current here pretty strong. Camped on a hill in a Beech thicket, all hands well tired and D—d cross. One of the scouts killed a deer. *Tuesday, May 23rd, 1775.* Proceeded up the River, found several rapids which obliged us to get out and haul our vessel up with ropes. The current stronger than yesterday. Saw several roads that crossed the River which they tell me are made by the Buffaloes going from one lick to another. (These licks are brackish or salt springs which the Buffaloes are fond of.) With hard labour suppose we have come twenty miles to-day. No signs of Indians. Camped on a stony hill near a Buffalo Lick. Saw several of them and killed two Calves and a Bull. Limestone impregnated with shells. Large Beech bottoms but our scouts inform me the Land is better a distance from the River. Believe G. Rice does not intend to go down the Ohio which will be a great disappointment to me. *Wednesday, May 24th, 1775.* Proceeded up the River, find the navigation worse, more rapids and strong current. Surrounded 30 Buffaloes as they were crossing the River, shot two young Heifers and caught two calves alive whose ears we marked and turned them out again. About noon Captn. Michael Cresop met us, informed us it is 100 Miles to Harwood's Landing the place our company intends to take up land. No danger of the Indians. Captn. Clark left us and went with Captn. Cresop. Clark always behaved well while he stayed with us.

*Wednesday, May 24th, 1775.* Land in general covered with Beech. Limestone in large flags. Few rivulets empty into the River, or few springs to be seen, which makes me suppose the country is badly watered. Camped at a place where the Buffaloes cross the River. In the night were alarmed with a plunging in the River. In a little time Mr. Johnston (who slept on board) called out for help. We ran to his assistance with our arms and to our great mortification and surprise found one of our Canoes that had all our flour on board sunk, and would have been inevitably lost, had it not been fixed to the other. We immediately hauled our shattered vessel to the shore and landed our things, tho' greatly damaged. It was done by the Buffaloes crossing the River from that side where the vessel was moored. Fortunately for Mr. Johnston he slept in that Canoe next the shore. The Buffaloes jumped over him into the other, and split it about fourteen foot.

Mr. Nourse and Mr. Taylor's servants usually slept on board, but had by mistake brought their blankets on shore this evening and were too lazy to go on board again or probably they would have been killed. *Thursday, May 25th, 1775.* Repairing our Vessel by putting in knees and calking her with the bark of the white Elm pounded to a paste, which is tough and glutinous, something like Bird-lime and answers the purpose very well. Some of the company shot a Buffalo Bull, saw several cross the River while we were at work. Two canoes full of men passed us down the River going to Fort Pitt. Am convinced Rice will not go with me, find he is a great coward. On inspection find our Flour is much damaged, obliged to come to an allowance of a Pint a man per day. Had we come to this resolution sooner it would have been better. Great quarrelling among the company.

*Friday, May 26th, 1775.* Proceeded up the River. Met 2 Canoes bound to Redstone. Shot an old Buffalo Bull that had his ears marked. Passed a bad rapid which took all our force to tow our Vessel up. Much tormented with Ticks, a small animal like a Sheeplouse, but very tough skin. They get on you by walking in the Woods in great numbers, and if you don't take care to pick them off in time they work their heads through the skin and then you may pull the body away but the head will remain in the skin, which is very disagreeable. If they are not removed in a short time they grow like the Ticks on a Dog. Beechy bottoms. Camped at the mouth of Elk Horn Creek. Our company still continues to be crabbed with one another and I believe will be worse as Bread grows scarce. *Saturday, May 27th, 1775.* This day got up several smart rapids. Thunder, Lightning and rain. Some high rocks and Cedar hills. Find Rice does everything in his power to quarrel with me, am determined not to give the first affront. *Sunday, May 28th, 1775.* Proceeded up the River. Saw a great many Buffaloes cross the River above us, all hands went ashore to surround them. I kept on the outside of them and shot a fine young Heifer, some of the rest shot a Cow and Calf. Our stupid company will not stay to jerk any, tho' we are in want of provisions. Camped on a gravelly Island. Beech bottoms and cedar hills with few rivulets.

*Monday, May 29th, 1775.* This morning George Rice (without any provocation) began to abuse me in a most scurrilous manner, threatened to scalp and tomahawk me. I was for bestowing a little manual labour upon him, but he flew to his Gun and began to load, swearing he would shoot me. I did the same, and had it not been for the timely interposition of my worthy Friend, Mr. Nourse, I believe one of us would have been killed. A great deal of abusive language was given on both sides, but nothing more. I have expected this for some time. He did it on purpose to get off his engagement to go down the Ohio, which it has effectually done. Proceeded a little way up the River to a great Buffalo crossing, where we intend to kill some meat. Our provision is almost out. *Tuesday, May, 30th, 1775.* This day Mr. Nourse, Mr. Taylor and Rice went to take a view of the Country. Mr. Johnston and I took a walk about 3 miles from the River, find the land pretty level, a blackish sandy soil. Timber chiefly Beech. In our absence those at the Camp caught a large Catfish which measured six inches between the eyes. We supposed it would weigh 40 pounds. Don't expect our company back tonight. *Wednesday, May 31st, 1775.* At the Camp washing and mending my clothes. In the evening Mr. Nourse and company returned and say the land a distance from the River, is the levelest, richest and finest they ever saw, but badly watered. *Thursday, June 1st, 1775.* Proceeded up the River, bad navigation, many rapids and strong currents. Saw a Gang of Buffaloes cross the River. Shot a Bull. Saw some Deer but killed none. Camped at a place where we found some Corn in a Crib, a Gun and some clothes, supposed to be left there by some people coming to take up land. Rocks, Cedar Hills and Beech Bottoms. *Friday, June 2nd, 1775.* This day met eight Canoes bound to Redstone and Fort Pitt. Went about 9 miles and camped, to hunt, shot at some Buffaloes, but killed none. Land good, weeds as high as a man. Pleasant weather. Our company continually quarrelling, but I have the good luck to please them all but Rice, whom I treat with contempt. *Saturday, June 3rd, 1775.* Proceeded up the River, till noon, when after being wet to the skin we camped about 10 miles below Harwood's Landing. Another Canoe passed us this day bound to Wheeling. Rocks, Cedar hills and Beech bottoms.

*Harwood's Landing — Sunday, June 4th, 1775.* Arrived at Harwood's Landing in the evening. Saw a Rattle Snake about 4 feet long. A bark Canoe at the landing. We have been Fourteen days in coming about 120 miles. My right foot much swelled, owing to a hurt I got by bathing in the River. Rocky and Cedar hills, along the banks of the River. My foot very painful. *Monday, June 5th, 1775.* This is called Harwood's Landing as it is nearest to a new Town, that was laid out last summer by Captn. Harwood, who gave it the name of Harwoodsburg about 15 miles from the Landing for which place Mr. Nourse,

Mr. Johnston, Taylor and Rice set out this morning. I would have gone with them, but my foot is so bad I am scarcely able to walk. Applied a fomentation of Herbs to assuage the swelling. Very little to eat and no possibility of getting any flour here. Must be without Bread very soon. *Tuesday, June 6th, 1775.* Mr. Nourse and company returned in the evening. He gives good account of the richness of the land, but says it appears to be badly watered and light timbered. They lodged in the town. Mr. Nourse informs me there is about 30 houses in it, all built of logs and covered with Clapboards, but not a nail in the whole Town. Informs us that the Indians have killed four men about nine miles from the town. This has struck such a panic that I cannot get anyone to go down the Ohio with me on any account. Determined to return by the first opportunity. My foot much better. Much provoked at my disappointment. *Wednesday, June 7th, 1775.* My foot much better. All of us that have Guns went hunting. Rambled over a great hill, saw a great deal of fine land, but no Game. Mr. Johnston left us and went to Harwoodsburg. *Thursday, June 8th, 1775.* This day divided our provisions, which came to 2 Quarts of flour, half a peck of Indian corn sprouted as long as my finger, one gallon of salt and about two pounds of Bacon per man. In the afternoon four men came to the landing who are bound up the River Ohio to Fort Pitt, they tell me that they have some flour and they are willing to take me in their company. Determined to go with them, but don't much like their looks. A confounded ragged crew. My foot almost well.

*Friday, June 9th, 1775.* About three o'clock this morning we were alarmed with a great noise in the River. The men I had agreed to go with were camped betwixt us and the River. They called to know whether any of our company were crossing the River as they saw two people in a Canoe endeavouring to get to the other shore. On examining we found two of our company missing, an indentured Servant belonging to Mr. Taylor and another that was come for Mr. Johnston's baggage from Harwood. They had taken all my flour and Mr. Johnston's and about two pounds of Gunpowder belonging to Johnston, but no Gun. The people at the landing threatened to fire on them if they did not return, upon which they went ashore and took to their heels. They had set all the Canoes adrift, except that they took with them, which luckily struck on a rock till one of the Company swam across the River and brought her over and my flour which they had got on shore, but in their hurry forgot. What can be their motive for running away in this wilderness Country, I cannot conceive. My new fellow-travellers got the *Charming Sally* from my old company, put our things on board, took leave of Mr. Nourse with whom I should have been glad to have returned, but he intends to go over land. This Gentleman has treated me with the greatest civility. My new company is Henry Tilling an Englishman, Thos. A. Briant an Irishman, John Clifton and Joseph Boassiers, Americans. Stopped about 30 Miles below the Landing at a hunting camp where we got some Buffalo meat.

*Kentucky River — Saturday, June 10th, 1775.* The people at the Camp we lodged at last night gave us some jerked meat. On inspecting our flour, found it does not amount in the whole to more than 15 pounds amongst 5 people. Must make no more bread but save our flour for soup. Proceeded down the River. These people behave very kind to me, I believe there is but two pair of Breeches in the company, one belonging to Mr. Tilling and the other to myself. The rest wear breechclouts, leggings and hunting shirts, which have never been washed only by the rain since they were made. Our Canoe very leaky. Determined to change her, the first opportunity. Camped at a Buffalo road. *Sunday, June 11th, 1775.* This morning killed a Buffalo Cow crossing the River. Fell down to Elkhorn Creek. Camped and jerked our meat, sprinkling it with salt which makes it more palatable. Found Captn. Hancock Lee camped at Elkhorn, surveying land. This is a new settlement by some Carolina Gentleman, who pretends to have purchased the Land from the Indians, but with what truth I cannot pretend to say as the Indians affirm they have never sold these lands. These Gentlemen claim all the Land on the S.W. side of this River to Green River, a tract of land about 200 Miles broad, and I suppose twice as long. They sell it about five pound sterling a thousand acres, subject to an annual quit rent of five shillings per thousand, no quit rents to be paid till the land has been possessed five years. It is surprizing what numbers of people has taken up lands on these terms, tho' they are generally of the most profligate sort, in short it is an asylum for rascals of all denominations. I believe the land is good in general, through the whole track, with several salt springs as I am informed.

An immense number of Buffaloes frequent them. Buffaloes are a sort of wild cattle, but have a large hump on the top of their shoulders all black, and their necks and shoulders covered with long shaggy hair with large bunches of hair growing on their fore thighs, short horns bending forward, short noses, piercing eyes and beard like a Goat. In the Summer the hair behind their shoulders is short as that on a horse. In the winter they are covered with long soft curling hair like wool, their tails are short with a bunch of long hair at the end. When they run they carry them erect. Some of them will weigh when fat 14 to 15 hundred and are good eating, particularly the hump, which I think makes the finest steaks in the world. They feed in large herds and are exceedingly fierce when wounded. Their sense of smelling is exquisite. If you get to leeward of them you may go up to them, or at least within shot, but if you are to windward they run long before they see you. They are fond of Salt or Brackish water. Springs of this sort have large roads made to them, as large as most public roads in a populous country. They eat great quantities of a sort of reddish Clay found near Brackish springs. I have seen amazing large holes dug or rather cut by them in this sort of earth, whether it is impregnated with Saline particles or not, I cannot determine. They do not roar like other cattle, but grunt like hogs. Got a large pine canoe out of some drift wood with great labour, but her stern is beat off and several bullet holes in her bottom, which we intend to repair to-morrow. Excessively hot.

*Monday, June 12th, 1775.* Repairing our Canoe by cutting the stern out of the *Charming Sally,* and putting it into her. Calked her and made her tight, believe she will answer very well, both stiff and light. Went to Captn. Lee's camp, who treated me very kindly with a dram of Whiskey and some bread, which at this time is a great luxury with me. Captn. Lee's brother gave me a Rattlesnake skin about four feet long. Very hot. *Tuesday, June 13th, 1775.* Fell down the River to a great lick where we intend to kill some meat. My company begin to quarrel among themselves, but behave well to me. *Wednesday, June 14th, 1775.* Very heavy rain last night, which we had no shelter from but a large tree. It made us wet lodging. Went to the Lick in the morning found no Buffaloes there, determined to go to Grinin's Lick. Fell down to Grinin's Lick, shot at some Buffaloes but killed none, tho' I am certain we must have wounded a great number. Five of us fired at a herd of two hundred odd not more than twenty yards. This is the largest Lick I ever saw. I suppose here is 50 acres of land trodden by Buffaloes, but there is not a blade of grass upon it. Incredible numbers come here to the Salt springs. Here is a number of salt and Brackish springs in a small compass, some of them so strong of the brine that the Sun forms the Salt round the edge of the Spring. Here were two Dutchmen, sent by the proprietors to make an experiment on the water of the strongest spring. They had made about a pint of Salt from sixteen Gallons of water. Some of Captn. Cresop's people had camped here for 4 days killing meat but intend to set out for Fort Pitt to-morrow. Our company intend to go with them and trust to Providence for provision. I think this a foolish act, but will not contradict them. Bought a Buckskin to make breeches.

## VI

## THE OHIO RIVER — THE INDIAN COUNTRY

*OHIO RIVER — Thursday, June 15th, 1775.* Intended to kill some meat at the Elephant Bone Lick. Proceeded down the River in company with nine of Captn. Cresop's people. Our company is increased to 14 persons and almost as many different nations, two Englishmen, two Irishmen, one Welshman, two Dutchmen, two Virginians, two Marylanders, one Swede, one African Negro, and a Mulatto. With the motley, rascally, and ragged crew I have to travel six hundred miles. I expect we shall have a great deal of quarrelling, but as we are in three Canoes it will be a means to keep them quiet. Got to the Mouth of the River about noon. Proceeded up the Ohio, where we killed a Buffalo and camped. *Friday, June 16th, 1775.* Very heavy rain last night, which made our lodging uncomfortable. Got under way this morning early, with wet clothes and hungry bellies. Obliged to pole up the River. This is done with poles about 12 feet long, the men stand in the vessel, set the pole against the bottom of the River, and push themselves along. It is a laborious exercise. Fortunately for me, none of our company can steer with a pole. I am obliged to sit and steer with a paddle. Killed another Buffalo on the Banks of the River. Our company quarrelled and the Irishman left us and went to Cresop's people, but returned to us at the Bone Lick where we camped.

*Saturday, June 17th, 1775.* This morning set out for the Elephant Bone Lick, which is only three miles S.E. of the River. However, we lost our way and I suppose travelled twenty miles before we found it. Where the bones are found is a large muddy pond, a little more than knee deep with a Salt spring in it which I suppose preserves the bones sound. Found several bones of a prodigious size, I take them to be Elephants, for we found a part of a tusk, about two foot long, Ivory to all appearance, but by length of time had grown yellow and very soft. All of us stripped and went into the pond to grabble for teeth and found several. Joseph Passiers found a jaw tooth which he gave me. It was judged by the company to weigh 10 pound. I got a shell of a Tusk of hard and good ivory about eighteen inches long. There is a great number of bones in a Bank on the side of this pond of an enormous·size but decayed and rotten. Ribs 9 inches broad, Thigh bones 10 inches diameter. What sort of animals these were is not clearly known. All the traditionary accounts by the Indians is that they were White Buffaloes that killed themselves by drinking salt water. It appears to me from the shape of their teeth that they were Grasseaters. There neither is or ever was any Elephants in North or South America, that I can learn, or any quadruped one tenth part as large as these was, if one may be allowed to judge from the appearance of these bones, which must have been considerably larger than they are now. Captn. Hancock Lee told me he had found a Tusk here that was six foot long, very sound but yellow. These tusks are like those brought from the Coast of Africa. Saw some Buffaloes but killed none. Several Indian paintings on the trees. Got plenty of Mulberries, very sweet and pleasant fruit but bad for the teeth. One of the company shot a Deer. The loudest Thunder and heaviest rain I ever saw this afternoon. Got to the Camp well wet and most heartily tired. A D—d Irish rascal has broken a piece of my Elephant tooth, put me in a violent passion, can write no more.

*Sunday, June 18th, 1775.* Left the Bone Lick. Got to the mouth of the Miamme River to dinner. Nothing but jerked meat without bread. Camped about eight miles above the Miamme. *Monday, June 19th, 1775.* Got under way early this morning. As we sat at dinner, saw two Buffalo Bulls crossing the River. When they were about half way over four of us got into a Canoe and attacked them in the River, the rest went along shore to shoot them, as soon as they came ashore. The River was wide and we had fine diversion fighting them in the water. The man in the head of the canoe seized one of them by the tail and he towed us about the River for half an hour. We shot him eight times, let him get ashore and he ran away. Our comrades ashore very angry with us and they have a great right to be so. Passed the mouth of the Little Miamme. In great fear of the Indians. Saw a Black Wolf pursuing a Faun into the River, the Faun we caught, but the Wolf got away. My company quarrels amongst themselves, but behave well to me. Camped late in the evening. *Tuesday, June 20th, 1775.* Very cold last night. N.W. wind. Camped early in the evening. *Wednesday, June 21st, 1775.* Cold in the night. Got up Le Fort's Falls, this is only a smart rapid scarcely perceivable when the River is high. Current very strong. Our people weary, not able to make more than 20 Miles per day in general. Camped early. *Thursday, June 22nd, 1775.* Proceeded up the River. Strong current. The River is twenty feet lower now than it was when we went down. *Friday, June 23rd, 1775.* Saw a Bear cross the River but did not get a shot at her. Got up to the Great Buffalo Lick where we intend to kill some meat, as ours is almost done. All hands much fatigued and the scarcity of provisions makes them very quarrelsome. They pay some respect to me, and I have hitherto prevented them fighting. Pleasant weather.

*Saturday, June 24th, 1775.* This morning set out to the Lick without breakfast. The reason was we had nothing to eat. Three of us stayed at the Lick till the afternoon waiting for the Buffaloes but saw none. When our out Hunters came loaded with meat and informed us they had killed a Buffalo about five miles off, set out and found it, and loaded ourselves and returned to the Camp, but never so much fatigued before. Having already experienced the want of victuals, was willing to guard against it for the future. I believe I have exerted myself more than I can bear. It is judged by the company that I brought between 70 and 80 pound of meat, exclusive of my Gun and Shot pouch. To add to my distress my shoesoles came off and I was obliged to walk bare foot for six miles. Find myself very unwell. Shot a Pole Cat. One of our Company missing. All the rest (except Tilling and myself) are going this evening, as they expect he is killed by the Indians. But I think he has lost himself in the Woods. Very arduous task to persuade them to stay, as they all expect to be killed before morning. *Sunday, June 25th, 1775.* Slept little last night, over-fatigued. This morning our company are for setting out immediately, confident that the man is killed. With much importunity prevailed on them to stay till evening, but could not persuade any of them to go to seek the man.  About sundown they all prepared for going, notwithstanding all that Mr. Tilling and I could say against it, but just as we were going aboard saw the man come along shore to our great joy.  It had happened as I supposed — he lost himself in the Woods and had rambled all night.  If we had left him, he must have perished. Very unwell.  *Monday, June 26th, 1775.*  Proceeded up the River.  Passed the mouth of the Sioto River on the N.W.  In fear of the Indians.  Camped early.  *Tuesday, June 27th, 1775.*  Very stiff current all day, heavy showers and very sultry.  It is a custom with our company, as soon as it begins to rain to strip naked and secure their clothes from the wet.  I have attempted it twice to-day, but the drops of rain are so disagreeable to my skin, that it obliged me to put on my shirt.  Killed a Faun.  Saw a Bear cross the River, but could not get a shot at her.  All hands very weary and very crabbed.

*Wednesday, June 28th, 1775.*  This morning started early in a very thick fog.  About three miles from our camp, the River was very broad and shallow a long way from the shore on that side we were on, which obliged us to keep out of sight of the shore for deeper water.  Opening a point of a Bar, saw 4 Canoes full of Indians about two hundred yards ahead of us, upon which we pushed for the shore, but to our great surprise saw six other Canoes full of Indians betwixt us and the shore so that we were entirely surrounded.  Everything was prepared for an engagement, all our lumber and a great part of our provisions were hoved overboard.  Out of twelve Guns five were rendered unfit for present use by the wet, mine happened to be in good order and I loaded her with an ounce bullet and seven swan shot.  The command of our Canoes was given to me. We had only two Guns on board fit for use, Mr. Tilling's and mine. Tom O'Brien in the scuffle let his fall in the River and got her filled with water. He laid down in the bottom of the Canoe, begun to tell his beads and prayed and howled in Irish. Boassier's Gun was wet and unfit for use. He followed O'Brien's example. Weeping, praying, said Ave Mary's in abundance, at the same time hugging a little wooden crucifix he pulled from his bosom most heartily. Jacob Nalen (a Swede) commanded a canoe had three rifle guns on board. Williams, the Welshman, commanded the other with two muskets. We held a short and confused council, wherein it was determined that Nalen should lead the Van, I in the centre, and Williams bring up the rear. The Indians had observed our confusion and lay on their paddleboxes 30 yards from shore. There were 23 Indians in the six Canoes betwixt us and the shore. All of them had poles or paddles, but our fears had converted them into Guns. These six we determined to attack as the River was shallow, if we by accident overset our Canoes we might wade ashore. The Canoes above us with 21 Indians bore down upon us, we made for the shore. I ordered Tom O'Brien to steer the Canoes within ten yards of Nalen's vessel and Boassier and Clifton to take their paddles. Clifton, tho' a young boy, behaved with the greatest resolution. Tilling's countenance was not in the least changed, his behaviour animated me very much. Boassiers and O'Brien lay crying in the bottom of the Canoes and refused to stir. I set the muzzle of my Gun to O'Brien's head, threatening to blow his brains out if he did not immediately take his paddle. It had the desired effect, he begged for his life, invoked St. Patrick, took his paddle and howled most horribly. Dangerous and desperate as we imagined our situation to be, I could not forbear laughing to see the condition of this poor fellow. Boassiers pretended to be in a convulsion fit. Mr. Tilling threw several canfuls of water in his face, but he refused to stir. I put a pistol bullet upon the load I already had in my Gun. I was determined to give some of them their quietus. I confess I felt very uneasy. When we got within thirty yards of them some of Nalen's crew hailed them and to our great satisfaction they told us they were friends. They had seen our confusion and laughed at us for our fears. It proved to be one Catfish, a Delaware Indian, and a party with him going to hunt. They had several Squaws or Indian women with them, some of them very handsome. We gave them some salt and Tobacco with which they seemed well pleased. Proceeded up the River very merry at the expense of our cowardly companions. Boassiers brags what he would have done had his Gun been in order. O'Brien says he was not fit for Death. All of them make some excuse or other to hide their cowardice. Heavy rain all afternoon. Camped five miles above Sandy Creek. Obliged to sleep upon a log, the ground is so wet and still continues to rain. *Thursday, June 29th, 1775.* The great Rains have raised the River about four feet last night, causing a strong current and laborious navigation. Saw another Canoe with Indians, but did not speak to them. Slept on a fallen tree — uneasy lodgings.

*Friday, June 30th, 1775.* Got to the Great Conhaway about noon, find the Fort evacuated. Saw some people that are settled about 5 miles above the mouth of the river, who inform us that the New Englanders have had a battle with the English troops at Boston and killed seven thousand. I hope it will prove that the English have killed several thousand of the Yankees. *Saturday, July 1st, 1775.* This morning John Clifton left us. He intends going home by land. He has behaved very well. Our provisions almost done, all our hooks and lines broken, all our feet so tender by standing continually wet that it is impossible for us to hunt, and the small quantity of provision we have is swarming with maggots. Our Flour expended and this night we have put the last of our Indian Corn to boil (about three half pints, sprouted as long as my finger). This we have always reserved for Sunday dinner with a little Elk fat rendered amongst it and thought it delicious. *Sunday, July 2nd, 1775.* Captn. Cresop's company had a mind to keep Sunday, but quarrelled about it and William Conner left them and came to us. They are all on wages and have some provisions left. We eat the last mouthful we had this morning, except a little stinking jerked beef full of maggots. Proceeded up the River past Hockhockin. About noon found a Buffalo Fish about six pound weight that an Eagle had just killed and brought ashore. Made a hearty meal of it. In the afternoon Boassier went to our Beef Barrel, but found it so bad, in a passion sent it overboard. Now we have not a morsel to eat. Slept on a rock without fire.

*Monday, July 3rd, 1775.* Got under way very early this morning, not a morsel to eat. Our people quarrelled very much, but behaved to me with great respect. Camped very late. *Tuesday, July 4th, 1775.* Got to mouth of the Little Conhaway about noon when I found myself very sick at the stomach for want of meat. Went ashore and got a little Ginseng root and chewed it which refreshed me exceedingly. In the evening got to one Doctor Briscoe's plantation about a mile from the River. It was night when we got there, found the house deserted, no Corn, Fowls, or meat of any kind. We all went into the Garden, dark as it was, to get Cucumbers or anything we could find that we could eat. Found a Potato bed and I ate about a dozen of them raw and thought them the most delicious food I ever ate in my life. Heavy and constant rain all day. Made a fire in the house, dried ourselves, and went to sleep. Very much fatigued. *Wednesday, July 5th, 1775.* This morning one of the Company went to the Canoe for our Kettle, the rest plundered about the plantation and got some young cabbages, squashes, and Cimbelines. This medley of vegetables we boiled all together, and seasoned with pepper and salt it made a most elegant repast. Proceeded to French Creek, where Cresop's people overtook us but would not give us a mouthful of victuals. Rain all day. One of our people sick, I gave half a dollar for about two ounces of Bread for him. *Thursday, July 6th, 1775.* Got to one Pursley's plantation where we got some Sour milk, but no bread. I dare eat none of it, got me Ginseng root. This is an excellent stomatic, went to sleep very hungry. Our sick man much better. *Friday, July 7th, 1775.* Got to a plantation belonging to one Rous a Dutchman, Bargained with the old Woman for as much mush as we all could eat (this is hasty pudding made of Indian meal) for about two dollars worth of Gunpowder. We had the Corn to grind on a hand mill and I thought it an age before we had done and the mush made. I suppose we might have eat till we had killed ourselves before we had satisfied our voracious appetites. The Old Woman prudently took our victuals away when we had eaten about a quart apiece. Have eaten no bread for twenty-eight days.

*Saturday, July 8th, 1775.* This morning one Captn.

David McClure came here on his way to Wheeling. He behaves civilly and offers me a place in his canoe to Wheeling. Mr. Tilling and Boassiers intend to go by land to Redstone. Tilling has always treated me with the greatest respect and kindness. This poor man was once a Lieutenant in the train of Artillery, but broke at New York for lancing a Colonel. He has taken up a good tract of land on the Kentucky. O'Brien and I went with Captn. McClure. One of his company shot 2 does. Plenty of meat and a little bread. Got to Captn. Rogers's plantation. *Sunday, July 9th, 1775.* Passed Grave Creek and Juniata Creek. Got to Fort Fincastle in the evening. No soldiers here but about 8 men from the neighbourhood, all drunk, and our company soon got in the same condition. A man had got Whiskey to sell. Captn. Cresop's people joined them and in a short time a general engagement begun. I got up into a loft and went to sleep. *Monday, July 10th, 1775.* Waiting for Captn. McClure, who is going within a little way of Mr. Shepperd's with a horse and will carry my baggage. Disagreeable company, fighting and quarrelling.

*Fort Fincastle — Tuesday, July 11th, 1775.* Waiting for Captn. McClure. Bought a belt of Wampum from him. Disagreeable situation. *Wednesday, July 12th, 1775.* Left the Fort and got to Mr. David Shepperd's. Saw an Alum mine near to Mr. Shepperd's, with a mine of good Coal in a Limestone rock. Hired a Horse from one of the neighbours to go to V. Crawford's. *Thursday, July 13th, 1775.* Left Mr. Shepperd's. Rambled the Woods and Wilds. Shot a Rattlesnake which had like to have bite my horse. It was about 4 feet long. Lodged at Catfish Camp. Great scarcity of provisions.

*West Augusta County — Friday, July 14th, 1775.* Left Catfish Camp, travelled over a great deal of fine land but very thinly inhabited. Crossed the Moningahaly River at Redstone Fort where I lodged with one Thos. Brown. Listing the best riflemen that can be got to go to Boston under Captn. Cressop for the humane purpose of killing the English Officers. Confusion to the Scoundrels. Here is a number of them here and I believe suspect me being a spy, they ask me so many impertinent questions. Very much fatigued this day. *Saturday, July 15th, 1775.* Left Redstone Fort and after losing myself several times, got to Captn. Thos. Gist's. Very kindly treated by Miss Nancy Gist, an agreeable young Woman who informs me that there has been two very severe engagements at Boston and great numbers killed on both sides. Forgot the part of an Elephant tusk at the Fort. *Sunday, July 16th, 1775.* Went to Major Crawford's, delivered some letters I had for him, gives me bad accounts of the Boston affair. Informs me Lord Dunmore had abdicated the Government of Virginia and gone on board a Man of War.

*Monday, July 17th, 1775.* Left Major Crawford's. Crossed the Yaughhagany River and went to Mr. V. Crawford's. In the evening went to Captn. Stephenson's to what they call a Reaping Frolic, usually make a feast when they get done reapings, very merry. *Tuesday, July 18th, 1775.* At Mr. V. Crawford's, Jacob Creek. These rascals have wore out all the clothes I left here, so that I am now reduced to three ragged shirts, two pair linen breeches in the same condition, a hunting shirt and jacket, with one pair of stockings. *Wednesday, July 19th, 1775.* Rode to Captn. Gist's, returned in the evening. Intend to stay here a week or two to recover myself. My late fatigues have reduced me exceedingly.

*Thursday, July 20th, 1775.* Very ill of the Gravel, felt some symptoms of it for two days, but now I am in violent pain. *Friday, July 21st, 1775.* Much worse, a most excruciating pain. Took a decoction of Roots prescribed by Mr. Crawford's Housekeeper, who uses me with the greatest care and tenderness. *Saturday, July 22nd, 1775.* Something easier this morning. Took some Tea made of the Roots of a small shrub which gave me almost immediate ease. Miss Grimes came to see me and cried most abundantly to see me in so much pain, as she said, but believe she has too much of the Irish in her. *Sunday, July 23rd, 1775.* Got pretty well again, but still continue to take the Tea. Captn. Prior Theobald came here to-day. Invites me to his house, but I don't intend to go. *Monday, July 24th, 1775.* Free from all symptoms of the Gravel. Walked about a little, but find myself weak.

*Tuesday, July 25th, 1775.* Intend to go into the Indian Country as soon as I am able, to dispose of the Silver Trinkets, I bought for that trade. I believe I shall be put to my shifts for cash to carry me there. *Wednesday, July 26th, 1775.* Rode up to the Laurel Mountain with some Young Girls to get Huckleberries. They are the same as our Bilberries, only grow in clusters. *Thursday, July 27th, 1775.* Went shooting and knocked down a Young Turkey. Nothing but whores and rogues in this country. *Friday, July 28th, 1775.* At Mr. Crawford's. Hot weather. *Saturday, July 29th, 1775.* The Rev. Mr. Belmain, only Church Minister in this County, came here to-day. Intends to give us a Lecture tomorrow. *Sunday, July 30th, 1775.*

Mr. Belmain preached under a large tree, a Political discourse.

*Monday, July 31st, 1775.* The people here are Liberty mad, nothing but War is thought of. Flux begins to rage in the neighbourhood. *Tuesday, August 1st, 1775.* Went with Mr. Belmain and Captn. Stephenson to Major Crawford's. *Wednesday, August 2nd, 1775.* Returned to V. Crawford's. Intend to go to Fort Pitt the first opportunity. I am now getting strong and healthy. *Thursday, August 3rd, 1775.* This morning went with Mr. V. Crawford and Mr. James Berwick a Manchester man to Major Crawford's, where we stayed all night. Bad news from Boston. The English drove to their ships and great numbers of them killed. I hope it is a lie.

*Friday, August 4th, 1775.* Agreed to go with Major Crawford to Mr. John Gibson's, an Indian Trader, about 12 miles below Fort Pitt. He is a man that has great interest amongst the Indians, consequently the best person to direct me how to dispose of my goods to the best advantage. Mr. Berwick lost his watch this evening. *Saturday, August 5th, 1775.* At Mr. Crawford's. Heavy rain. *Sunday, August 6th, 1775.* At Mr. Crawford's. Heavy rain for forty-eight hours without intermission. *Monday, August 7th, 1775.* At Mr. Crawford's waiting for Major Crawford. I believe he is a dilatory man and little dependence to be put in him. *Tuesday, August 8th, 1775.* Very uneasy to wait here, doing nothing. Am afraid I shall be too late to return home this fall. Went with Miss Crawford and Miss Grimes to John Minton's. When we came to a small Creek we had to cross the girls tucked up their petticoats above their knees and forded it with the greatest indifference. Nothing unusual here, tho' these are the first people in the Country.

*Wednesday, August 9th, 1775.* Mr. Berwick and I set out this morning to Major Crawford's, but met him at his Mistress's. This woman is common to him, his brother, half brother, and his own Son, and is his wife's sister's daughter at the same time. A set of vile brutes. He informs me the Congress have discarded all the Governors on the Continent and taken all affairs Civil and Military into their management. Independence is what these Scoundrels aim at. Confusion to their schemes. *Thursday, August 10th, 1775.* At Captn. Stephenson's. Instructed his people to make a stack of wheat. Farming in a poor uncultivated state here. Captn. Stephenson an honest, worthy man. Went to V. Crawford's in the evening. No prospect of Major Crawford going to Gibson's soon. Determined to set out for Fort Pitt on Monday next. *Friday, August 11th, 1775.* Last night Miss G. came. A fine blooming Irish Girl. The Flesh overcame the Spirit.

*Saturday, August 12th, 1775.* No prospect of getting money for Bills upon Mr. Kirk here. This evening Captn. James Wood arrived here from the Indian town. He had been sent to invite the Indians to a Treaty at Fort Pitt to be held on the tenth of September. The Convention of Virginia had employed him. He says that an English Officer and a French man from Detroit had been at all the Indian towns to persuade the Indians not to go to any Treaty held by the Colonists. But tells us his superior eloquence prevailed and all the different nations he has been at will certainly attend the Treaty. *Sunday, August 13th, 1775.* Mr. Berwick was kind enough to let me ride his horse to Fort Pitt, where I am to deliver him to a certain

Mr. John Meddison. Left Mr. V. Crawford's and with him I left my watch, Buckles, Breast Buckles, Stock Buckle and silver buttons, with a paper directing how I would have them disposed of if death should happen to my lot, as everyone tells me that I am running a great risk of being killed by the Indians. I am not afraid of meeting with bad usage from them. Got to Mr. John De Camp's at night.

*Fort Pitt — Monday, August 14th, 1775.* Left Mr. De Camp's. Dined at Turtle Creek. Arrived at Fort Pitt in the evening with only two Dollars in my pocket and very shabby dress. Put up my horse at the best Inn in town, know the Landlady to be a Tory, Sister-in-law to Major Connoly. *Tuesday, August 15th, 1775.* Delivered the horse to Mr. Mattison, applied to four people in town to get cash for my Bills on Mr. Kirk, but my appearance prevents my success. Offered to sell my silverware to them, but the Rascals knowing my distress will not give me more than half its value. Exceedingly uneasy. *Wednesday, August 16th, 1775.* A great deal of company in town, being Committee day. No one willing to supply me with a little cash, tho' I have applied to every man in town where there is a probability of getting any. Oh, the disadvantages of a ragged dress! Very uneasy. *Thursday, August 17th, 1775.* Very low-spirited. At supper had a political dispute with Mr. John Gibson. Find him much prejudiced against me by the malevolent aspersion of that double-faced villain, B. Johnston. No prospect of getting money here. Made my situation known to the Landlord desiring credit for my board till the Treaty, when some Gentleman of my acquaintance will be there and loose me. Told me he paid ready money for his provisions. By the influence of his wife got credit.

*Friday, August 18th, 1775.* Never till now did I put any confidence in Dreams. Last night I went to sleep with a mind as much confused as a skein of silk pulled the wrong way. The behaviour of my landlord had been a principal cause. But find I have a good friend in my Landlady, who wears the breeches. Dreamed that there was a friend that would relieve me near at hand. I woke with a gleam of hope and waited on Mr. John Anderson, the only person in town that I had omitted. He generously proffered me any cash I might want, to find me a Horse, and go with me into the Indian Country, serving as an interpreter and guide. *Friday, August 18th, 1775.* This Gentleman is an Indian Trader and has business at their Towns. Tells me he had observed my situation for some days and intended to offer me his assistance this day had I not spoke to him. Got some money from him to pay my Landlord. When he found that I had got a Friend his tone altered and it did not signify anything if I did not pay him till the Treaty. I made use of his own words to him, told him as he paid ready money for his provisions consequently he must expect the same from me. His wife abused him a good deal about his meanness, called him a pitiful rascal in abundance.

*Saturday, August 19th, 1775.* Waiting for Mr. Anderson. Employed an Indian Woman to make me a pair of Mockeysons and Leggings. This evening two of the Pennsylvania Delegates to Treat with the Indians arrived here, escorted by a party of paltry Lighthorses. Colnl. Arthur St. Clair and Colnl. James Wilson. Supped and spent the evening with them. My Landlady remarkably kind to me, owing to my political sentiments agreeing with hers. She is by nature a most horrid Vixen. *Sunday, August 20th,*

*1775.* Waiting for Mr. Anderson. he is detained by the Indians coming to trade. *Monday, August 21st, 1775.* Mr. Anderson informs me that the Indians are not well pleased at anyone going into their Country dressed in a Hunting shirt. Got a Calico shirt made in the Indian fashion, trimmed up with Silver Brooches and Armplates so that I scarcely know myself. Crossed the Allegany River and went about two miles and camped at a small run to be ready to start early in the morning. We had forgotten a tin kettle in Town. I went back for it while ✓ Mr. Anderson made a fire, returning in the dark lost my way and got to an Indian Camp, where I found two Squaws, but they could not speak English. By signs made them understand what I wanted and they put me right.

*Indian Country — Tuesday, August 22nd, 1775.* A very heavy fog this morning. We had got two bottles of Rum, two loaves of Bread, and a Bacon Ham along with us. Agreed to take a Dram to prevent us catching the Fever and Ague, but drank rather too much and most stupidly forgot our provisions. Got to Logg's Town about noon, crossed the River and went to Mr. John Gibson's. Lodged there, but would not make our wants known for fear of being laughed at. We crossed the River in a Canoe made of Hickory Bark, stretched open with sticks. *Wednesday, August 23rd, 1775.* Proceeded on our journey, but not one morsel of provision. Crossed Great Beaver Creek at Captn. White-Eye's house. This is an Indian Warrior of the Dellawars Nation. Camped at Little Beaver Creek with three Indian Squaws and a man. Nothing to eat but berries such as we found in the woods. Find Mr. Anderson a good hearty companion. One of the Indian Squaws invited me to sleep with her, but I pretended to be sick. She was very kind and brought me some plums she got in the woods.

*Thursday, August 24th, 1775.* Parted with the Indians. Met Captn. Killbuch, an Indian Warrior. Camped at White Oak run. Got plenty of Red plums and wild Cherries which is our only food. *Friday, August 25th, 1775.* Very heavy rain all day. Lost our horses, but an Indian brought them to us in the evening for which we gave him a pair of leggings. Breakfasted, dined and supped on Plums and Wild Cherries. Here are wild Plums in great abundance, about the size of our common white plums in England, some Red, others White and very well flavoured. The Cherries are small and black, very sweet, and grow in Bunches like Currants.

*Saturday, August 26th, 1775.* Set out early this morning, travelled very hard till noon, when we passed through the largest Plum Tree Thicket I ever saw. I believe it was a mile long, nothing but the Plum and Cherry Trees. Killed a Rattlesnake. Just as the Sun went down we stopped to get our Supper on some Dewberries (a small berry something like a Gooseberry). Mr. Anderson had gone before me and said he would ride on about two miles to a small run where he intended to camp, as soon as I had got sufficient. I mounted my Horse and followed him till I came to a place where the road forked. I took the path that I supposed he had gone and rode till it began to be dark, when I imagined myself to be wrong, and there was not a possibility of me finding my way back in the night. Determined to stay where I was till morning, I had no sooner alighted from my horse, but I discovered the glimmering of a fire about four hundred yards from me. This rejoiced me exceedingly, supposing it was Mr. Anderson.

When I got there, to my great disappointment and surprise found three Indian women and a little boy. I believe they were as much surprised as I was. None of them could speak English and I could not speak Indian. I alighted and marked the path I had come and that I had left, on the ground with the end of my stick, made a small channel in the earth which I poured full of water, laid some fire by the side of it, and then laid myself down by the side of the fire, repeating the name of Anderson which I soon understood they knew.

The youngest Girl immediately unsaddled my Horse, unstrapped the Belt, Hoppled him, and turned him out, then spread my Blankets at the fire and made signs for me to sit down. The Oldest made me a little hash of dried Venison and Bear's Oil, which eat very well, but neither Bread or Salt. After supper they made signs I must go ✓ to sleep. Then they held a consultation for some time which made me very uneasy, the two eldest women and the boy laid down on the opposite side of the fire and some distance away. The youngest (she had taken so much pains with my horse) came and placed herself very near me. I began to think she had some amorous design upon me. In about half an hour she began to creep nearer me and pulled my Blanket. I found what she wanted and lifted it up. She was young, handsome, and healthy. Fine regular features and fine eyes, had she not painted them with Red before she came to bed.

*Sunday, August 27th, 1775.* This morning my Bedfellow went into the woods and caught her horse and mine, saddled them, put my Blanket on the saddle, and prepared everything ready, seemingly with a great deal of good nature. Absolutely refused my assistance. The old Woman got me some dried venison for Breakfast. When I took my leave returned the thanks as well as I could by signs. My Bedfellow was my guide and conducted me through the woods, where there were no signs of a road or without my knowing with certainty whither I was going. She often mentioned John Anderson and talked a great deal in Indian. I attempted to speak Indian, which diverted her exceedingly. In about an hour she brought me to Mr. Anderson's camp, who had been very uneasy at my absence and employed an Indian to seek me. I gave my Dulcinea a match coat, with which she seemed very well pleased. Proceeded on our journey and about noon got to an Indian Town called Wale-hack-tap-poke, or the Town with a good Spring, on the Banks of the Muskingham and inhabited by Dellawar Indians. Christianized under the Moravian Sect, it is a pretty town consisting of about sixty houses, and is built of logs and covered with Clapboards. It is regularly laid out in three spacious streets which meet in the centre, where there is a large meeting house built of logs sixty foot square covered with Shingles, Glass in the windows and a Bell, a good plank floor with two rows of forms. Adorned with some few pieces of Scripture painting, but very indifferently executed. All about the meeting house is kept very clean.

In the evening went to the meeting. But never was I more astonished in my life. I expected to have seen nothing but anarchy and confusion, as I have been taught to look upon these beings with contempt. Instead of that, here is the greatest regularity, order, and decorum, I ever saw in any place of Worship, in my life. With that solemnity of behaviour and modest, religious deportment would do honour to the first religious society on earth, and put a bigot or enthusiast out of countenance. The parson was a Dutchman, but preached in English. He had an Indian interpreter, who explained it to the Indians by sentences. They sung in the Indian language. The men sit on one row of forms and the women on the other with the children in the front. Each sex comes in and goes out of their own side of the house. The old men sit on each side the parson. Treated with Tea, Coffee, and Boiled Bacon at supper. The Sugar they make themselves out of the sap of a certain tree. Lodged at Whiteman's house, married to an Indian woman.

*Monday, August 28th, 1775.* Left Wale-hack-tap-poke. Crossed the Muskingham and went to Kanantohead, another pretty Moravian Town, but not so large as Wale-hack-tap-poke. About eight miles asunder. Crossed Muskingham again and a large plain about 3 miles over without tree or shrub and very level. Saw several Indian Cabins built of bark. Got to Newcomer Town about noon. This has been a large town, but now is almost deserted. It is on the Muskingham, built without any order or regularity. I suppose there is not twenty houses inhabited now. Crossed the Muskingham again, and another large plain. Met several Indians coming from a Feast dressed and painted in the grandest manner. Lodged at White-Eye's Town only three houses in it. Kindly treated at a Dutch Blacksmith's, who lives with an Indian Squaw. Got a very hearty supper of a sort of Dumplings made of Indian Meal and dried Huckleberries which serves instead of currants. Dirty people, find it impossible to keep myself free from lice. Very disagreeable companions. *Tuesday, August 29th, 1775.* Left White-Eye's town. Saw the bones of one Mr. Cammel, a White man, that had been killed by the

Indians. Got to Co-a-shoking about noon. It is at the forks of the Muskingham. The Indians have removed from Newcomer Town to this place. King Newcomer lives here. Sold part of my goods here to good advantage. Crossed a branch of Muskingham and went to Old Hundy, this is a scattering Indian settlement. Lodged at a Mohawk Indian's house, who offered me his Sister and Mr. Anderson his Daughter to sleep with us, which we were obliged to accept.

*Wednesday, August 30th, 1775.* My bedfellow very fond of me this morning and wants to go with me. Find I must often meet with such encounters as these if I do not take a Squaw to myself. She is young and sprightly, tolerably handsome, and can speak a little English. Agreed to take her. She saddled her horse and went with us to New Hundy about 3 miles off, where she had several relations who made me very welcome to such as they had. From there to Coashoskis, where we lodged in my Squaw's Brother's, made me a compliment of a young wolf but I could not take it with me. *Thursday, August 31st, 1775.* At Coashoskis. Mr. Anderson could not find his horse. Sold all my goods for Furs. In the afternoon rambled about the Town, smoking Tobacco with the Indians and did everything in my power to make myself agreeable to them. Went to see the King. He lives in a poor house, and he is as poor in dress as any of them, no emblem of Royalty or Majesty about him. He is an old man, treated me very kindly, called me his good friend, and hoped I would be kind to my Squaw. Gave me a small string of Wampum as a token of friendship. My Squaw uneasy to see me write so much.

*Friday, September 1st, 1775.* At Coashoskin Mr. Anderson found his horse. Saw an Indian Dance in which I bore a part. Painted by my Squaw in the most elegant manner. Divested of all my clothes, except my Calico short breechclout, leggings, and Mockesons. A fire was made which we danced round with little order, whooping and hallooing in a most frightful manner. I was but a novice at the diversion and by endeavouring to act as they did made them a great deal of sport and ingratiated me much in their esteem. This is the most violent exercise to the adepts in the art I ever saw. No regular figure, but violent distortion of features, writhing and twisting the body in the most uncouth and antic postures imaginable. Their music is an old Keg with one head knocked out and covered with a skin and beat with sticks which regulates their times. The men have strings of Deer's hoofs tied round their ankles and knees, and gourds with shot or pebblestones in them in their hands which they continually rattle. The women have Morris bells or Thimbles with holes in the bottom and strung upon a leather thong tied round their ankles, knees and waists. The jingling of these Bells and Thimbles, the rattling of the Deer's hoofs and gourds, beating of the drum and kettle, with the horrid yells of the Indians, render it the most unharmonious concert, that human idea can possibly conceive. It is a favourite diversion, in which I am informed they spend a great part of their time in Winter. Saw an Indian Conjuror dressed in a Coat of Bearskin with a Visor mask made of wood, frightful enough to scare the Devil. The Indians believe in conjuration and Witchcraft. Left the Town, went about two miles. Camped by the side of a run. A young Indian boy, son of one Baubee, a Frenchman, came after us and insists on going with us to Fort Pitt. Find myself very unwell this evening, pains in my

head and back. Nancy seems very uneasy about my wel-
fare. Afraid of the Ague.

*Saturday, September 2nd, 1775.* Got to White-Eye's
Town to breakfast. Saw the Indian Warmarks made by
Captn. Wingimund, a Dellawar Warrior which Mr. Ander-

*Indian Warmarks.*

son and Capt. White-Eyes explained to me. These hiero-
glyphic marks are the history of his whole warfare. The
rude resemblance of a Turtle on the left hand is the
emblem by which his Tribe or Nation is known. The
Cross and the two Halfmoons are the Characters by which
he is personally distinguished among his nation. That
figure on the right hand is the Sun. Those strokes under
it signify the number of men he had with him when he
made this mark, their leaning to the left signifies that they
have their backs towards the Sun and are bound to the
Northward. Those marks on the Lefthand under the
Turtle signify the number of scalps and prisoners he has
taken and of what sex. Those marked thus X are scalps,
those $\overset{*}{X}$ men prisoners and those marked thus $\overset{\circ}{X}$ women

prisoners. The rough sketches of Forts in the middle are what he has helped to attack, but what their names were I cannot learn. Called at several Indian Villages. Crossed the River and got to Newcomers Town. Very sick. Nancy is gone to fetch an old Indian woman to cure me as she says, therefore I must lay by my pen.

*Sunday, September 3rd, 1775.* Last night, Nancy brought an Indian Squaw which called me her Nilum. i.e. Nephew, as Mr. Anderson told me, and behaved very kindly to me, She put her hand on my head for some time, then took a small brown root out of her pocket and with her knife chopped part of it small, then mixed it with water which she gave me to drink, or rather swallow, being about a spoonful, but this I evaded by keeping it in my mouth till I found an opportunity to spit it out. She then took some in her mouth and chewed it and spit on the top of my head, rubbing my head well at the same time. Then she unbuttoned my shirt collar and spat another mouthful down my back. This was uncomfortable but I bore it with patience. She lent me her Matchcoat and told me to go to sleep. Nancy was ordered not to give me any water till morning, however, I prevailed on the good-natured creature to let me take a vomit that Mr. Anderson had with him as soon as the old woman was gone, which has cured me, tho' the old woman believes that her nostrum did it. Obliged to stay here this day, somebody has stolen one of Mr. A's horses. *Monday, September 4th, 1775.* Saw an Indian scalp. Heard an Indian play upon a Tin Violin and make tolerable good music. Went to Kanaughtonhead, walked all the way, my horse loaded with skins. Camped close by the Town. Nancy's kindness to be remembered.

*Tuesday, September 5th, 1775.* At Kanaughtonhead.

Went to the meeting where Divine service was performed in Dutch and English with great solemnity. This Chapel is much neater than that at Wale-hack-tap-poke. Adorned with basket work in various colours all round, with a spinet made by Mr. Smith the parson, and played by an Indian. Drank Tea with Captn. White-Eyes and Captn. Wingenund at an Indian house in Town. This Tea is made of the tops of Ginsing, and I think it very much like Bohea Tea. The leaves are put into a tin canister made water tight and boiled till it is dry, by this means the juices do not evaporate. N. did not choose to go into the town, but employed herself in making me a pair of Mockesons. *Wednesday, September 6th, 1775.* Left Kanaughtonhead. Mr. Anderson bought several cows there which he intends to take to Fort Pitt. Camped within two miles of Wale-hacktappoke.

*Thursday, September 7th, 1775.* Got to Walehacktap-poke to breakfast. N. refused to go into the Town, knowing that the Moravians will not allow anyone to cohabit with Indians in their town. Saw an Indian child baptized, eight Godfathers and four Godmothers, could not understand the ceremony as it was performed in Indian. *Friday, September 8th, 1775.* At Walehacktappoke. Find my body invaded with an army of small animals which will be a little troublesome to dislodge. Saw an Indian sweathouse. It is built of logs about eight feet by five and about two foot high, with a small door and covered all over with earth to keep in the steam. The patient creeps into the house wrapped in his Blanket, when his friends put in large stones red hot and a pail of water, then make up the door as close as possible, the patient throws the water upon the hot stones till the house is filled with hot steam and vapour. He continues in this little hell as long as he is able to bear it, when the door is opened and the patient instantly plunged into the River. This method of treating the Smallpox has been destructive to many of them. Bought a blanket made of a Buffalo skin.

*Saturday, September 9th, 1775.* Left the town. Mr. Anderson, N. and I went to the Tuscarora town. Then got lost in the Woods and rambled till dark, when we camped by the side of a little run. Very merry this afternoon with our misfortune. *Sunday, September 10th, 1775.* Rambled till noon when we found ourselves at Bouquet's old Fort now demolished. Went to an Indian Camp, where Mr. Anderson met with an old wife of his, who would go with him, which he agreed to. We have each of us a ·/ Girl. It is an odd way of travelling, but we are obliged to submit to it. Met with Mr. Anderson's people in the evening, camped by the side of Tuscarora Creek. Saw the vestige, the Tuscarora old town, but now deserted. *Monday, September 11th, 1775.* Mr. Anderson and I with our Ladies proceeded, and left the people to bring the skins and cattle which he had purchased. Travelled over a great deal of bad land. About sundown Mr. A. called out, " A Panther." I looked about and saw it set in a tree about twenty yards from me. Fired at it on horseback and shot it through the neck. It is of a Brown colour and shaped like a cat, but much larger. It measured five foot nine inches from Nose end to Tail end. Camped and skinned the Panther. This exploit has raised me in N. esteem exceedingly, tho' I claim no merit from it, being merely accidental. *Tuesday, Sept. 12th, 1775.* Our ·/ Squaws are very necessary, fetching our horses to the Camp and saddling them, making our fire at night and cooking our victuals, and every other thing they think will please us. Travelled over several barren mountains, some of them produce great plenty of wild Grapes. Lodged in an old Indian Camp. Bad water. *Wednesday, Sept. 13th, 1775.* Met John Gibson and an Indian going to hasten the Indians to the Treaty. Dined at Mr. Gibson's. Camped at the mouth of a small run, ten miles from Fort Pitt.

*Fort Pitt — Thursday, September 14th, 1775.* Got to Fort Pitt about noon. Left our Girls amongst the Indians that are coming to the Treaty. Great numbers of people in Town come to the Treaty. Terrible news from the Northward, but so confused I hoped there is little truth in it. *Friday, September 15th, 1775.* Very few of the Indians come in yet, the commissioners have been waiting for them a week. Shall be obliged to stay here some time to see the Treaty. *Saturday, September 16th, 1775.* Got acquainted with Mr. Ephraim Douglas, an Indian trader. Found him sensible and an agreeable companion. N. finished my Leggings and Mockeysons, very neat ones.

*Sunday, September 17th, 1775.* Here are members of Congress to treat with the Indians, Delegates from the Conventions of Virginia and Pensylvania for the purpose, and Commissioners from the Convention of Virginia to settle the accounts of the last campaign against the Indians. All Colns., Majors, or Captains and very big with their own importance. Confound them altogether. Colonial disputes are very high between Virginia and Pensylvania and if not timely suppressed will end in tragical consequences. *Monday, September 18th, 1775.* Spent the day in company with Mr. Douglas. *Tuesday, September 19th, 1775.* No news of the Indians, the Commissioners are afraid they will not come at all. *Wednesday, September 20th, 1775.* N. uneasy at parting with me. Obliged to promise her to return in two moons. *Thursday, September 21st, 1775.* Great commotion amongst the people about the boundaries of Pensylvania and Virginia, imprisoning the Magistrates in the Pensylvania Interest. Expect some lives will be lost on the occasion. *Friday, September 22nd, 1775.* Begin to be very uneasy to stay here doing nothing, but cannot get my affairs settled as the Furs have not yet come. *Saturday, September 23rd, 1775.* In the afternoon with Mr. Douglas and some of the Pensylvania party to see a rejectment served. A disagreeable scene between the parties. *Sunday, September 24th, 1775.* Nothing but quarrelling and fighting in every part of the town. *Monday, September 25th, 1775.* Informed that the Shawnee Indians were at Logstown. Went over the Alligany River with Mr. Douglas to get Island Grapes. This is a small grape and grows on low vines on the gravelly beeches and Islands in the River. But the most delicious Grape I ever eat.

*Tuesday, September 26th, 1775.* This morning N. informed me that the Indians would come to the Council fire. About noon the Shawnees and Dellawars Indians with one of the Ottawa Chiefs crossed the River in two Canoes, about thirty in number. They were met at the River side by the Delegates and Garrison under arms, who saluted them with a Volley, which the Indian Warriors returned, then proceeded to the Council house, dancing, beating the drum, and singing the Peace Song, all the way. When they got to the Council house the Dancing ceased and all took their places according to seniority, and a profound silence ensued for the space of ten minutes. One of their old men then got up and spoke a few words to the Delegates, signifying that he hoped they should brighten the chain

of Friendship and gave them a small string of white wampum, several others spoke and gave Wampum. Then they
lighted a pipe and smoked with everyone in the house out
of one pipe. The Delegates had an artfull speech prepared
for them and adjourned the business till to-morrow. The
Indians seem a little confused.

*Wednesday, September 27th, 1775.* The Treaty re-
newed to-day when the Ottawa Chief made one of the
best speeches I ever heard from any man. Determined to
get a copy of it if possible. My Landlady informs me that
I am likely to be took up for a Spy by the Delegates.
*Thursday, September 28th, 1775.* My peltry arrived this
day, which I sold to Mr. Anderson, but find I shall be a
loser upon the whole. Determined to leave the town on
Monday. *Friday, September 29th, 1775.* The Indians
seem displeased at something. Meet at the Council house
every day.

*Saturday, September 30th, 1775.* Went over the River
and bought a Porcupine Skin of an Indian. It is something
like our Hedgehog at home, only the quills are longer, the
Indians dye them of various colours and work them on
their trinkets. Mr. Edward Rice promised me his horse
to carry me to V. Crawford's on Monday. Sold my Gun
to Mr. James Berwick, who gave me a copy of the Indian
speech. Saw the Indians dance in the Council house. N.
very uneasy, she weeps plentifully. I am unhappy that this
honest creature has taken such a fancy to me.

*Sunday, October 1st, 1775.* Took leave of most of my
acquaintances in town. Mr. Douglas gave me an Indian
Tobacco pouch made of a Mink Skin adorned with porcupine quills. He is desirous of keeping a correspondence
with me, which in all probability will be for the interest

of us both. I have conceived a great regard for the Indians and really feel a most sensible regret in parting from them, however contemptible opinion others may entertain of these honest poor creatures. If we take an impartial view of an Indian's general conduct with all the disadvantages they labour under, at the same time divest ourselves of prejudice, I believe every honest man's sentiments would be in favour of them. As soon as an Indian comes into the world he is tied with his back to a board which serves for bed and cradle, and by putting a string through the end of the board next his head is very conveniently conveyed from place to place on his Mother's back. He is kept in this position till half a year old, but often plunged in the water in Summer and rolled in the Snow in Winter. He is then set at liberty to walk as soon as he can. Their Youth is never troubled with severe Pedagogues to whip their senses away, for they are entirely unacquainted with letter or figures. The little knowledge they have of past times is handed to them by hieroglyphics or tradition, subject to numberless errors and misrepresentations. Hunting is their diversion as well as support, and in this they are initiated early in life.

There is established in each Nation a Species of Government which I cannot just now find a name for. It is neither despotic, Aristocratical, Democratical, but rather a compound of the two last. Their Kings have no more honour or respect paid them than another man, and is obliged to hunt for his living as well as the rest. Except in Council, he has a right to speak first, and if he be an old man in whose ability they can confide, his advice is generally observed. In War he acts as General. When anything of consequence is to be done, the whole nation is convened at the Council house built for that purpose. Everyone has a right to speak, but it is generally left to the old men to debate the matter, as they pay the greatest attention to the voice of wisdom which experience has conferred on the aged. Everything is conducted with the greatest regularity and decorum, silence and deliberation, only one speaks at once, and then the most profound silence and attention is observed.

Those famed for oratory have an opportunity of displaying their talents to the greatest advantage. They express themselves in a bold figurative style, accompanied with violent gestures, tho' exceedingly natural and well adapted to what they are saying and in general as expressive as their words. Their dress, attitude and firmness of countenance (when speaking) even to a person ignorant of their language, strike his mind with something awful and his ideas with something great and noble. The following speech shows they are not wanting in words:

### *Speech of Shaganaba, the Ottawa Chief.*

" Fathers: From the information of the people at Detroit with distrust I accepted your invitation, and measured my way to this Council fire with trembling feet. Your reception of me convinces me of this falsehood and the groundlessness of my fears. Truth and they have long been enemies. My Father and many of our Chiefs have lately tasted of Death. The remembrance of that misfortune almost unmans me, and fills my eyes with tears. Your kind condolence has lightened my Heart of its heavy burden, and shall be transmitted to my latest posterity." Here he gave a string of White Wampum. " Fathers, I rejoice to hear this day what I have heard, and do assure you it shall be faithfully delivered to my Nation. Should you want to speak to me in future, I shall joyfully attend and now thank you for the present invitation. The particular favour shewed me and the Gun you have given me for the kindness I shewed your Brother, Young Fields, claim my warmest acknowledgements. I am conscious I did but my duty. He who barely does his duty merits no praise. If any of your people visit mine, whether curiosity or business be their motive, or if unwillingly compelled by the strong hand of the Victor, they shall find the same entertainment your Brother found. You inform me if my people visit yours they shall meet with an hospitable welcome. My fears are done away. I have not one doubt remaining. I will recommend it to my Young men to visit and get acquainted with yours. Fathers, what has passed this day is, too deeply engraved on my heart for time ever to erase. I foretell that the Sunny rays of this day's peace shall warm and protect our Children's Children from the storms of misfortune. To confirm it I give you my Right hand, that hand which never yet was given, but the heart consented, that never shed Human blood in peace or spared an enemy in War, and I assure you of my Friendship with a Tongue which never yet mocked at Truth, since I was of age to know that Falsehood was a crime."

I think this speech would do honour to an orator of the first magnitude, allowance being made for the beauty it loses in translating. The power of their King is rather persuasive than coercive. He is rather reverenced as a Father than feared as a King. He has neither Revenue Officers, or prison or can put anyone to death or conflict any corporal punishment on any of his people. One act of injustice would pull him from the head of affairs forever. No hereditary honour titles amongst them, an Indian has no method to render himself of consequence among his companions, but by his superiority of personal qualifications of body or mind, and which are far from being such fools as they are generally imagined to be. Though they have not the advantage of learning, they by the light of natural reason distinguish right from wrong with the greatest exactness. They never mean deceit themselves and detest it in others, nor ever place confidence a second time where it has been once abused. Indeed those that have conversed much with the whites have learned several things from them, that the natural honesty of their nature would never have thought of.

In all their trades with the Europeans they are imposed on in the greatest manner. Their sensibility is quick and their passions ungoverned, I may say ungovernable, and it is not to be wondered at if they make returns in kind whenever it is in their power. It is said they are cruel and barbarous and I believe they exercise some cruelties, the thought of which makes human nature shudder, but this is to be attributed to their national customs. It is a general opinion with White men that their difference in colour, and advantages of education give them a superiority over those poor people which Heaven and Nature never designed. They are beings endowed with reason and common sense and I make not the least doubt but they are as valuable in the eyes of their Maker as we are, our fellow creatures, and in general above our level in many virtues that give real preeminence, however despicably we think of or injuriously we treat them.

Their persons are tall and remarkably straight, of a copper colour, with long black hair, regular features and fine black eyes. The dress of the men is short, white linen or calico shirts which come a little below their hips without buttons at neck or wrist and in general ruffled and a great number of small silver brooches stuck in it. Silver plates about three inches broad round the wrists of their arms, silver wheels in their ears, which are stretched long enough for the tip of the ear to touch the shoulder, silver rings in their noses, Breechclout and Mockeysons with a matchcoat that serves them for a bed at night. They cut off their hair except a lock on the crown of the head and go bareheaded, pluck out their beards. The women wear the same sort of shirts as the men and a sort of short petticoat that comes no lower than the knee, leggings and Mockeysons, the same as the men. Wear their hair long, curled down the back in silver plates, if they can afford it, if not tied in a club with red gartering. No rings in the nose but plenty in the ears. Both men and women paint with Vermillion and other colours mixed with Bear's Oil and adorn themselves with any tawdry thing they think pretty. Their language is soft, copious and expressive. God in the Delawar is Wale-hak-ma-neta, the Devil, Menta, Bread, Augh-pone. They cannot curse or swear in their own language, are obliged to the Europeans for that vice.

Religion they have little amongst them and that seems to have something of the Jewish manner in it. They have some particular dances at the full and change of the moon, and sometimes pay a sort of adoration to the Sun. At certain periods the women absent themselves from society for a few days and will not suffer anyone to touch a rag of their clothes or eat with them. Before they join their friends again they wash all their clothes and purify every vessel they have made use of with fire. Marriage is little observed, as they live together no longer than they can agree. The woman keeps all the children. Wives are absolute slaves to their husbands. It is very rare for a couple to live all their life together without changing. Polygamy is not allowed. They pay great respect to the dead, particularly those that have rendered themselves conspicuous in War. Their houses are built of Logs or Bark with the fire in the middle and benches on each side the house which serve for chairs, beds, and tables. In Summer they chiefly live in the woods, in Bark tents, smoke much tobacco mixed with the leaves of Sumack which is very pleasant. Inclined much to Silence, except when in liquor which they are very fond of, and then they are very loquacious committing the greatest outrages on each other. The women always hide all offensive weapons as soon as the men get intoxicated, and it is observed that they never all get drunk together, one of them will keep sober to take care of the rest. There is upwards of thirty different nations nearly similar in customs and manner, none of them very numerous. Since spirituous liquors were introduced amongst them they have depopulated fast. Smallpox has made terrible havoc.

*Monday, October 2nd, 1775.* Am informed that the Delegates intend to examine my papers. I will prevent the scoundrels, if possible. Settled my affairs with Mr. John Anderson, who has behaved more like a Father than a common acquaintance. Made him a compliment of my silver buckles and agreed to keep up a correspondence. Parting with N. was the most affecting thing I have ever experienced since I left home. The poor creature wept most plentifully. However base it may appear to conscientious people, it is absolutely necessary to take a temporary wife if they have to travel amongst the Indians. Left Fort Pitt. Dined at widow Myers. Got to Mr. John De Camp's.

*West Augusta, Virginia — Tuesday, October 3rd, 1775.* At Mr. John De Camp's, who absolutely refuses to let me go away till to-morrow. *Wednesday, October 4th, 1775.* Left Mr. De Camp's, lost my way several times, but got to V. Crawford's in the evening. *Thursday, October 5th, 1775.* At V. Crawford's. Performed the part of a Clergyman at the funeral of an infant. At the Grave the parents and friends Wept and drank Whiskey alternately. V. Crawford promised to hire me a horse to carry me over the mountain before I went to Fort Pitt, but I believe he never intends to perform. *Friday, October 6th, 1775.* Went to Captn. Gist's to see if he could assist me with a horse. He treated me very kindly, but could not furnish me with a horse. Lodged there. *Saturday, October 7th, 1775.* Returned to V. Crawford's. Find V. wants to take advantage of my necessity. Experience teaches me adversity is the touchstone of friendship. *Sunday, October 8th, 1775.* At V. Crawford's very uneasy, my clothes wore out and my money almost expended. I have made an unfortunate summer's work of it, but cannot tax myself with extravagance, but with a great deal of imprudence in the choice of my companion Rice.

*Monday, October 9th, 1775.* On my way to Major Crawford's saw the vestiges of an old fortification. It appears to me that this country has been inhabited by a race of people superior in military knowledge to the present Indians. In different parts of the country there are the vestiges of regular fortifications, and it is well known the Indians have not the least knowledge of that art. When, or by whom, these places were built. I leave to more able antiquarians than I am to determine. Fortunately for me Zachariah Connel is going over the Mountain to-morrow and will find me a horse to go along with him. Returned to V. Crawford's.

*Allegany Mountain* — *Tuesday, October 10th, 1775.*
Left V. Crawford's, whom I believe to be a scoundrel. Set
out with Mr. Zac. Connel for Winchester. Lodged at the
Great Meadows at one Lynch's Tavern in company with
Colnl. Lee, Colnl. Peyton, Colnl. Clapham, Colnl. Black-
burn, Colnl. McDonald and Mr. Richard Lee. All of them
Commissioners from the Virginia Convention, for settling
the accounts of the last Indian War. A set of niggardly
beings. Great want of beds, but I am well content with
the floor and my blanket. *Wednesday, October 11th, 1775.*
Crossed the Falling Timbers, Yaough-a-ga-ny River, at
the Great Crossing Laurel mountain. Breakfasted at Rice's
Tavern. Then over the winding ridge. Crossed the Maryland line, and Negro Mountain. Lodged at Tumblestones
Tavern on the top of the Allegany Mountain. *Thursday,
October 12th, 1775.* Crossed the little meadow mountain,
Shades of Death and the Savage Mountain. Breakfasted at
Tittle's Tavern. Then to Greg's Tavern, Fort Cumberland
now deserted and demolished on Wills Creek and Potow-
meck River. Got to Old Town in Maryland, 14 miles
from Fort Cumberland. Lodged at one Rollins's Tavern.

## VII

## BACK IN VIRGINIA—NEWS OF THE REVOLUTION

*FROM Old Town to Mr. Wm. Gibb's—Friday, October 13th, 1775.* This is a pretty little town for such an inconvenient situation. Some good land about it first settled by Cressop an Englishman from Skipton in Craven. Crossed the Potowmeck River at the conjunction of the North and South Branch. Met a Woman with two small children in great distress, on whom I bestowed my last shirt except that I had on, crossed the Spring Gap Mountain and dined at Rinker's Tavern. Got to Mr. Gibb's in the evening. Mr. G not at home. Two young ladies lodged there who gazed at me as if I was a wild man of the Woods. They and my ragged breeches caused me to spend a disagreeable evening.

*Redmont, Berkeley County, Virginia—Saturday, October 14th, 1775.* Got up early this morning and mended my breeches with a piece of my shirt lap. Shaved and made myself as decent as my circumstances would admit. After settling with Mr. Connel, I have only one penny left. No money to be got at Mr. Gibb's as he is not at home. Went to Mr. Nourse's, who makes me welcome and will assist me to Leesburg. *Sunday, October 15th, 1775.* At Mr. Nourse's very genteelly entertained. Major Gates's lady here on a visit who insisted on me going to Church, ragged as my dress was. Mr. Nourse read prayers, no parson.

*Leesburg, Loudoun County, Virginia.* — *Monday, October 16th, 1775.* He lent me a horse to Leesburg, where I arrived in the evening. Lodged at Mr. Moffit's. *Tuesday, October 17th, 1775.* Went to Captn. Douglas. Agreed to pay one half of the expenses I have been at and confirm the bargain, but this I will defer for sometime, till there is a probability of these disputes being ended. *Wednesday, October 18th, 1775.* Slept very little last night, it being the first night I have slept in a bed since the 28th. April last. Got a Boy and horse from Captn. Douglas to carry me to Alexandria. Returned Mr. Nourse's horse by Mr. F. Keys. Set out for Alexandria in company with Mr. Charles Little. Dined at Mosses. Lodged at Mr. Little's about 5 miles from Alexandria.

*Alexandria, Virginia* — *Thursday, October 19th, 1775.* Got to Alexandria to dinner. Found Mr. Kirk very well. He was glad to see me, expected that I was killed by the Indians. A letter from my Father dated Sept. 16th, '74 which makes me very unhappy, with one from Mr. Latham of the same date. Everything is in confusion, all exports are stopped and hardly a possibility of getting home. I have nothing to support me and how to proceed I do not know. I am in necessity obliged to rely on Mr. Kirk's kind promises. This is disagreeable, but I must submit to it. *Friday, October 20th, 1775.* Slept very little last night owing to my agitation of mind. To add to my distress, the Moths have eaten two suits of my clothes to pieces. Nothing but War talked of, raising men and making every military preparation. A large army at Boston, another in Canada and another at or about Norfolk in Virginia. This cannot be redressing grievances, it is open rebellion and I am convinced if Great Britain does not send more men here and subdue them soon they will declare Independence C.T.M.P. *Saturday, October 21st, 1775.* I am now in a disagreeable situation, if I enter into any sort of business I must be obliged to enter into the service of these rascals and fight against my Friends and Country if called upon. On the other hand, I am not permitted to depart the Continent and have nothing if I am fortunate enough to escape the jail. I will live as cheap as I can and hope for better times. *Sunday, October 22nd, 1775.* No Church.

*Monday, October 23nd, 1775.* News that Lord Dunmore was coming up the River with four thousand men to destroy the town. I am determined to get on board the King's Ship as soon as possible. *Tuesday, October 24th, 1775.* The inhabitants begin to remove their most valuable effects out of town, but I think it will prove a false alarm. *Wednesday, October 25th, 1775.* Exceedingly uneasy. Mr. Kirk does everything in his power to make me unhappy. *Thursday, October 26th, 1775.* News that Lord Dunmore had landed at Norfolk and seized 50 Guns and spoilt all the cannons there. *Friday, October 27th, 1775.* Supped and spent the evening at Captn. Ramsay's. Great political dispute with him. *Saturday, October 28th, 1775.* Mr. Kirk went to Leesburg and left me to take care of his house and people. Very unwell this evening. *Sunday, October 29th, 1775.* A violent pain in my breast this morning, took a dose of Salts which has taken it away.

*Monday, October 30th, 1775.* The people here are ripe for a revolt, nothing but curses and imprecations against England, her Fleets, armies, and friends. The King is publicly cursed and rebellion rears her horrid head. The people in this Colony and the province of Maryland are in general greatly in debt to the Merchants in England, and

think a revolt would pay all. *Tuesday, October 31st, 1775.*
Understand I am suspected of being what they call a Tory
(that is a Friend to my Country) and am threatened with
Tar and Feathers, Imprisonment and the D—l knows what.
Curse the Scoundrels. *Wednesday, November 1st, 1775.*
News that 300 people on the Eastern shore in Maryland
had gone over to Lord Dunmore. The Committee took
an account of the Flour in town as they apprehend his Lordship will pay them a visit. *Thursday, November 2nd, 1775.*
Nothing remarkable. *Friday, November 3rd, 1775.* Determined to talk about the time as little as possible and
slip away as soon as I can get an opportunity. *Saturday,
November 4th, 1775.* Captn. McCabe came down and
brought me a letter from Mr. Kirk. *Sunday, November
5th, 1775.* No preaching here, for people are too much
taken up with the War.

*Monday, November 6th, 1775.* News that the King's
Ships had burnt Falmouth in New Hampshire. Some New
England Masters of Vessels that lie here, being the anniversary of the Gunpowder Plot, had the Pope, Lord North,
Barnard, Hutchinson, and the Devil burnt in effigy after
carting them through the town with Drums and Fifes.
*Tuesday, November 7th, 1775.* Nothing remarkable.
*Wednesday, November 8th, 1775.* Want of employment
and my disagreeable situation make my life miserable.
Something must be done to get a living. *Thursday, Nov.
9th, 1775.* At dinner had a long dispute with Doctor Jackson about the origin of the present proceedings. I believe
he was employed to draw me into a political dispute. I proceeded with great caution and temerity. Most of the company agrees that I had the better of the argument. But
never so much embarrassed in my life.

This convinces me that, though parents take ever so much pains to inculcate every virtue in the minds of their Children, they commit a great error by treating them too long as mere children. I can experimentally prove that this system is attended with the worst consequences. A severe restraint over youth, unless those in whom bad dispositions are apparent, is the surest method to make blockheads of them, for they are thereby prevented learning to think and by appearing to make little of their opinion, smother every ray of genius and almost every qualification they profess and give them such a diffidence of themselves as will make them appear, though possessed of the best understandings, unpolished clowns. A young man always under the eye of a severe parent and by his rigour restrained from enjoying those amusements to which youth are naturally addicted and from which a little indulgence would wean him, no sooner becomes his own master, than, hurried on by those gratifications which his imagination has represented so delicious to him he generally plunges into excesses, which in a short time dissipate his fortune, ruin his health, and too often bring him an untimely martyr to his grave. Another ill consequence attending this conduct is that it is impossible to know their disposition without allowing them the liberty of acting as they choose in things of no material consequence. I mean, when they are arrived at the age of eighteen or twenty, for at that time of life, their passions are just ripening, when the bent and turn of their minds, the good or bad dispositions, will be seen and are easily brought to perfection or in a great measure extinguished. I am led into this train of thoughts by the many embarrassments this system has frequently laid me under at different periods and am convinced it will be a great obstruction to my future proceedings or advancement in life. When I am in company with people of equal or superior abilities or those of an unconstrained behavior, tinctured with a large share of assurance, my diffidence and temerity is so great that it renders me ridiculous, even when the discourse happens to turn upon a topic I understand as well as any of them. (Mem. Never to enter into Political disputes again till I have more impudence or am in a free country.)

*Friday, November 10th, 1775.* This War is carried on by the Americans in the most curious manner. The name of liberty is most vilely prostituted. Under this sanction the Congress have persuaded the people to believe that paper Bills paid by them are transmuted into real Gold and Silver after it has received their infallible emblem and benediction. There are some few heretics which dispute the orthodoxy of this doctrine, but if it is in the power of prisons and persecution to convince them of their mistaken notions I believe it will not be wanting. Their emblems and mottoes on their bills are well adapted. On the 8 Dollar bills there is the figure of a harp with this motto — *Majora minoribus consonant* (The greater and smaller ones sound together). On the 4 Dollar bills is impressed a Wild Boar running on the spear of the hunter with this motto — *Aut mors, Aut Vita Decora* (Either Death or life is glorious). On the three Dollar bills is drawn an Eagle on the wing, pouncing on a Crane, who turns upon his back and receives the eagle on the point of his long bill which pierces the eagle's breast, with this motto — *Exitus in dubio est* (The event is uncertain). On the 5 Dollar bills we have a thorny bush, which a hand seems attempting to eradicate. The hand seems to bleed, as if pricked by the spines. The motto is, *Sustine vel abstine* (Which may be rendered, Bear with me or let me alone — or thus, Either support or leave me). On the 6 Dollar bills is the figure of a Beaver gnawing a large tree, with this motto, *Perseverando* (By perseverance). On the 2 Dollar bills is the figure of a hand and flail over sheaves of wheat with this motto, *Tribulatio ditat* (Thrashing improves it). On the one Dollar bills is the plant Acanthus sprouting on all sides under a weight placed upon it with the motto, *Dipressa resurgit* (Tho' oppressed it rises). The 7 Dollar bills have for their device a Storm descending from a Black heavy Cloud with this motto *Serenabit* (It will clear up). The 30 Dollar bills have a wreath of Laurel on a marble monument or Altar, the motto, *Si recte facies* (If you act rightly). The Congress have issued two million of Dollars in these bills for the support of the present War. It is to be sunk by the sale of Land, in Terra Incognita. *Saturday, Nov. 11th, 1775.* News — Chumbly taken. *Sunday, Nov. 12th, 1775.* Mr. Kirk returned home and is well pleased with my management in his absence. *Monday, Nov. 13th, 1775.* Mr. V. Crawford called to see me and Lodged with me at Mr. Kirk's. *Tuesday, Nov. 14th, 1775.* Nothing remarkable. *Wednesday, Nov. 15th, 1775.* No prospect of getting home this winter, as I am suspected of being a Spy. I am very narrowly watched. Agreed to go to Leesburg to assist Mr. Kirk's bookkeeper to settle his books, but this must be kept a profound secret that I am anyways employed by him, tho' I receive no wages, only my board, such is the fashion of the times. *Thursday, Nov. 16th, 1775.* No news. Hope General Howe has given them a drubbing, makes them so quiet.

*Leesburg, Virginia — Friday, November 17th, 1775.* Left Alexandria. Dined at Mosses. Got to Leesburg in the evening. Lodged at Mrs. Sorrel's with Mr. Cavan. *Saturday, Nov. 18th, 1775.* At Leesburg, spent the evening with Captn. Douglas, Mr. Johnston, Mr. I. Booker, and Cavan at a Turkey feast in the neighbourhood. *Sunday, Nov. 19th, 1775.* Went to Church or Courthouse which you please, in the forenoon, spent the evening at Mr. George Ancram's. *Monday, Nov. 20th, 1775.* Spent the evening at Captn. McCabe's. Great disturbance for want of Salt. *Tuesday, Nov. 21st, 1775.* Nothing remarkable. *Wednesday, Nov. 22nd, 1775.* Find Cavan to be a good-natured, sensible young man, and his sentiments agree with mine. Spent the evening at George Johnston's. *Thursday, Nov. 23rd, 1775.* Very uneasy. Dam the rascals. He thinks no more of them than I do. *Friday, Nov. 24th, 1775.* News — That St. John's was taken and 500 prisoners in it and that Major Connolly was taken in disguise, at Frederick Town in Maryland. *Saturday, Nov. 25th, 1775.* Spent the evening at Captn. McCabe's in company with Captn. Douglas and Cavan. *Sunday, Nov. 26th, 1775.* A Methodist meeting in town. *Monday, Nov. 27th, 1775.* Spent the evening at Mr. Johnston's with Hugh Neilson and Cavan. *Tuesday, Nov. 28th, 1775.* Nothing worth notice. *Wednesday, Nov. 29th, 1775.* Dined at Captn. McCabe's. Spent the evening at the store in company with Captn. McCabe and Captn. Speake and all of us got drunk. *Thursday, Nov. 30th, 1775.* Dined at Captn. Douglas's, being the anniversary of St. Andrews the titular saint of the Scotch, in company with Captn. McCabe, Messrs. Cavan, Booker, Johnston, Neilson and McIntire. We had one of the best dinners I have ever seen in America. Spent an agreeable day, but find myself low-spirited, in short, almost stupid sometimes, continually unhappy. *Friday, Dec. 1st,*

*1775.* Dined at Captn. Douglas's. Got to town in the evening, which I spent with an honest Quaker, one Matthews. News that Quebec was taken by the Rebels, but I believe it to be a D—d lie. *Saturday, Dec. 2nd, 1775.* Nothing remarkable. *Sunday, Dec. 3rd, 1775.* No preaching in town.

*Monday, December 4th, 1775.* Left Leesburg, in company with Mr. Matthews and Mr. James Booker. Dined at Nolan's Ferry, where we crossed the Potowmeck and went to Frederick Town in Maryland. This is a smart town, a small manufactory of Stockings and Guns, a Dutch Church and an English one with a poorhouse and several very good buildings. The inhabitants are chiefly Dutch. It is 25 miles from Leesburg. Lodged at Carlton's Tavern. *Tuesday, Dec. 5th, 1775.* Went to see Major Connolly, who is prisoner at Frederick Town, but obliged to get one of the Committee men to go with me. They would not trust us alone. Found him in good spirits. He was bound to Detroit and had one Smith and Cameron with him to raise a Regmt. there and meet Lord Dunmore at Alexandria in the spring. Left Frederick Town. Dined at Noland's Ferry, got to Leesburg at night. *Saturday, Dec. 9th, 1775.* Nothing remarkable these four days. *Sunday, Dec. 10th, 1775.* Went to Church, spent the evening at Mr. Johnston's with the Rev. Mr. David Griffiths and several Gentlemen. *Monday, Dec. 11th, 1775.* Court day, no business done, everything in confusion. Wrote to Fort Pitt by V. Crawford. *Tuesday, Dec. 12th, 1775.* Nothing remarkable. *Saturday, Dec. 16th, 1775.* Nothing worth mentioning this week. *Sunday, Dec. 17th, 1775.* Went to hear Bombast, Noise and Nonsense, uttered by a Methodist and an Anabaptist preacher. Spent the evening at Mr.

G. Johnston's. *Thursday, Dec. 21st, 1775.* Nothing but lies in papers. *Friday, Dec. 22nd, 1775.* Spent the evening at Captn. McCabe's in company with George West Esq. Find him a volatile, flighty man. *Saturday, Dec. 23rd, 1775.* Very cold day, freezing and snowing. *Sunday, Dec. 24th, 1775.* Went with Captn. McCabe to Mr. West's about five miles from town. No news for several days.

*Pea Hill, Loudoun County — Monday, December 25th, 1775.* Christmas Day, which we spent at Mr. West's. *Tuesday, Dec. 26th, 1775.* After dinner went to Mr. Wm. Elzize, but returned to Mr. West's at night. *Wednesday, Dec. 27th, 1775.* The sharpest frost last night I ever knew, we slept in a very small room and had a large fire. It froze the wine in the pot, which did not stand more than five foot from the fire. Left Pea Hill. Mr. West treated us with the greatest civility. Went to town.

*Leesburg — Thursday, December 28th, 1775.* A Methodist meeting in town, great numbers of people came in sleighs. They are something like our sleds. *Friday, Dec. 29th, 1775.* No news. An invitation to Captn. Douglas, on Monday next. *Saturday, Dec. 30th, 1775.* Nothing remarkable., *Sunday, Dec. 31st, 1775.* This is the last day of the year 1775, which I have spent but very indifferently. In short I have done nothing, but wore out my clothes and constitution, and according to the present prospect of affairs, the New Year bears a forbidding aspect. I am here a prisoner at large. If I attempt to depart and don't succeed, a prison must be my lot. If I do anything to get a living, perhaps I must be obliged to fight against my King and Country, which my conscience abhors. I will wait with patience till summer and then risk a passage.

*Garralland, Loudoun County — Monday, January 1st, 1776.* Went to Garalland, seat of Captn. Wm. Douglas. A great deal of agreeable company and very merry. *Tuesday, Jan. 2nd, 1776.* At Garralland Dancing and playing at Cards. In the evening several of the company went in quest of a poor Englishman, who they supposed had made Songs on the Committee, but did not find him. *Wednesday, Jan. 3rd, 1776.* Went to Leesburg. Spent the evening at Mr. Johnston's. *Thursday, Jan. 4th, 1776.* Alarmed with some symptoms of the Itch. *Friday, Jan. 5th, 1776.* This being my birthday, invited Captn. McCabe, H. Neilson, W. Johnston, Matthews, Booker and my particular Friend P. Cavan to spend the evening with me. We have kept it up all night and I am at this time very merry.

*Saturday, January 6th, 1776.* Spent the evening at Mr. Johnston's with our last night's company. He is going to camp. All of us got most feloniously drunk. Captn. McCabe, Hugh Neilson and I kept it up all night. *Sunday, Jan. 7th, 1776.* Went to bed about two o'clock in the afternoon, stupidly drunk. Not been in bed or asleep for two nights. *Monday, Jan. 8th, 1776.* My last two days' conduct will not bear reflection. The uneasiness of my mind causes me to drink deeper when in company to elevate my spirits. Fatal remedy indeed. *Saturday, Jan. 13th, 1776.* Nothing remarkable this week. *Sunday, Jan. 14th, 1776.* Went with Captn. McCabe to dine with Mr. Matthew Cammel about two miles from Town. Returned in the evening. No news. *Monday, Jan. 15th, 1776.* Spent the evening at Captn. McCabe's with Captn. I. Speake, who gave us certain accounts that Norfolk was burnt on the 1st of the present month and that there is a Vessel repairing at

Alexandria bound for London with passengers. Determined to go down and take a passage to-morrow.

*Alexandria, Virginia — Tuesday, January 16th, 1776.* Left Leesburg in company with Captn. Speake. Dined at Mosses Ordinary. Got to Alexandria. Mr. Kirk informs me that the vessel will not be permitted to go to England or Ireland. No hopes of going in her. Mr. Kirk advises me to keep my intention of going home a secret or I am certain to be imprisoned. D—m the Rascals. *Wednesday, January 17th, 1776.* Drank Coffee at Captn. Harper's. Spent the evening at Captn. Speake's with Captn. F. Speot and Dennis Ramsay. Two conceited ignorant fops. No news, except it be lies. *Thursday, Jan. 18th, 1776.* A many of my old acquaintances looks very cool upon me because I will not be as great scoundrels as themselves. *Friday, Jan. 19th, 1776.* A pamphlet called "Commonsense" makes a great noise. One of the vilest things that ever was published to the world. Full of false representations, lies, calumny, and treason, whose principles are to subvert all Kingly Governments and erect an Independent Republic. I believe the writer to be some Yankey Presbyterian, Member of the Congress. The sentiments are adopted by a great number of people who are indebted to Great Britain. *Saturday, Jan. 20th, 1776.* An odd adventure this evening. The Follies of life are innumerable. *Monday, January 22nd, 1776.* Nothing but Independence talked of. *Tuesday, Jan. 23rd, 1776.* Last night the River froze over. Dined at Captn. Conway's with Mr. Buckhamhan. Drank Coffee at Mr. John's. *Wednesday, Jan. 24th, 1776.* Left Alexandria. Dined at Mosses. Got to Leesburg in the evening. D.G. *Friday, Jan. 26th, 1776.* Nothing but Independence will go down. The Devil is in the people.

*Saturday, Jan. 27th, 1776.* This evening Mr. Cavan and I salved for the Itch, and got very merry. Curse the disorder. *Sunday, Jan. 28th, 1776.* Received a letter from Mr. Kirk advising that Lord Dunmore was coming up the River as soon as the Ice would permit him and desiring us to send him all the Waggons that we can get. I wish his Lordship a safe arrival.

*Monday, January 29th, 1776.* All in confusion. The Committee met to choose Officers for the new company that are to be raised. They are 21 in number, the first men in the County and had two bowls of toddy, but could not find cash to pay for it. Spent the evening at Captn. Mc.Cabe's. *Tuesday, Jan. 30th, 1776.* Preparing for the reception of Mr. Kirk and his people. Mr. Hugh Neilson spent the evening at the store. News, that Quebec was not taken, but that Montgomery had stormed it. He was killed and his rabble defeated. *Wednesday, Jan. 31st, 1776.* Nothing remarkable. *Friday, February 2nd, 1776.* Find our Landlady to be a thief. Determined to watch her narrowly. *Saturday, Feb. 3rd, 1776.* Spent the evening at the Tavern with Messrs. Neilson Booker, & Cavan. Mr. Kirk's goods arrived in town. *Sunday, Feb. 4th, 1776.* Methodist meeting in town. *Monday, Feb. 5th, 1776.* Spent the evening at the Tavern with Mr. V. Crawford. *Tuesday, Feb. 6th, 1776.* Went with Mr. Crawford to Captn. Douglas's, but returned to town in the evening. *Wednesday, Feb. 7th, 1776.* This day the town was alarmed with a Horse Stealer being pursued through the streets several times. The poor fellow had neither saddle or bridle, but got away by swearing he had won the race.

*Thursday, February 8th, 1776.* News, that General Lee was sent with 5000 men to reinforce the Rebel Army at

Quebec. Spent the evening with Mr. B. Call. *Saturday, Feb. 10th, 1776.* Nothing remarkable. *Sunday, Feb. 11th, 1776.* Went with Mr. Cavan and Mr. Thos. Matthews to a Quaker meeting, about 7 miles from town. This is one of the most comfortable places of Worship I was ever in, they had two large fires and a Dutch stove. After a long silence and many groans a Man got up and gave us a short Lecture with great deliberation. Dined at Mr. Jos. Janney's one of the Friends. Got to Leesburg at night. *Monday, Feb. 12th, 1776.* Court day. Great confusion, no business done. The populace deters the Magistrates and they in turn are courting the rebels' favour. Enlisting men for the Rebel Army upon credit. Their paper money is not yet arrived from the Mine. *Tuesday, Feb. 13th, 1776.* Mr. Kirk arrived in town, informs me there is some hopes of a reconciliation. I wish it may be true.

*Wednesday, February 14th, 1776.* Some thoughts of attempting to make Nitre out of the floors of Tobacco houses. If I can effect it, it will gain me a little favour with the people and assist me in my escape from this hateful country. Mentioned it to Mr. J. Booker, who is willing to join me. *Thursday, Feb. 15th, 1776.* Spent the evening at Captn. McCabe's with Mr. Kirk and Cavan. *Friday, Feb. 16th, 1776.* Breakfasted at Mr. McCrea's with Mr. Kirk, who advises me to attempt the Nitre. Mr. K. returned to Alexandria. *Saturday, Feb. 17th, 1776.* Got some earth and fixed tubs, as I was going to make lye, of Ashes, which I intend to let stand two days before I draw it. *Sunday, Feb. 18th, 1776.* Dined at Captn. Douglas returned to town in the evening. *Monday, Feb. 19th, 1776.* Spent the evening at the Tavern with Messrs. Neilson Cavan, Booker, one Doctor, Mr. Nichols and

Doctor Mc.Ginnis. A confounded mad frolic. *Tuesday, Feb. 20th, 1776.* Very sick with my last night's debauch. Temperance is a most finished virtue. *Wednesday, Feb. 21st, 1776.* Boiled my lye (and set it to cool, but am doubtful of success). *Thursday, Feb. 22nd, 1776.* My success is greater than I expected. Am certain I can bring it to bear after a few trials. Went with Mr. Booker and H. Neilson to Garralland. *Friday, Feb. 23rd, 1776.* Returned to Leesburg this morning. Mr. Cavan went to collect debts and left me to take care of the store. *Sunday, Feb. 25th, 1776.* Nothing remarkable.

*Monday, February 26th, 1776.* A report that Commissioners have arrived at Philadelphia to settle affairs with the Congress. Mr. Cavan returned. *Tuesday, Feb. 27th, 1776.* Nothing remarkable. *Wednesday, Feb. 28th, 1776.* Spent the evening at the store with Captn. George Johnston and Mr. Jas. Jannay. Captn. Johnston informs me they killed 82 of the King's troops at the great Bridge near Norfolk without having one man on their side killed or wounded. This is very strange, if it be true. *Thursday, Feb. 29th, 1776.* Spent the evening with Captn. Johnston. Politics the general topic and independence seems to be his favourite scheme and I believe it will be declared very soon. Exceedingly cold. *Friday, March 1st, 1776.* Some talk of a Reconciliation, but am afraid it is not well grounded. Very unwell to-day.

*Saturday, March 2nd, 1776.* Spent the evening at the Tavern in company with Booker, Cavan, Rispes, and Doctor McGinnis, but was obliged to go home to bed sick. *Sunday, March 3rd, 1776.* Violent pains all over my body. Some symptoms of a nervous fever. *Monday, March 4th, 1776.* Applied to the Doctor, who assures me it is a complication of the Nervous Fever and Rheumatism. Gave me physic. *Wednesday, March 20th, 1776.* Have been confined to my room in violent pain. A little better to-day, and able to walk about my room. This is the first day I have been able to write since the 4th. of the month. *Thursday, March 21st, 1776.* Much better, but very weak. Taking a decoction of the woods. My spirits are good and I hope I shall get over this bout. News that the Great Sanhedrim, the Congress, had given the Colonies liberty to trade with all nations but Great Britain and its Islands, and that they had begun to Bombard Boston. *Friday, March 22nd, 1776.* Free from pain, wrapped myself up and went to see the general musters of the Militia in town, about 700 men but few arms. Great confusion among them. *Saturday, March 23rd, 1776.* Am afraid I got cold yesterday, violent pain in my back and head. *Sunday, March 24th, 1776.* Confined to my room. The Doctor scolds me and brings more of his Damd nostrums. *Friday, March 29th, 1776.* Confined to my room these past five days, and greatest part of the time to my bed, unable to help myself. I am a little better to-day, able to walk about the room, but look like the picture of Famine.

*Saturday, March 30th, 1776.* Something better. News, that the Rebels had defeated the King's friends under the command of General Mc.Donald at Widow More's Creek in South Carolina. Part of Genl. Lee's Bodyguard went through here. *Sunday, March 31st, 1776.* News, that the English had evacuated Boston and gone to Sea. Hope it is a lie. *Monday, April 1st, 1776.* A great deal better but weak. Still continue to take the Doctor's slops and he is for confining me another week to my room. Mr. Kirk has written several kind letters to me, but Cavan's kindness I

shall never be able to repay. *Tuesday, April 2nd, 1776.*
Captn. McCabe and Mr. West came to see me and stayed
late. Attending on them is of bad consequence to me at
this time. *Wednesday, April 3rd, 1776.* Sitting up last
night has caused a relapse, confound them both. *Tuesday,
April 9th, 1776.* Confined to my room for five days.

*Wednesday, April 10th, 1776.* Took a violent sweat
last night, which has eased me of all pain and restored the
use of my limbs. No news. *Thursday, April 11th, 1776.*
Find myself much better. Confound the stupid Blockhead that he could not prescribe a sweat sooner. I can
walk about and eat heartily.

*Friday, April 12th, 1776.* Agreed with Mr. James
Booker to join him in making Saltpetre. He is to find
wood, earth, and Negroes to work, and a house proper
to boil it in. I am to find Boilers, tubs, and have the management of the work and go equal shares in the profit.
And pay him for my board at *The Cattail.* Bought a large
kettle and three Rum Hh^{ds}. to make tubs of and sent them
to the place. I shall not be able to go to Sea if I had an
opportunity this three months. This will take off all suspicion and I can live cheaper than in town, admit I make
nothing by the business. *Saturday, April 13th, 1776.*
Much better. Rode to *The Cattail,* about a mile from
town. Set four Tubs with earth for Saltpetre, returned at
night. Believe my ride has done me good. *Sunday, April
14th, 1776.* Nothing but Methodist meetings in every
part of the town. *Monday, April 15th, 1776.* I am now
free from pain, but very weak and feeble and not fit for
anything. Mr. Kirk is coming here, I am determined to
go to *The Cattail. Tuesday, April 16th, 1776.* Preparing

to go to *The Cattail*, Captn. Douglas and Captn. McCabe came to see me and spent the evening with me.

*Cattail, Loudoun County, Virginia — Wednesday, April 17th, 1776.* Left Leesburg. Went to *The Cattail.* Set my tubs arunning, but think it is too weak. *Thursday, April 18th, 1776.* Got my pot fixed to boil the lye and other necessary matters. *Friday, April 19th, 1776.* Began to boil, but find I must construct some method of fixing the Volatile Salts or I shall make very little Nitre. *Saturday, April 20th, 1776.* Set the tubs with fresh earth and put about half a bushel of wood ashes in the bottom of each. I am not able to bear much fatigue. *Sunday, April 21st, 1776.* Mr. Neilson and Mr. Cavan came to see me. My hair begins to come off. *Monday, April 22nd, 1776.* A violent headache, not able to do anything. *Tuesday, April 23rd, 1776.* Much better. Boiling lye with the ashes in it, find it answers better than expectation. *Wednesday, April 24th, 1776.* Dined at Thomson Mason's Esq. Riding is of service to me if my strength would bear it. *Thursday, April 25th, 1776.* Set more tubs and one with ashes above the lye. I intend to mix. *Friday, April 26th, 1776.* Went to Captn. Douglas's. Returned at night. *Saturday, April 27th, 1776.* Mixed the Nitrous Lye and the wood ash lye together which breaks like curds, but makes purer Nitre and more of it. *Sunday, April 28th, 1776.* Dined with Mr. Kirk, who has come to live in Leesburg. He does everything to encourage me, with great profession of friendship. *Tuesday, April 30th, 1776.* At Town very unwell.

*Wednesday, May 1st, 1776.* News. That a fleet fitted out by Congress under the command of a certain Esack Hopkins, a Yankee man, had made a descent on New Providence in the West Indies, and took a considerable quantity of cannon and military stores. In their passage back had met with the Glasgow Man of War and made her run away. *Thursday, May 2nd, 1776.* Find by mixing the Nitrous Lye with about one third part strong Wood Ash Lye fixes the Nitre and prevents its flying off in air. *Friday, May 3rd, 1776.* Am afraid my partner will be dilatory. *Saturday, May 4th, 1776.* Experiments tried to-day, but none answers so well as that on Thursday last, which I am determined to pursue. *Sunday, May 5th, 1776.* Went to town, which is rather more than I can well bear, am so weak. Mr. Kirk lent me his mare for the Summer. No news. *Saturday, May 11th, 1776.* Employed at home all this week. I shall make bread and something more. *Sunday, May 12th, 1776.* Went to town. Returned in the evening. *Thursday, May 16th, 1776.* Employed for several days at home. News that Mr. John Goodrich a Merchant in Norfolk, was confined in Williamsburg jail with 100ᵂᵗ. of Irons upon him. This is persecution with a witness.

*Friday, May 17th, 1776.* This day is appointed by the Great Sanhedrim to be kept an Holy Fast throughout the Continent, but we have no prayers in Leesburg. The Parson is gone into the Army. *Saturday, May 18th, 1776.* Employed at home. No news. *Sunday, May 19th, 1776.* Went to town. Nothing but Methodist preaching-hypocrisy and nonsense. *Monday, May 20th, 1776.* Employed at home. *Tuesday, May 21st, 1776.* Dined at Mr. Kirk's. Bespoke some new clothes, as mine begin to be shabby and it is absolutely necessary to keep up a genteel appearance, tho' I can badly afford it. *Thursday, May 23rd, 1776.* Employed at home yesterday and to-day. *Friday, May*

*24th, 1776.* After I had finished my work for the day was seized with a most violent pain in my back and head. A great riot in town about Torys. Mr. Cavan obliged to hide himself. *Saturday, May 25th, 1776.* The pain continues, but not with such violence as at first. *Sunday, May 26th, 1776.* Something better, rode to town. Got a Vomit from Mr. Kirk, which I intend to take in the morning. *Monday, May 27th, 1776.* Took the Vomit, which has given me some ease at the Stomach. *Tuesday, May 28th, 1776.* A pain in my head and Feverish. Have nothing proper to nourish me or anything to be got. Curse the Country. *Friday, May 31st, 1776.* Very ill and exceedingly low-spirited these three days. Nobody to dress a mouthful of victuals fit for a dog to eat. *Saturday, June 1st, 1776.* Weak and fainty with pain in my limbs. *Sunday, June 2nd, 1776.* Something better, went to town and dined with Captn. McCabe. *Monday, June 3rd, 1776.* Set 4 tubs of fresh earth.

*Tuesday, June 4th, 1776.* Dined at Mr. Mason's, where I saw the part of a Horned Snakeskin about 5 foot long. This is the most venomous Snake that is known. It is covered with scales like a fish, Black and white on the back, the belly white with a small hair in its tail like a cockspur from whence it takes its name. It does not crawl on its belly like other snakes, but tumbles tail over head and by that means strikes its Horn into its enemy, which is of such a poisonous nature it is instant death. I have been informed by several credible persons, some of them offers to swear, that if it strikes its horn into a tree in full leaf it withers and dies in twenty-four hours. I never saw this, but have not the least reason to doubt the truth of it. They had cut the head off this snake. They tell me it had small horns and was about 9 foot long. When they had disabled it, it roared like a Calf.

The Rattlesnake is scaly, the back variegated with black and yellow, in an angular manner, the belly white, the head Black and Green with the brightest eyes I ever saw in any creature on earth. It has a power of extending its mouth at pleasure furnished with 4 teeth crooked like a Cat's claw. With these they bite and introduce the venom which is of a yellow colour into the wound. They only use them as weapons of defence, as they never masticate their food, but swallow Rabbits and Birds whole, after they have anointed them with their Saliva. Their Rattle is a sort of dry horny substance, joined together very curiously. It is said they have an additional one every year. I have seen some with ten of them, they generally rattle at your approach and are easily avoided. People that travel much in the Woods wear leggings of coarse woollen cloth, which their teeth cannot get through. Neither these or the Horned Snake propagate by eggs, but bring their young entire. They all disappear in winter. Here are several other Snakes, the Coppersnake is very like the Rattlesnake but no rattle, whose bite is venomous. The Glasssnake, the Gaitersnake and Blacksnake, these three last are not hurtful. The Glassnake if you strike it, it breaks to pieces.

*Wednesday, June 5th, 1776.* Went to town to instruct the workmen how to erect a pump in Mr. Kirk's Distillery. No news for this week past. *Thursday, June 6th, 1776.* Employed at home, very much indisposed. *Friday, June 7th, 1776.* Mr. Kirk sent for me to dine with him and proposed me joining him in the Potash making which he persuades me I am capable of managing, but I declined it, as I am determined to leave this country as soon as I can. *Saturday, June 8th, 1776.* Employed at home. *Sunday, June 9th, 1776.* Went to town in the afternoon. Mr. Kirk advises me to take a decoction of the Woods, which he is kind enough to prepare. *Saturday, June 15th, 1776.* Employed at home all the week. Am taking the decoction. Very weak and feeble, believe I use too much exercise. *Sunday, June 16th, 1776.* Went to town. Dined with Mr. Kirk. *Saturday, June 22nd, 1776.* Employed in my business this week. News that the Yankee Privateers or rather Pirates have taken three Jamaica ships worth £100,000. D—m the ungrateful, double-tongued scoundrels. Certainly the Spirit of the Nation will now be roused. *Sunday, June 23rd, 1776.* Went to town and heard a Methodist Sermon. *Saturday, June 29th, 1776.* Employed at home all this week. Find I can by hard labour make as much as will pay my board. Begin to get strength, tho' very slowly. No news this week. *Sunday, June 30th, 1776.* No preaching of any sort. Mr. Kirk and the Doctor advise me to bathe in cold water every morning.

*Monday, July 1st, 1776.* News, that Washington had discovered a plot laid for his life and that of all the staff Officers at New York. One of the Conspirators was hanged and several of the others confined in jail. No news of any troops arriving from England. Made myself a bath. *Saturday, July 6th, 1776.* Employed at home. Find great benefit from the cold bath. *Sunday, July 7th, 1776.* Dined at Mr. Kirk's in company with Mr. Booker. No news. *Monday, July 8th, 1776.* Directing Mr. Kirk's people how to make a Hayrick.

*Tuesday, July 9th, 1776.* At Mr. Kirk's. News that the Sanhedrim had declared the thirteen united Colonies Free and Independent States. That this was intended by the Northern Colonies from the first, I am well convinced and the two following Letters confirm me in that opinion.

*Anonymous letter to the Hon*ble*. James Warren, Watertown, near Boston.*

DEAR SIR,

In confidence I am determined to write freely to you this time, a certain great fortune and piddling genius, whose fame has been loudly trumpetted, has given a silly cast to our whole proceedings. We are between Hawk and Buzzard. We ought to have had in our hands a month ago the whole legislative, executive and judicial of the whole Continent and have completely modelled a constitution, to have raised a Naval Power and opened all our Ports wide, to have arrested every Friend to Government on the Continent and held them as hostages for the poor victims in Boston. And then opened the door as wide as possible for Peace and Reconciliation. After this they might have petitioned and negotiated and addressed & & & if they would. Is all this extravagant? Is it wild? Is it not the soundest Policy?

One Piece of news — Seven hundred weight of Powder arrived here last night. We shall send along some as soon as we can. But you must be patient and frugal.

We are last in the extensiveness of our Field of business. We have a Continental Treasury to establish, a Paymaster to choose, and a Committee of Correspondence or Safety or Accounts, or something I know not what, that has confounded us all day.

Shall I, hail you Speaker or Counsellor or what? What kind of an Election had you? What sort of Magistrates do you intend to make? Will your new Legislative and Executive feel bold or irresolute? Will your judicial, hand and whip and Fine and Imprison without scruples? I want to see our distressed Country once more, yet I dread the sight of devastation.

You observe in your letter, the oddity of a great man. He is a queer creature, but you must love his dogs if you love him, and forgive a thousand whims for the sake of the soldier and the Scholar.

The following is a letter from Mr. John Adams to his wife Abigail in which the letter to Mr. Warren was enclosed.

*Philadelphia, July 24th, 1775.*

MY DEAR,

It is now almost three months since I left you, in every part of which my anxiety about you and the children as well as my country have been extreme.

The business I have had upon my mind has been as great and important as can be entrusted to Man, and the difficulty and intricacy of it is prodigious. When 50 or 60 men have a Constitution to form for a great Empire at the same time that they have a Country of fifteen hundred Miles extent to fortify, Millions to arm and train, a Naval power to begin, an extensive commerce to regulate, numerous Tribes of Indians to negotiate with, a standing Army of Twenty-seven thousand men, to raise pay, victual and Officer. I really shall pity those 50 or 60 men. I must see you e'er long. Rice has written me a good letter and so has Thaxter for which I thank them both. Love to the Children. I.A.

P.S. I wish I had given you a complete history from the beginning to the end of the Journey of the behaviour of my Compatriots. No mortal could equal it. I will tell you in future, but you shall keep it secret. The fidgets, the whims, the caprice, the Vanity, the Superstition, the Irritability of some is enough to —

Both these Letters were intercepted by the King's Officers and published in Draper's *Massachusetts Gazette* in August last.

*Wednesday, July 10th, 1776 — Saturday, July 13th, 1776.*

Employed at home. Still continue the cold Bath a
great benefit from it. This cursed Independence ha
me great uneasiness. *Sunday, July 14th, 1776.* Drank Tea
at Mr. Kirk's. *Monday, July 15th, 1776.* Employed at
home. *Tuesday, July 16th, 1776.* Went to Captn. Douglas's. Returned in the evening. *Saturday, July 20th, 1776.*
Employed at home for several days. I am now got almost
strong enough to shoot a Yankee Man. *Sunday, July 21st,
1776.* News that Lord Howe was arriving at New York
with a large fleet and a numerous Army. God send him good
health. *Monday, July 22nd, 1776.* News that the *Roebuck* was coming up to Alexandria. *Thursday, July 25th,
1776.* At home, finished the last of my earth, and my
partner will not clear out the other Tobacco houses.

*Friday, July 26th, 1776.* Dined at Mr. Mason's, who
proffers to give me a letter of recommendation to the Governor Henry for liberty to go on board the Fleet in the
Bay. I have no other choice to get home but this. *Saturday, July 27th, 1776.* At Town. A general muster of the
Militia. Great confusion among them. Recruiting parties
offer 10 Dollars advance and 40s per month. *Sunday, July
28th, 1776.* At home. *Wednesday, July 31st, 1776.* At
home these three days employed in refining Saltpetre.
*Thursday, August 1st, 1776.* Refining Nitre. I have made
several experiments but have hit on one that answers well,
by putting the crude Nitre into a pot and fluxing it till it
has the appearance of milk, then let it cool and put to every
pound of Nitre three pints of water, boil it a little and sit
to shoot. It made a beautiful appearance like Icicles, white
as Snow and transparent as glass. From $7\frac{1}{2}$ pounds of crude
Nitre I have got $4\frac{1}{2}$ pound pure. News that Lord Dunmore was driven from Gwinn's Island and the Fleet had

left the Bay. I am now at a loss again. Determined to go to New York and endeavour to get to the Army. *Friday, August 2nd, 1776.* At home. I am now got pretty healthy again, but very uneasy. Believe I am one of the most unfortunate dogs on earth. Intend to go with Mr. Cavan to Mr. Wm. Neilson's.

*Saturday, August 3rd, 1776.* Went with Cavan to Mr. Neilson's about 15 miles from town. He calls this place Scotland and I think it is well named. *Sunday, August 4th, 1776.* Left Mr. Neilson's. Crossed the Blueridge and Shanando River, went to Mr. Nourses at Piedmont, Berkely County. *Monday, August 5th, 1776.* Went with Mr. and Mrs. Nourse to Colnl. Saml. Washington's, Brother to the General. Drank some Whiskey Grog and came back. *Tuesday, August 6th, 1776.* Left Mr. Nourse's. Dined at Mr. Frank Willis's, got to Mr. Neilson's at night. Mr. H. Neilson gave me some Rattlesnake teeth. *Wednesday, August 7th, 1776.* At Mr. Neilson's, who is the most industrious man I have seen in Virginia, but an ugly place to cultivate. *Thursday, August 8th, 1776.* Left Mr. Neilsons, got to *The Cattail* at night.

*Friday, August 9th, 1776.* At town. Dined at Mr. Kirk's. *Saturday, August 10th, 1776.* Directing Mr. Kirk's people how to top the Hayrick. Lodged at Mr. Kirk's. *Sunday, August 11th, 1776.* At home. No news this week. *Saturday, August 17th, 1776.* At home all this week, employed in dressing Faunskins. Am determined to go to New York. I must either escape that way or go to jail for Toryism. *Sunday, August 18th, 1776.* Mr. Kirk sent for me to ask my advice about a Mare he has sick. Believe she will die. Am certain she has the maw worms. *Monday, August 19th, 1776.* This morning found the

Mare dead. My conjecture was right. The worms had eaten through her maw. Mr. Kirk proffers to lend me his horse to New York. *Tuesday, August 20th, 1776.* Went to Mr. Joseph Jennings. Got a letter of introduction from him to Messrs. Warder & Sons in Philadelphia, returned in the evening.

*Wednesday, August 21st, 1776.* Went to Captn. Douglas. Settled my affairs with him. Called at Mr. Mason's, who says he will give me a letter of recommendation to some of the members of the Congress. Don't act fairly by Mr. Mason, not to let him know my designs. *Thursday, August 22nd, 1776.* Settled my affairs with Mr. James Kirk and parted with great concern, as he has behaved to me with the greatest respect and kindness, but dare not tell him of my design. Left my chest and clothes to the care of my good Friend P. Cavan, who is the only person privy to my intentions. I owe nothing to anyone but Mr. Kirk. His horse I intend to return by Mr. Cooper. *Friday, August 23rd, 1776.* Left Leesburg in company with Mr. Alexander Cooper, a Storekeeper in town. Called at Mr. Mason's, who gave me letter to Messrs. Francis Lightfoot Lee, Thos. Stone, Thos. Jefferson, and John Rogers Esq., all members of the Congress. Dined at Frederick Mansceyson Creek. Lodged at Bentley's Tavern. Find us in County Maryland.

# VIII

## ATTEMPT TO LEAVE — SUSPECTED
## AS A SPY

*Y*ORK TOWN, *Pennsylvania — Saturday, August 24th, 1776.* Left Bentley's Tavern. Crossed Little Pipe Creek at a Bridge. Breakfasted at Tanny Town, small place, inhabitants chiefly Dutch. Crossed the Pennsylvania line. Puter-Littlis, town very small. Dined at Mr. Callister's in Hannover town, which is a smart little town with a Church, chiefly Dutch people. Lodged at York Town, the sign of *The Brewhouse,* the Landlord is a Dutchman with a confounded hard name and a D—m dirty house. This is a pretty large town. Some manufactories in Iron. Pleasant and well laid out, the inhabitants Dutch and Irish. Droll adventure this evening.

*Pennsylvania, — Sunday, August 25th, 1776.* Left York Town. Breakfasted at *The Sign of the Plough,* a Dutch house about 3 miles from Y.T. Crossed Susquehanna River at Wright's Ferry. River about 1¼ miles broad. Dined at Lancaster, *The Sign of the Two Highlandmen.* Landlord's name Ross. This is a large town, but the situation is disagreeable between two hills, several good buildings and some manufactories of Guns and Woollen, but no navigation. Four hundred English prisoners here. Crossed Conistogo Creek. Lodged at *The Sign of the Duke of Cumberland,* the Landlord is a Scotch-Irish Rebel Colonial and his house is dirty as a Hog's stye. Land good in general. Farmers rich and industrious.

Irish and Dutch inhabitants. *Monday, August 26th, 1776.* Left *The Duke of Cumberland,* which is one of the dirtiest houses I ever put my foot in. Breakfasted at *The Waggon,* the Landlord a rigid Irish Presbyterian. Dined at *The Cross Keys.* Lodged at *The Spread Eagle,* a clean Dutchman's house. Land broken and hilly, but the Farmers seem rich, good stock, and their land well cultivated. Passed 5 companies going to camp. *Tuesday, August 27th, 1776.* Left *The Spread Eagle.* Crossed Schulkill Ferry, got to Philadelphia to breakfast. In our journey from Leesburg I have seen only 3 signs hanging, the rest pulled down by Soldiers. Making my observations. Lodged at *The Black Horse* in Market Street.

*Philadelphia — Wednesday, August 28th, 1776.* Viewing the Town. Delivered my letters to Mr. Warder, who received me very kindly and invited me to dine with him. Introduced me to several Gentlemen of his acquaintance. All Quakers. Spent the evening at *The Sign of the Black Horse* with Mr. Joseph Brewer — Clerk to Mr. Jeremiah Warder. Don't like my lodgings, full of Irish Colnls., Captns., and Convention men, most of them profoundly ignorant and as impertinent as any Skipkinnet. These are here for the purpose of making a new code of Laws for the Province. O, Happy people indeed that has such wise guides. *Thursday, August 29th, 1776.* Viewing the Town. Dined at Mr. Brewer's with Mr. Buchhannan, an Irish Gentleman. Find him a sensible, polite man. In the afternoon met with Phillip Morchington, who keeps a pretty large store here. Spent the evening with him and one Thos. Thornbur from Skipton and one Gresswold, a distiller in town, at the *City Tavern.* Thornbur and Gresswold two sensible men, but Morchington is an extravagant fop. Great preparations for War, and great numbers of ragged soldiers come into town. News that the English had defeated them on Long Island and taken a thousand prisoners. *Friday, August 30th, 1776.* Mr. Buchhannan went with me to every place of note in town. Dined at Marchington's Lodgings. Spent the evening with Messrs. Brewer & Buchhannan. Both *Sgnik Sdneirf*.

*Saturday, August 31st, 1776.* Waited on Mr. Francis Lightfoot Lee and Mr. Thos. Jefferson with my letters, who behaved with the greatest complaisance and politeness, proffered to get me a pass from the Congress by virtue of which I may travel where I please. Mr. Buchhannan went with me to the Fishing house on the River Schuylkill about 5 miles from town. Here is a small collection of Marines and Indian curiosities, but don't think it a good one. Snuff mills and paper mills. Several elegant Country seats.

*Sunday, September 1st, 1776.* Went with Mr. Brewer and Mr. Buchhannan by water to see the Fort, Gondolas, and Chevaux-de-Frise or rather the Vis-a-de-Frise about 7 miles below the city. The Fort is on a low dirty Island at the conflux of the Schuylkill with the Dellawar, only a shell, not finished part of it picketed and three Blockhouses, there is eight 32 pounders well situated to cover the Vis-a-de-Frise. A large boom across the River. Thirteen Gondolas — some carried 4 Guns, some 2 and some one, trifling things rowed with oars — and a floating Battery, which mounts 14 heavy cannons, very formidable. On our return dined at Gloster town in New Jersey. Fine view of the city from the River.

*Monday, September 2nd, 1776.* Waited on Mr. Jefferson, who gave me a pass written by Mr. John Hancock, Pres. of the Congress. Went with P. Marchington to German town, about 9 miles from Philadelphia. A long rambling place, a considerable manufactory of coarse stockings, inhabitants chiefly Dutch. Determined to go to New York and make my escape to the English Army. Marchington will send the horse to Leesburg. In short, I have no other alternative, if I stay amongst the *Sleber*, I must go to *Liaj*. Great numbers — I believe half the people in town — are *Sgnik Sdneirf*. Some of the people have hung Washington, Putnam, and Mifflin on their sign post in public.

*Tuesday, September 3rd, 1776.* This is a large, rich, populous and regular town. The Delaware River is on the North side the town and Schuykill River on the South West. Streets run parallel with the Delaware River, others in direct lines which forms it in squares. The streets are sixty foot wide, except Market Street which is an hundred, but the Market house is set in the middle of this street which entirely spoils the beauty of it. These are paved with brick and kept very clean with walks on each side for the foot people. Well supplied with pumps, very level, and so remarkably straight there is nothing to obstruct your view from one end of the town to the other. Three English Churches, Christ Church, St. Paul's and St. Peter's, and two Dutch Lutheran Churches. Nine dissenting meeting houses, two Roman Chapels, Four Quaker meeting houses, and a Swedish Church. All neat plain buildings but none of them elegant ones. The State house is a good building but does not make a grand appearance. Here all public business is done. Now the nest of the great and mighty Sanhedrim. Near this is the New Jail, a good and large stone building now occupied with *Sgnik Sdneirf*. A Handsome brick Hospital, but not large. Here is a good building they call a Bettering House, where all strolling and disorderly people are confined to labour till they can give a sufficient account of themselves. Here is a College for the education of Youth. It makes no great appearance, and how it is endowed I cannot tell. The Buildings are Brick, very plain, convenient and neat, no very grand edifices as the Quakers have the management of public affairs. Here is a large and plentiful Market, but chiefly supplied from the Jerseys. It is a Corporation town, governed by a Mayor and 20 Aldermen and Common Councilmen. Everything is kept in the greatest order. Here is Barracks for 7 or 8 thousand men. They build as fine Ships here as any part of the World and with as great dispatch. There are four continental Frigates built here in a few months, two of them 111 foot keel and two 96, as fine vessels as I ever saw. I suppose they will be ready for sea in a month, if they can get hands to man them. This is the most regular, neat and convenient city I ever was in and has made the most rapid progress to its present greatness. Spent the day with Mr. Buchhannan.

*Wednesday, September 4th, 1776.* Spent the day with Mr. Buchhannan and Mr. Thornbur. Great many ships laid up and unrigged at the wharfs. Took my passage in the Stage for New York. Left the Horse in care of Marchington to send him to Leesburg if I don't return in 6 days. *Thursday, September 5th, 1776.* Set out from Philadelphia about 5 o'clock this morning in a vehicle neither coach nor waggon but between both. It holds 15 persons and is not uneasy travelling. Breakfasted at *The Wheatsheaf* 12 miles. Crossed Shammory Ferry. Stopped at Bristol, a small town opposite Burlington where we changed Horses, 20 miles from Philadelphia.

*Prince-town, New Jersey — Thursday, September 5th,*

*1776.* Crossed Delaware River at Trenton Ferry. Dined at Trenton, this is a small town and very little trade. Through a small town or rather village called Maidenhead. Lodged at Prince-town. This is a neat Little town with an Elegant College for the education of Youth. I believe there are 60 rooms in it for the students, each room has two closets and two beds, a Chapel, Library and Schoolroom. Cellars and storerooms complete. Saw the Orrery and Electrical Machine made by the famous David Writtenhouse. Electrical machine and apparatus not complete. Doctor Witherspoon. Lodged at *The Sign of Hudibras.*

*Newark, New Jersey — Friday, September 6th, 1776.* Left Prince-town. Passed thro' Kingstown. Breakfasted at Brunswick. This is a small trading town, situated on Rareaton River, which is navigable to the town for small craft. Crossed Rareaton River, several pleasant seats along the Banks. Land good. Changed horses at Woodbridge and paid the other half of the fare, 11s. here and 10s. at Philadelphia. This is a small, neat town. Dined at Elizabeth town, this is a small town of some trade. Lodged at Newark. This is nothing more than a Village. Country populous in general but now in distraction. Land along the Rivers good. Hills rather poor. Believe one of the company is a Spy upon my actions.

*New York, Saturday, September 7th, 1776.* Left Newark. Crossed Passihack or Second River, then Hackensack River, then North River at Powlershook Ferry. River about 1½ miles wide. Landed in New York about nine o'clock, when one Collins, an Irish merchant, and myself rambled about the town till three in the afternoon before we could get anything for breakfast. At length we found a little Dutch tippling house and persuaded the old woman to get us something to eat. It was a stew of pork bones and cabbage so full of Garlic, nothing but necessity would have compelled me to eat it, my companion would not taste another mouthful. Nothing to be got here. All the inhabitants are moved out. The town full of Soldiers. Viewing the town and fortifications and contriving means to effect my escape, but despair of it, the Rivers are too well guarded.

This town is the best situated for trade of any place I ever saw. It is on a point of Land with wharfs two thirds of the way round the town and very near the Sea. The town is not so regular as Philadelphia, nor so extensive, neither has it so many good buildings, but more elegant ones both public and private. Here are three English Churches, the old Trinity Church, St. Paul's and St. George's Chapel, two Dutch Churches, four dissenting meeting houses, one Quaker Meeting, and a Jews' Synagogue and a French Church. A College and Hospital, two elegant buildings. There was a fine equestrian statute of his Majesty, but the *Sleber* has pulled it down and cast it into Bullets. The Statue of the Earl of Chatham is still standing unhurt in the attitude of an apple woman, dressed like a Roman Orator. I am not a judge, but don't think it clever. The liberty pole, as they call it, is covered with Iron bars. Streets fortified with small batteries towards the River. My fellow-traveller, Mr. Collins, and I should have lodged in the streets, had we not luckily met one Godard, Postmaster, who got us a sorry lodging at the Hull Tavern. From the top of this house have a prospect of Long Island, Staten Island, Governor's Island, Bedlow's Island and Gilbert's Island, three last small ones. All the British Fleet and part of the Army make a fine appearance, but it is utterly out of my power to get to them. I never, till now, thought of it, but honour forbids it, as I am enabled to travel by the interest of Mr. Mason. Was I to make my escape, he might be reflected on.

*Newark, New Jersey — Sunday, September 8th, 1776.* Left New ,York early this morning. Crossed the North River to Powlershook. While we waited for the Stage, viewed the *Sleber* Fortifications here. They are made of earth, but what number of Guns or what size I cannot tell. No admittance into the Fort. The Troops stationed here are Yankee men, the nastiest Devils in creation. It would be impossible for any human creature whose organs of smelling was more delicate than that of a hog to live one day under the Lee of this Camp, such a complication of stinks. Saw a Yankee put a pint of molasses into about a gallon of Mutton Broth. The Army here is numerous, but ragged, dirty, sickly, and ill-disciplined. If my countrymen are beaten by these ragamuffins I shall be much surprized. Their Fleet is large and it is said their Army is numerous. New York must fall into their hands, their batteries on Long Island command the town. Heard a smart cannonade crossing the Ferry this morning, supposed to be at Hellgate. The Fleet is within 2 miles of the town. Got to Newark to dinner. Great scarcity of provisions, the roads full of soldiers. Very uneasy. Must be obliged to go into Canada or stay in this D—d Country.

*Prince-town, New Jersey — Monday, September 9th, 1776.* Left Newark. Breakfasted at Elizabeth town. Dined at Brunswick. Lodged at Prince-town. Great numbers of soldiers on the road. Our company chiefly Irishmen.

*Philadelphia — Tuesday, September 10th, 1776.* Left Prince-town. Breakfasted at Trenton. Dined at Bristol, where we changed horses. Got to Philadelphia in the evening. Lodged at one Mrs. Stretch's in Second Street, my old lodging took up. Spent the evening with the French Officers that are prisoners here, taken at St. John's. Very polite gentlemen, but exceedingly cautious. Town full of soldiers. *Wednesday, September 11th, 1776.* Dined at Mr. Brewer's. Spent the afternoon with Mr. Buchhannan. Lodged at Mrs. Stretch's. My designs are frustrated. Spend a good deal of money to no sort of purpose. I must return to Virginia and endeavour to get to Canada. *Thursday, Sept. 12th, 1776.* Determined to set out to Virginia to-morrow. Dined at Mrs. Stretch's. Supped and spent the evening at *The Golden Fleece* in company with Marchington, Gresswold, Brewer and Thornbur, all *Sgnik Sdneirf*, very merry. News that General Prescott and General McDonald were exchanged for G. Sullivan and G. Sterling, *Sleber* took at Long Island.

*Christiana Bridge — Friday, September 13th, 1776.* Left Philadelphia in company with Messrs. Marchington & Gresswold. Crossed Schuylkill at Grey's Ferry. Through Derby, a little place. Dined at Chester, a smart little town on the Delawar River. Here Marchington and Gresswold left me and I joined an Irish Tailor metamorphised into a Captn. and an Irish Blacksmith his Lieutenant. Both going to Baltimore. Passed Brandywine Mills. Here are 8 of them in a quarter of a mile, so convenient that they can take the grain out of the Vessels into the Mills. Wilmington, a pretty town on the River, then Newport a trifling place. Lodged at Christiana Bridge, a little town situated on a Creek of the same name.

*Bushtown, Maryland — Saturday, September 14th, 1776.* Breakfasted at the head of Elk. The River falls into

Chessapeak Bay and is only 12 miles from Christiania Bridge. Fed our horses at Charlestown, a small place at head of the Bay and seems to be on the decline. Crossed Susquehannah River at the Lower Ferry. Dined at the Ferry house. Lodged at Bushtown or Hartford, which you please, this is a small and poor town. Land poor in general all along the road. My companions rank Paddys. The Captn. talks as if he was able to take General Howe in two days with his company.

*Elkridge Landing — Sunday, September 15th, 1776.* Breakfasted at Skyer's Tavern. Dined at Baltimore. This is the principal trading town in Maryland. It is regularly laid out and tolerably well built, but the situation is exceedingly inconvenient. Ships can't come within a mile of the town to a place called Fell's point where they are sent up in flats to town. About a mile below Fell's point is the Fort lately built, but I did not go to it. Saw the Buckskin Frigate of thirty-six guns just built. A fine vessel. Lodged at Elkrige Landing, a small Village. Great number of iron works. Land poor in general. Very unwell, excessively hot weather and uneasiness of mind have brought on a fever.

*Bladensburg, Maryland — Monday, September 16th, 1776.* Much better, slept a little last night. Breakfasted at an indifferent house about 10 miles from the Landing. Got to Bladensburg in the afternoon. Lodged at Mr. Wm. Sidebottam's. From Marple Bridge the road badly furnished with inns and some of the poorest land I have yet seen.

*Alexandria, Virginia — Tuesday, September 17th, 1776.* Fed my horse at George-town, this is a smart town on the Potowmack River on the Maryland side. Crossed the

River. Got to Alexandria. Spent the evening with Mr. Wm. Elzey and George Muir. Lodged at Mr. Flemming's.

*Leesburg, Virginia — Wednesday, September 18th, 1776.* Left Alexandria in company with Harry McCabe. Dined at the Falls Church. Got to Leesburg in the evening. Found my old friend P. Cavan ill of the fever and ague. Lodged at Captn. Taylor's.

*Cattail, Loudoun County, Virginia — Thursday, September 19th, 1776.* Mr. Kirk insisted on me dining with him. Expected I was gone aboard the Fleet. I am sorry it was not so. Lodged at *The Cattail. Friday, Sept. 20th, 1776.* Dined at Mr. Kirk's. Very unhappy. *Saturday, Sept. 21st, 1776.* At town. Mr. Booker returned this evening. *Sunday, Sept. 22nd, 1776.* Dined at Mr. Mason's. *Monday, Sept. 23rd, 1776.* Mr. Kirk sent for me this morning to assist him. Mr. Cavan is sick of the fever and ague. *Wednesday, Sept. 25th, 1776.* At Mr. Kirk's. News that General Howe had got possession of New York. Lodged at *The Cattail. Friday, Sept. 27th, 1776.* At Home. Employed two days in doing nothing at all. Very disagreeable business. *Saturday, Sept. 28th, 1776.* Went to town in the morning. After dinner went to Kite's Island. Spent the evening and slept at Mr. Cartwright's. *Sunday, Sept. 29th, 1776.* At home, if I have such a place. *Monday, Sept. 30th, 1776.* At *Cattail,* too much time for reflection. I am now disappointed in my favourite plan of getting home and it is reported that the Indians have begun to commit outrages on the back inhabitants, so that my Canada scheme is rendered abortive. I have nothing to trust to but Providence, and I have but little faith in that.

However, I am determined to rot in a Jail rather than take up arms against my native country.

*Tuesday, October 1st, 1776.* Went with Mr. James Booker to Mr. Matthew Campbell's. Spent the evening there and got most feloniously drunk. This is a bad preface to the new volume of my diary. Drunkenness the first remark. *Wednesday, Oct. 2nd, 1776.* At home, sick with my last night's debauch. O! Temperance, temperance, thou best of virtues, what pains we take to ruin our constitutions by these nocturnal excesses. *Saturday, Oct. 5th, 1776.* Employed I can't tell how, a worthless life indeed. *Sunday, Oct. 6th, 1776.* Mr. Booker and I went to the Quaker Meeting, but were too late, tho' it would have been equally as well as if we had been sooner, for the spirit did not move any of them to speak. Can't conceive what service the people can receive by grunting and groaning for two or three hours without speaking a word. This is a stupid religion indeed. Dined at Mrs. Baker's with a *Sleber* Officer. Got home in the evening. *Monday, Oct. 7th, 1776.* At Leesburg, returned in the evening. No news. *Tuesday, Oct. 8th, 1776.* Went to Kite's Island on no good design. Lodged at Mr. Cartwright's. Did not meet with success. The fruits of idleness are, intemperance and a numberless train of evils.

*Wednesday, October 9th, 1776.* At home. No Newspapers the last week. I suppose the rascals have had bad luck of late and are afraid it should be known to the public.

*Thursday, October 10th, 1776.* Went to town to assist Mr. Kirk. Mr. Cavan is sick. The 6th Regt. of Virginians are camped here on their way to the Northward. A set of dirty, ragged people, badly clothed, badly disciplined and badly armed. *Friday, Oct. 11th, 1776.* Salt sells here at Forty shillings, Currency, per Bushel. This article usually sold for four shillings. If no Salt comes in there will be an insurrection in the Colony. *Saturday, Oct. 12th, 1776.* Spent part of the evening at Mr. McCrey's in company with Messrs. Kirk, Booker, McCabe and Campbell. McCabe went with Kirk and me home where we entered into political disputes and McCabe and I quarrelled. (Mem. Never to enter into political disputes for the future, if I can avoid it, especially with *Slebers.*) *Sunday, Oct. 13th, 1776.* Mr. Kirk, Messrs. McCabe, Campbell, Dow, Dean and Cavan dined and spent the evening with me at *The Cattail.* Mathematical disquisition the chief subject of discourse, this afternoon. Far preferable to the cursed politics. *Thursday, October 17th, 1776.* At home this week. Intend to go to Alexandria to-morrow, as I am informed there is a Sloop bound for Bermudas. Will endeavour to get a passage in her. There is no other method of getting out of this hateful country.

*Alexandria, Virginia — Friday, October 18th, 1776.* Dined at Mosse's Ordinary. Got to Alexandria in the evening. Lodged at Mrs. Hawkins's. *Saturday, Oct. 19th, 1776.* Saw the Master of the Sloop, who informs me he is bound to Bermudas if he meets with none of the King's Ships. He is in an illicit trade, his port precarious, his passage extravagant, and he appears to be an ill-natured morose man. Am determined not to go with him. Dined at Mr. John Muir's, a merchant in town. This gentleman is looked on as the pattern of hospitality and generosity, but I am far from thinking him a good man. It is true he keeps an excellent table, a glass of good wine, punch &&, but he is an epicure himself and likes a companion along with his bottle. His humanity is not to be commended. He has five children by a negro woman, slave to a Gentleman in town. They are all slaves for life. He sees them daily wanting the common necessaries of life, without taking the least pity or compassion on their wretched condition. The man who can bear to see his own flesh and blood in this horrid situation without being most sensibly affected is lost to every feeling of humanity and is a degree worse than a brute.

*Sunday, October 20th, 1776.* No service at Church to-day. Religion is almost forgotten or most basely neglected. In short, the Parsons are not willing to expound the Gospel to people without being paid for it, and there is no provision made for the Episcopal Clergy by this new code of Laws, therefore Religion as well as Commerce is at a stand. Indeed, the few that pretend to preach are mere retailers of politics, sowers of sedition and rebellion, serve to blow the cole of discord and excite the people to arms. The Presbyterian Clergy are particularly active in supporting the measures of Congress from the Rostrum, gaining proselytes, persecuting the unbelievers, preaching up the righteousness of their cause and persuading the unthinking populace of the infallibility of success. Some of these religious rascals assert that the Lord will send his Angels to assist the injured Americans. They gain great numbers of converts and I am convinced if they establish their Independence that Presbyty will be the established religion on this Continent. Spent the evening with Mr. Robert Muir and Mr. Kirk.

*Monday, October 21st, 1776.* This morning I am told that the Committee of this town will not permit me to depart this Colony as they look upon me to be a Spy and that I must be obliged to give security or go to jail. Whether this is done to get me to enlist into their service or some rascal has informed against me I cannot tell. Intended to have gone to Leesburg to-night, but some villain has stolen my surtout coat. Spent the evening at Mr. William Harthorn's.

*Cattail, Loudoun County, Virginia.— Tuesday, October 22nd, 1776.* Mrs. Hawkins promised to pay for my coat, but don't believe her. Left Alexandria. Called at Goodwin's Mill. Lodged at Mosses Ordinary. *Wednesday, Oct. 23rd, 1776.* Got to *The Cattail* to dinner. Mr. Booker gone to Alexandria. I am housekeeper myself. *Saturday, Oct. 26th, 1776.* These three days I have spent most disagreeably — nothing to do and all alone. When I reflect on my present situation it makes me miserable. I am now in an enemy's country, forbidden to depart. Little to subsist upon and dare not do anything to get a living, for fear of getting myself ranked as an inhabitant and be obliged to carry arms against my native country. My interest and inclination, unhappy alternative indeed, to turn parricide or starve. Am determined to go amongst the Indians. I look upon them to be the more humane people of the two. *Sunday, Oct. 27th, 1776.* Went to town to a Methodist meeting.

*Monday, October 28th, 1776.* General Muster of the County Militia in town, about 600 men appeared underarmed, with Tobacco sticks in general. Much rioting and confusion. Recruiting Officers for the *Sleber* Army offer Twelve Pounds bounty and 200 acres of land when the War is over, but get very few men. *Tuesday, Oct. 29th, 1776.* At town. Dined with Captn. G. Johnston a violent *Sleber. Wednesday, Oct. 30th, 1776.* Dined at Mr.

Thornton Mason's, who advises me to petition the Congress for permission to go home. Promises to give me letter of recommendation to some members of Congress. *Thursday, Oct. 31st, 1776.* Went to Mr. Peter Car's. Droll adventure there, don't know how it will terminate. Got some silver dollars at 6⅙ per dollar.

*Friday, November 1st, 1776.* Dined at Mr. Kirk's, who persuades me to stay till Spring, but for what reason I cannot tell. Am in doubt whether his advice proceeds from friendship or interested motives. From him I have my present support, by his interest I have been kept out of Jail, and without his approbation I cannot go, and to stay and be dependent on him for bread and liberty is worse than Egyptian bondage. Determined to petition the Congress at all events. *Saturday, Nov. 2nd, 1776.* Dined at Mr. Kirk's, who is still harping on the old string. He now insists on me staying the Winter, endeavours to persuade me that there will be an end to these disputes this Fall. I see no probability of it therefore will not stay if I can help it. *Sunday, Nov. 3rd, 1776.* At town, no Church. Mr. Kirk uses every argument in his power to prevail on me to stay. Indeed he is angry with me that I won't. I am resolved to persevere, be the consequence what it will. I might as well be in the infernal regions as in this country where my sentiments are known. Every rascal looks on me as an enemy to him and except I could tacitly submit to every insult or divest myself of the faculties of sight, speech and hearsay, must be miserable. *Monday, Nov. 4th, 1776.* Went to town, and agreed with Josiah Moffit to carry my Chest to Philadelphia. He goes next week. *Tuesday, Nov. 5th, 1776.* Mr. Kirk promises to go with me into Berkely to-morrow. I am under sundry obligations to Mr. Nourse

It would be wrong to go and not acquaint him with it, as he, by me, has an opportunity of writing to his Friends.

*Piedmont, Berkley County, Virginia — Wednesday, November 6th, 1776.* Left Leesburg in company with Mr. Kirk. Dined at Key's Ferry. Lodged at Mr. Nourse's, who was very glad to see us. My companion seems to have taken a great fancy to Miss Nourse. If there was a little more parity in years, it might do very well to make a match. *Thursday, Nov. 7th, 1776.* Got to Mr. Gibb's in the afternoon. Mr. Kirk seems to have taken particular notice of Miss Nourse. Hope it may amount to something in time. Spent an agreeable evening with two Irish ladies, the Miss Reynolds, that was at Mr. Gibbons. *Friday, Nov. 8th, 1776.* Went to Winchester with Messrs. Kirk and Gibbs. Dined there and spent the evening with Colnl. Jacob Alligood, who is a prisoner here. Most of the Company got drunk. Going to Mr. Gibbs, Mr. Kirk fell from his horse and let him get away. At Mr. Gibbs, Kirk and I got into a political dispute which terminated in a quarrel, but made it up before we went to bed. *Saturday, Nov. 9th, 1776.* For the sake of the ride went to Winchester to enquire for Mr. Kirk's horse, but heard nothing of him. Breakfasted with Alligood, who informs me I am suspected of being a Tory and Spy. Rat the scoundrels. Dined and spent the afternoon at Mr. John Reynolds, an Irish Gentleman who is settled as a Farmer here and is in a fine way to make a fortune by it. Lodged at Mr. Gibbs. No news of the horse, suppose somebody has stolen him. This is the pernicious effect of drunkenness.

*Pennyroyal Hill, Frederick County, Virginia — Sunday, November 10th, 1776.* Mr. Kirk's uneasiness for the loss of his horse disturbed me last night and very ill became a man of his sense to make himself so exceedingly unhappy about such trifles, tho' I believe it is unavoidable in him, he is by nature fretful. About eight o'clock the boy came with his beast and restored him to his usual good humour. Mr. Gibbs' family, Mr. K. and I dined at Mr. Reynolds and spent an agreeable afternoon. *Monday, Nov. 11th, 1776.* Left Mr. Gibbs. Dined at Mr. John Kite's. This Gentleman is falling a victim to his Bacchanalian excesses. Lodged at Mr. Nourse's.

*Cattail, Loudoun County, Virginia — Tuesday, November 12th, 1776.* Left Mr. Nourse's with some regret. He gave me letters to my care for Charles Fouace Esq., Admiralty Office, Mr. Hughes, Linen Draper, York street, Covent Garden, and Mrs. Seaman, Honiton, Devon. Dined at Key's Ferry. Mr. Henry Peyton was shot through the body attempting to take a deserter from the *Sleber* Army. Got to *The Cattail* in the evening. *Wednesday, Nov. 13th, 1776.* Employed in preparing for my departure. *Thursday, Nov. 14th, 1776.* Mr. Booker and I went to Mr. William Neilson's a particular friend of mine an industrious man and a *Sgnik Dneirf*. Lodged there. *Friday, Nov. 15th, 1776.* Returned to *The Cattail* in the evening. *Saturday, Nov. 16th, 1776.* Went to town. Josiah Moffit tells me to have my things ready by next Saturday.

*Sunday, November 17th, 1776.* Went to Mr. Campbell's, from there to town and dined with Mr. Cavan. Mr. Kirk at Captn. McCabe's, sorry for it. *Monday, Nov. 18th, 1776.* Mr. Booker and I spent the evening at Mr. Campbells very merrily. This Gentleman is falling a sacrifice to the sports of Venus. *Tuesday, Nov. 19th, 1776.* Packing up my things. Mr. Booker is going to live near Williamsburg. A very mad frolic this evening. Set the house on fire three times and broke Mr. Drean's leg (a Gentleman that Mr. Booker had brought to spend the evening with us), got drunk and committed a number of foolish actions. *Wednesday, Nov. 20th, 1776.* Sick with my last night's intemperance. Went to town and took lodgings at Mr. Sorrel's till I set out for Philadelphia. Will not live at Mr. Kirk's any longer. *Thursday, Nov. 21st, 1776.* Dined at Mr. Thos. Rispes and sold him my Saltpetre apparatus. Paid Mr. Booker for my board and spent the evening with him at *The Crooked Billet. Friday, Nov. 22nd, 1776.* Preparing for my journey. Hired a horse from Mr. T. Rispes.

*Saturday, November 23rd, 1776.* News that General Howe was on his march to Philadelphia and drives the *Sleber* before him. Believe it to be true, if I may be allowed to judge from the countenance and behaviour of the Fire-brands. *Sunday, Nov. 24th, 1776.* Spent the evening with Mr. Booker and Mr. Dean at *The Crooked Billet.* All the newspapers are stopped, none are allowed to be given to the public. A certain sign that the rascals are defeated.

*Leesburg, Virginia — Monday, November 25th, 1776.* This morning took my farewell of Mr. James Booker, who is going to be Overseer to a Gentleman near Williamsburg. This young man is one of the most curious characters I have ever met with. He is proud and affable, ostentatious and niggardly, a beau and a sloven, by turns. Whether the Moon has any influence over his passions, or he was born under some capricious Planet, I cannot pretend to determine. Spent the evening at Mr. Kirk's, who uses every means in his power to detain me here this Winter, but I am determined to go if there is a possibility of getting away.

*Tuesday, Nov. 26th, 1776.* Settling my affairs. News that General Howe is at Brunswick in the Jerseys, the *Sleber* Army flying towards Philadelphia and that the Congress has removed from Philadelphia to Baltimore. Brave news indeed.

## IX

## A WINTER OF DISCONTENT

*W*EDNESDAY, *November 27th, 1776.* The Committee met to-day. Am informed it is to search my papers, if not to take me up and imprison me, but will be prepared for them. *Thursday, Nov. 28th, 1776.* This morning three of the Committee men waited on me and informed me that the Committee did not think it prudent to let me go out of the Country at this time and hoped that I would give my word of honour not to depart this Colony for three months. Otherwise they would confine me. I was obliged to do the first as the lesser evil of the two. They were polite enough not to search my chest. Spent the evening at Mr. Kirk's, who seemed very glad that I was obliged to stay. This affronted me, we both got drunk and quarrelled about State affairs.

*Alexandria, Virginia — Friday, November 29th, 1776.* Very sick with my last night's debauch, and very sorry for my last night's conduct. My present disagreeable confinement, the loss of three years of the most valuable part of life, the disappointments and misfortunes I have met with since I left my native Country, and what is worst of all, the certainty of being reproached with obstinacy and extravagancy on my return. These bitter reflections will intrude themselves involuntarily, and create a lowness of spirit which too often is the cause of me drinking more than is of service. I must and will call my resolution and fortitude to my aid, or I shall insensibly sink into the Sot or the Drunkard. A character so despicable ought to be avoided with the greatest care. Mr. Kirk and I made up the quarrel this morning. Must not quarrel with him. He confesses that he did every thing in his power to intoxicate me, on purpose to raise my spirits. I will not borrow my spirits in that manner for the future. Left Leesburg. Dined at Mosses Ordinary. Got to Alexandria. Spent the evening with Mr. McCrey. *Saturday, Nov. 30th, 1776.* This morning went to Mrs. Hawkins, expecting to get paid for my coat, supposing that she was not informed that I was forbid to depart the Colony, but the D—d Jade tells me that I am a Tory and she won't pay me a Farthing. This is provoking, but I cannot help myself. Spent the evening with Mr. McCrey.

*Leesburg, Loudoun County, Virginia—Sunday, December 1st, 1776.* Left Alexandria. Dined at Mosses. Got to Leesburg at night. News that the English have taken Fort Washington and 2500 prisoners in it. This is the strongest Fortification they had, it is on the North end of New York Island. They have long boasted that all the forces belonging to Great Britain could not take it. What is it that Englishmen cannot do whenever they choose to exert themselves? It is said they have deserted Fort Lee. If this be true I hope the rascals will soon be humbled. *Monday, Dec. 2nd, 1776.* Troubled with the Rheumatism in my arms. *Tuesday, Dec. 3rd, 1776.* Abundance of Political puffs and lies told to amuse the public. It is a matter of dispute with me whether the Whigs or Torys are the greatest propagators of falsehood.

*Wednesday, December 4th, 1776.* A Dutch mob of about 40 horsemen went through the town to-day on their way to Alexandria to search for Salt. If they find any they will take it by force. All of them armed with swords or large clubs. This article is exceedingly scarce, if none comes in the people will revolt. They cannot possibly subsist without a considerable quantity of this article. The people in general live on Salt meat in the Summer. The excessive heat renders the keeping of fresh meat very difficult, even for one day, and the thinness of inhabitants and markets prevents them killing little else but young hogs and fowls. They likewise give Salt to their Horses, Cattle, Hogs and Sheep almost every day in the Summer. The cattle are exceedingly fond of it, so much that they will follow you anywhere for a lick of it and it is so essentially necessary that they will not thrive without it. *Thursday, December 5th, 1776.* Exceedingly unhappy, was it not for the company of a few friends I should be completely miserable. *Friday, Dec. 6th, 1776.* This day the Dutchmen returned from Alexandria without doing the least mischief, the poor wretches have got about three pints of Salt per man. They are told that there will be plenty in a little time. But I hope his Majesty's Ships will prevent it coming into the Bay. Spent the evening at Mr. Kirk's in company with Captn. McCabe and Mr. George West. T.K. had a scuffle with McCabe. It is true they were both in liquor, but whether Mr. Kirk's anger was bent against Mr. McCabe or not, is a mystery to me. I kept perfectly sober and left them as soon as I could. *Saturday, Dec. 7th, 1776.* Mr. Kirk is very uneasy concerning his conduct last night. Sobriety is a noble virtue.

*Sunday, December 8th, 1776.* News, by private letters, the public papers are stopped, that General Howe was at Woodbridge in the Jerseys. God send him a safe and speedy arrival in Philadelphia. It is said the *Sleber* are flying before him. *Monday, Dec. 9th, 1776.* This morning I was remarkably low-spirited. About three o'clock in the afternoon Mr. Hugh Neilson came and insisted on my spending the evening at *The Billet.* I have spent it with a vengeance with Flemming, Patterson, Cleone More, Captn. Wm. Johnston and H. Neilson. Sent them all to bed drunk and I am now going to bed myself at 9 in the morning as drunk as an honest man could wish. *Tuesday, December 10th, 1776.* Got up at 2 in the afternoon. Got drunk before 10, with the same company I was with yesterday and am now going to bed at 2 in the morning, most princely drunk indeed. I saw all my companions in bed before I left them, but most damnable drunk. A fine course of life truly, drunk every night, this is tampering with the Devil to it. *Wednesday, Dec. 11th, 1776.* Much indisposed this morning. I hear my pet companions and brothers in iniquity coming upstairs, but am determined to keep sober to-day. *Thursday, Dec. 12th, 1776.* Last night was the worst we have had since we first commenced the trade of drunkards. Mr. Kirk and P. Cavan joined us. We instituted a foolish society by the name of the Blackeyed Club. I was President and Mr. More Secretary. All of us got most intolerably drunk. This is the first day that I have had any time for reflection this week. Uneasiness of mind first engaged me in this last debauch. Good company induced me to continue it and now a bitter reflection, an aching head, a sick stomach, a trembling hand and a number of disagreeable concomittants that are annexed to this detestable vice causes me to quit the pursuit. Drunkenness is certainly one of the most odious vices that mankind can possibly be guilty of, the consequences are so exceedingly pernicious to our Health, our happiness and interest.

[ 175 ]

It is astonishing that any being endued with the faculty of thinking, should take such pains to divest himself of reason, that knowingly and willingly he will destroy his constitution and sink himself below the level of a brute. Mr. Kirk came and spent the evening at my lodgings.

*Saturday, December 14th, 1776.* News that General Howe is at Trenton in the Jerseys, from Philadelphia. It is certain the Congress has left Philadelphia and are now at Baltimore. Great numbers of recruiting parties are out to raise men, but can scarcely get a man by any means, tho' their bounty is 12£. None will enlist that can avoid it. They get some servants and convicts which are purchased from their Masters, these will desert the first opportunity. The violent *Slebers* are much dispirited. The Politicians (or rather timid Whigs) give all up for lost. And the Torys begin to exult. The time is out that the Flying Camp was enlisted for, and it is said that they refuse to serve any longer, tho' they have been solicited in the strongest terms. This will make a great deficiency in their Army, the loss of Ten Thousand men. I am convinced that if General Howe will push to Philadelphia the day is his own. Find it will be best for me to remove out of town for a little while or I may stand a chance of going to jail as I am too often abusing these rascals. Am determined to go into Berkely. *Sunday, Dec. 15th, 1776.* Dined with Mr. Kirk. After dinner went to Mr. Neilson's. *Monday, Dec. 16th, 1776.* Left Mr. Wm. Neilson's in company with Mr. Hugh Neilson, who lent me a horse. Crossed the Shanando River and got to Mr. Francis Willis. Spent the evening with Mr. John Cook, Captn. Throgmorton and Doctor Armstrong, son of General Armstrong. All violent *Slebers,* but a little discouraged.

*Piedmont, Berkley County, Virginia — Tuesday, December 17th, 1776.* Went to Mr. Nourse's. He was much surprised to see me, supposed that I had been gone. Insists on me spending the Christmas with him. *Wednesday, Dec. 18th, 1776.* Exceedingly unhappy, everyone here is industriously employed, and I am living for no use in creation, except it be to eat and drink. The pleasure that this numerous family enjoys and the company and conversation of each other, the apparent harmony, peace and quietness that subsists amongst them, call thoughts of a very unpleasing nature to my mind, and make me miserable. Everyone does the utmost to keep up my spirits and make the time pass agreeable. Miss Kitty Nourse is not the most backward in this particular. She is one of the most sensible, agreeable and well-bred girls, that I have seen since I left England. Added to these, industry, economy (which by the by, is a virtue very seldom to be met with in either Male or Female in this country) wit, good nature, and a handsome person altogether renders her a reliable and agreeable companion. Was I fixed in my place of life and nothing at home, should think myself happy. To prevent any disagreeable passion intruding, am determined to leave the house to-morrow. *Thursday, Dec. 19th, 1776.* Went with Mr. Nourse to a sale of Horses, the property of the late Jacob Kite, who was killed by the Cherokee Indians last summer. Sold amazingly high, a Horse that I could buy in England for £10 would sell here for £40. Went with Mr. Gibbs home. Mr. Nourse seems affronted, but he is not acquainted with my true reasons. Obliged to tell him lies.

*Pennyroyal Hill, Frederick County, Virginia — Friday, December 20th, 1776.* Went to Mr. Reynolds. Dined there. Returned to Mr. Gibbs. *Saturday, Dec. 21st, 1776.* At Mr. Gibbs. Mr. Perry came here, a gentleman from Maryland that has purchased an Estate here. *Sunday, December 22nd, 1776.* Mr. Gibbs, Mr. Perry and I dined at Doctor McDonald's. A very polite gentleman. *Monday, Dec. 23rd, 1776.* Dined and spent the afternoon at Mr. Reynolds. *Tuesday, Dec. 24th, 1776.* At Mr. Gibbs. Directing his workmen how to make a pump for his still-house. *Wednesday, Dec. 25th, 1776.* Christmas Day, but very little observed in this country, except it is amongst the Dutch. *Thursday, Dec. 26th, 1776.* The Snow fell last night two feet thick and level. This is the greatest fall of snow I have seen in this country. *Friday, Dec. 27th, 1776.* Dined at Mr. Reynolds's, in company with Mr. and Mrs. Gibbs and Mr. Perry. Spent an agreeable afternoon. What still adds to the pleasure, is, the certain account of Genl. Lee's being taken prisoner. It is by a private letter and I have not the least doubt of its being true. *Sunday, Dec. 29th, 1776.* A violent pain in my breast and side for two days. Afraid of pleurisy. *Monday, Dec. 30th, 1776.* Much better. Went with Mr. Gibbs to Winchester. News that General Howe had retreated to Brunswick, Washington had harassed his rear, taken a good many prisoners and played the devil. *Tuesday, Dec. 31st, 1776.* This is the last day of the old Year, which I have spent in worse than Egyptian bondage. No prospect of altering my situation speedily. Spent the day at Mr. Reynold's.

*Wednesday, January 1, 1777.* This is the first day of the New Year, which I am afraid will be spent, by me, to as little purpose as the two last have been. I am now in a disagreeable and precarious situation. I dare do noth-

ing to get bread, cannot return to my native country. The
means of my support depends on the whim and caprice of
a Friend. In fear of going to Jail every day on account
of my political principles, and no prospect of this unnatural rebellion being suppressed this Year. Am determined to make my escape the first opportunity. Spent the
day very happily at Mr. Gibbs with a few of his friends,
dancing and making ourselves as merry as Whiskey, Toddy
and good company will afford. *Thursday, Jan. 2nd, 1777.*
Spent the day at Mr. Reynolds. *Friday, Jan. 3rd, 1777.*
At Mr. Gibbs. Misfortunes and present vagabond life
cause great uneasiness of mind. *Saturday, Jan. 4th, 1777.*
Left Mr. Gibbs, who has treated me with the greatest
kindness and hospitality and insists on me returning back
and spending a month with him before I leave the country.
Dined at Mr. Francis Willis's. Crossed the Shanandoe
River and the Blue Ridge, got to Mr. William Neilson's
in the evening.

*Scotland, Loudoun County, Virginia — Sunday, January
5th, 1777.* This happens to be Mr. Neilson's Birthday, as
well as mine, We spent it as happily as our situation would
admit. We are of the same opinion in political matters,
which makes it the more agreeable. *Monday, Jan. 6th,
1777.* News that Washington had taken 760 Hessian prisoners at Trenton in the Jerseys. Hope it is a lie. This
afternoon hear he has likewise taken six pieces of Brass
Cannon. *Tuesday, Jan. 7th, 1777.* The news is confirmed.
The minds of the people are much altered. A few days
ago they had given up the cause for lost. Their late
successes have turned the scale and now they are all liberty
mad again. Their Recruiting parties could not get a man
(except he bought him from his master) no longer since

than last week, and now the men are coming in by companies. Confound the turncoat scoundrels and the cowardly Hessians together. This has given them new spirits, got them fresh succours and will prolong the War, perhaps for two years. They have recovered their panic and it will not be an easy matter to throw them into that confusion again. Volunteer Companies are collecting in every County on the Continent and in a few months the rascals will be stronger than ever. Even the parsons, some of them, have turned out as Volunteers and Pulpit Drums or Thunder, which you please to call it, summoning all to arms in this cursed babble. D— them all.

*Wednesday, January 8th, 1777.* This is a most unhappy country. Every necessary of life is at an extravagant price, some of them indeed is not to be had for money. Poor people are almost naked. Congress or Committee of Safety or some of those infernal bodies have issued an Order that every one that is fortunate enough to be possessed of two coats is to give one to their naked soldiers. Grain now begins to bear a good price, owing to such great quantities being distilled and the small proportion that is in the ground. I am persuaded there will be a famine very soon as well as a War. *Saturday, Jan. 11th, 1777.* Very cold weather for three days. Almost stupid for want of employment. *Sunday, Jan. 12th, 1777.* News that the *Slebers* Ships had taken 30,000 suits of clothes, that were intended to clothe Our Army for the Winter. Believe it is a lie. However, it serves the rascals' purpose to entice the people to enlist. *Tuesday, Jan. 14th, 1777.* News, that Washington had entirely routed our Army and the few that had escaped had been obliged to take refuge on board the ships. This must certainly be a lie. *Wednesday,*

*Jan. 15th, 1777.* I am exceedingly kindly treated here, and am very happy in the company of Mr. Neilson, but the thought of receiving such unmerited kindness from an entire stranger, whom in all probability it will never be in my power to repay, makes me uneasy. *Thursday, Jan. 16th, 1777.* Intend to go to Leesburg to-morrow. I am unhappy every where. The late news has increased my anxiety to be at home that I may have an opportunity to be revenged of these miscreants.

*Leesburg, Loudoun County, Virginia — Friday, January 17th, 1777.* Left Mr. Neilson's. Got to Leesburg to my old lodgings. Dined and spent the evening at Mr. Kirk's, who begs me to make him the model of a machine for driving piles into the River to build wharfs upon. Their late successes have made him believe that they will have a free and open trade to all parts of the World very soon. Such is the instability of human affairs. Six weeks ago this gentleman was lamenting the unhappy situation of the Americans and pitying the wretched condition of their much-beloved General, supposing his want of skill and experience in military matters had brought them all to the brink of destruction. In short, all was gone, all was lost. But now the scale is turned and Washington's name is extolled to the clouds. Alexander, Pompey and Hannibal were but pigmy Generals, in comparison with the magnanimous Washington. Poor General Howe is ridiculed in all companies and all my countrymen abused. I am obliged to hear this daily and dare not speak a word in their favour. It is the Damd Hessians that has caused this, curse the scoundrel that first thought of sending them here. *Saturday, Jan. 18th, 1777.* Dined at Mr. Kirk's. I lead a most worthless lazy life and cannot help it at present. *Sunday,*

*Jan. 19th, 1777.* Spent it as I do the rest of my time, doing nothing. *Tuesday, Jan. 21st, 1777.* Preparing materials for the model. *Thursday, January 23rd, 1777.* Curiosity and company induced me to spend the evening at a place of no great credit. The various scenes I saw may be of great service to me sometime or other. *Friday, Jan. 24th, 1777.* Salt sold to the people at 6d. per quart by order of the great Committee of Safety. Every tithable in the family is allowed a quart and no more. Even this seems to please the people. I believe they are all mad. *Saturday, Jan. 25th, 1777.* Employed in making the model, obliged to be joiner and smith myself.

*Sunday, January 26th, 1777.* Dined with Mr. Kirk. Eleven English prisoners arrived and are to be stationed here, all of them soldiers. Have been summoned to mount guard over them, but absolutely refused. I suppose this will be a Committee affair, but I am determined to go to jail myself rather than guard an English prisoner. *Tuesday, Jan. 28th, 1777.* Finished the model, which answers exceedingly well. It is an inch to a foot, calculated for one man to raise a 1000 weight, twenty feet which falls on the head of the Pile. Summoned again, but refused to go. *Wednesday, Jan. 29th, 1777.* The Captn. of towns Militia excused my appearance on guard. To my great surprise find one of them to be Mr. John Gee. He that married Miss Nancy Worthington. *Thursday, Jan. 30th, 1777.* News that Fort Washington was retaken by the Yankees. *Friday, Jan. 31st, 1777.* News that New York was deserted by the English, but believe it is a lie. The *Sleber* has a surprizing run of good luck if all be true.

*Saturday, February 1st, 1777.* Mr. Gee and Mr. Hugh Neilson dined and spent the evening with me. Mr. Gee tells me he was settled at New York as a merchant, at the first of these troubles, had made his sentiments known which made him obnoxious to the populace. When it was known that General Howe intended to go to New York he was very industrious amongst the King's Friends and had raised a company of rangers under the famous Major Rodgers. This was known to the Committee before General Howe's arrival at New York. He was seized by the mob, carried by them on a sharp rail through the town, cut with knives and much bruised with clubs. Afterwards put in a dungeon or dark prison where they kept him three days without victuals. Then he was removed to Morristown in the Jerseys, from thence (on the approach of our Army) to Philadelphia. From Philadelphia to Baltimore where in their great confusion he got amongst the soldiers and now passes for clerk to the 71st. Regt. He is in a wretched condition, scarcely clothes sufficient to cover his nakedness, and very dirty. I have given him a shirt, hunting shirt, jacket and blanket, as they have only three blankets in the whole company. Mr. Neilson has given him leather to make himself a pair of breeches and I will get them made.

*Sunday, February 2nd, 1777.* News that Washington and his Myrmidons had defeated a large body of our troops at Prince-town in Jersey. This is very surprizing that there should be any of our Army at Prince-town when it was affirmed for fact, that they were drove a shipboard. *Tuesday, Feb. 4th, 1777.* My landlady has got nothing to burn or anything to eat that is fit for a Christian. To pay 12 shillings a week is very hard, without I get the real necessaries of life. Am determined to go to Captn. Douglas. *Wednesday, Feb. 5th, 1777.* Spent part of the evening with Mr. Gee at *The Crooked Billet.* Afraid he is a Sot.

If that be the case he will be miserable. Mr. Cavan came to my lodgings on purpose to drink Gin. I made him very merry before he went away. This is the first time I have seen him in liquor. *Thursday, Feb. 6th, 1777.* Dined at Mr. Kirk's with Captn. Wm. Sandford a Continental Officer. News that Fort Lee was retaken. *Friday, Feb. 7th, 1777.* Left Leesburg and went to Captn. W. Douglas.

*Garralland, Loudoun County, Virginia — Sunday, February 9th, 1777.* Dined with Thomson Mason Esq., who is laid up with the Gout. No news these three days. A Methodist preaching here. In the evening the parson and I had a long discourse about the New Faith, as he calls it. Find him a sensible man not so much biggoted as some of them are. *Sunday, February 16th, 1777.* In the course of the last six days I have read more religious authors and had more discourse about religion than in all my life before. Captn. Douglas uses his utmost endeavours to make a proselyte of me, but I cannot find that Whitefield's road to Heaven is one jot better or nearer than Martin Luther's. Therefore, will continue in the opinion under which I was educated. *Tuesday, Feb. 18th, 1777.* News that three of his Majesty's Ships are in the Bay. Determined to go on board some of them if possible as soon as I can meet with an opportunity. *Friday, Feb. 21st, 1777.* Three days at Garralland. More religious discourse with the usual effect. *Saturday, Feb. 22nd, 1777.* Went to Leesburg. Dined at Mr. Kirk's. News that Washington was taken. This is too good news to be true. Returned to Garralland at night. *Sunday, Feb. 23rd, 1777.* . News confirmed that Ships are in the Bay. My parole will be out soon and then I will give the rascals the slip. *Monday, Feb. 24th, 1777.* Went to town with Captn. Douglas and his family to a Methodist meeting. Lieut. Ancram informs me that I am likely to be brought into trouble for reporting that Washington was taken prisoner. Can give up my authors. Dined at Mr. Rispes'.

*Tuesday, February 25th, 1777.* Expected to have had a Methodist meeting here to-day. The Company, or Congregation, of Canting, Whining Hypocrites met, but the Parson disappointed them. I am sorry that Captn. Douglas should be such a dupe to these religious quacks. He keeps a good table, is a good-natured man, easily led, and rather unsteady in his religious principles, always glad to see or converse with these Fag-end-of-the-Scripture mongers, and as long as his house is open to them they will haunt him as bad as they tell us the Devil haunts their meetings. They are a set of the noisiest fellows I ever heard. Instead of enforcing their arguments, they only exalt their voices. *Thursday, Feb. 27th, 1777.* One of these Parsons has had a long confab with me to-day. He is one of the most effected bigoted little puppies I ever met with. Out of his great kindness has made old Pluto a compliment of me. *Friday, Feb. 28th, 1777.* This is a Fast Day appointed by the Great Sanhedrim to return thanks for their late successes, and beg a continuation of them. It is ordered to be kept sacred by all. Every one to go to Church or Meeting. I have not been. It seems to be like Oliver Cromwell's proceedings.

*Saturday, March 1st, 1777.* Went with Captn. Douglas and Mr. Flemming Patterson to see Mr. Josiah Clapham. He is an Assembly Man, Colonel of the county and Justice of the Peace on the present establishment. He is an Englishman from Wakefield in Yorkshire, much in debt at home, and in course a violent *Sleber* here. Has made himself very popular by erecting a Manufactory of Guns, but it is poorly carried on. His Wife is the most notable woman in the County for Housewifery, but I should like her much better if she would keep a cleaner house. He has got a very good plantation, takes every mean art to render himself popular amongst a set of ignorant Dutchman that are settled in his neighbourhood. Dirty in person and principle. Returned to Garralland at night. *Sunday, March 2nd, 1777.* No news this week. Intend to go to Leesburg tomorrow. If I stay much longer here I may be the means of making a certain person in the family unhappy, tho' very inadvertently on my part and I believe involuntarily on theirs. This would be an unpardonable as well as an ungrateful act in me, who has been so kindly treated in this agreeable family.

*Leesburg, Virginia — Monday, March 3rd, 1777.* Went to Leesburg. Saw a review of Captn. Wm. Johnston's company, a set of rascally servants and convicts most of them just purchased from their masters. A ragged crew indeed. Captn. Douglas is angry with me for leaving his house, but he is ignorant of the cause. *Tuesday, March 4th, 1777.* I have had the misfortune to affront one of the Committee men, by not giving his Daughter a kiss when I was introduced to her. This has offended the old man so much, that I am informed by my friends he has several spys to watch my actions. If anything treasonable is discovered (as he is pleased to term it) I am to be prosecuted to the utmost of the Laws. Sorry I did not give the ugly Jade a kiss and have escaped the censure of this ostentatious blockhead. If I don't proceed with caution shall not get away this summer.

*Thursday, March 6th, 1777.* Laying schemes how to

get out of this hateful place, something like building castles in the air. I intend to go to Alexandria to see if I can get any recompense for my coat and collect some other small debts that are due to me. Perhaps something may happen in my favour by and by. *Friday, March 7th, 1777.* Left Leesburg. Dined at Mosses Ordinary. Got to Alexandria. Lodged at Mr. Flemming's. *Saturday, March 8th, 1777.* This morning went to Mrs. Hawkins about my coat, much insulted by her son, an Adjutant in the *Sleber* Army. Called an English Tory, and every bad name the puppy could think of, and dared not resent it. Had I made the least quarrel, the jail must have been my portion. However, I got ten dollars for my coat and think myself very well that I got anything. Neither law or justice in this country. Dined at Mr. Flemming Patterson's, an honest Scotchman. Lodged at Mosses Ordinary. *Sunday, March 9th, 1777.* Much disturbed last night, by the groans of a Methodist Parson who slept in the next room. Got to Leesburg to dinner. A company of soldiers that had been raised in the County, marched out of town on their way to the Jerseys.

*Monday, March 10th, 1777.* Court day. Several Recruiting parties, but they got very few men. Indeed the County and Country in general is pretty well thinned. Have avoided all company to-day as much as possible. In the afternoon Colonels Green and Greyson came to my lodgings with Mr. Mason, told me they had seen my model of the Pile Machine which pleased them so much that they made me an offer of an Engineer's Captn. Commission in their Army which, with the perquisites belonging to it, is three dollars per day. They paid me a great many encomiums on my mechanical abilities and did everything in their power to persuade me to engage in the noble struggle for liberty as they are pleased to call it. I excused myself with all the politeness I was master of, or could possibly muster at this time, told them I could not bear the thoughts of taking up arms against my native country, and was much obliged to them for the honour they would confer upon me, but as it is incompatible with my present sentiments must pardon my not accepting the offer. They were pleased to make me some genteel compliment about my steadiness and resolution, at the same time blended with some bitter reflections on my countrymen which rather nettled me. *Tuesday, March 11th, 1777.* News that the *Sleber* had killed 500 of the English near Brunswick, only with the loss of two men. This must certainly be a lie. *Wednesday, March 12th, 1777.* Dined at the Tavern with Captn. W. Johnston, for dinner and two bowls of Toddy paid 8/6 this I can very ill afford, but it is necessary for me to keep up appearances.

*Thursday, March 13th, 1777.* Some thoughts of going amongst the Indians and either living amongst them till these disturbances are settled or making my escape into Canada through the Indian Country. This will be attended with a many disagreeable inconveniences. To go into Canada without hard money will answer no purpose without I enlist as a common soldier. This I am not willing to do. Am determined to go to the Indians and live amongst them, very certain that I can live happy and I am ashamed and afraid to return home in the situation that I came out. Tho' my misfortunes have been unavoidable, I know that I shall be censured for misconduct. *Friday, March 14th, 1777.* Went to Captn. Douglas. Saw them making sugar out of the sap of the sugar maple. They boil it till the wattery particles evaporate and the sugar remains at the bottom of the pot. Four gallons of water will make a pound if it is early in the spring. Something like Muscovada Sugar, I believe not quite so strong.

*Saturday, March 15th, 1777.* Dined with Mr. Mason, who promises to give me every assistance in his power to return home. Proposes giving me a letter of introduction and recommendations to the Governor of Virginia by his permission to go on board the Man of War in the Bay. This is the most probable method of getting home, but will not attempt it till the next month. Rather too cold to stay on board the ships without better and warmer clothes than I am master of at present. *Sunday, March 16th, 1777.* Heard a Sermon preached by the Revd. David Griffith. A political discourse. Indeed, there is nothing else to be expected now. Spent the evening at the Tavern with Mr. Cleone More, Mr. Kirk and Captn. McCabe, but left them as soon as I could with decency. Tavern charges extravagant. *Monday, March 17th, 1777.* Went with Mr. Henry McCabe to dine at Mr. William Elyey's, Senator for this district. Very genteelly entertained by Mrs. Elyey. Mr. Elyey not at home. *Tuesday, March 18th, 1777.* Dined at Captn. Douglas's. Spent the evening at the Tavern with Colonel Angus McDonald who informs me that the Indians are broken out and killed several people about Fort Pitt. Must not go there this summer.

*Scotland, Loudoun County, Virginia — Wednesday, March 19th, 1777.* Left Leesburg and went to Mr. Neilson's. Mr. Griffith and his lady are here and a most violent *Sleber*. He is Doctor and Chaplain to one of their Regmt. *Saturday, March 22nd, 1777.* At Mr. Neilson's. Great tumults and murmurings among the people, caused by them pressing the young men into the Army. The people now begin to feel the effects of an Independent Government and groan under it, but cannot help themselves, as they are almost in general disarmed. May God continue and increase their confusion.

*Leesburg, Virginia — Sunday, March 23rd, 1777.* Left Mr. Neilson's, got to town, found Mr. Kirk laid up with the Gout. He desires me to direct the workmen how to make a pump to work by a pendulum. I am under sundry obligations to this gentleman that claim my warmest gratitude, promised to undertake it. *Monday, March 24th, 1777.* This morning begun to work at the pump with a Prussian carpenter and two Negroes. Went to the Sawmill to get some wood proper for the work. Dined at Mr. Elyey's. The Miss Elyeys very sensible but not killing beauties. *Tuesday, March 25th, 1777.* Dined at Captn. Douglas's, and agreed with a man to furnish me with a pair of horses to Williamsburg. Intend to set out the 10th. of next month. I have no other method of getting anything with me except it is on horseback.

*Wednesday, March 26th, 1777.* This morning got engaged in a terrible fray. Six waggoners attacked Mr. Dean in his store, all of them armed with whips. He called to me for assistance. I got a good stick and knocked two of them down when Mr. Cavan came to our assistance. The battle then became general. Four to six, we had rather the advantage of them in weapons, tho' not in number, and gave them a good drubbing. Cavan has broken one of the men's arms and I have bared another's scull for about six inches long, and hurt another very much. Have seized two of the ringleaders. Mr. Dean is very much hurt, fainted several times with loss of blood. The two men

give security for their future good behaviour and pay the
Doctor and other expenses which I believe has cost them
about six pounds. Am very uneasy about the man that I
hurt so very bad. *Thursday, March 27th, 1777.* Find myself a little sore with the bruises I got yesterday. Mr.
Dean is much hurt and in bed. This is the happy fruits
of Independence, the populace are grown so insolent, if you
do not tacitly submit to every insult or imposition they
think proper, they immediately call you a Tory and think
that if you have that stigma upon your character they have
a right, nay, even take it to be a meritorious act to knock
your brains out. *Friday, March 28th, 1777.* Employed
in directing the workmen about the pump, find them profoundly ignorant. (Mem. never to employ a negro if white
man is to be got.) The people here are much bigoted to
their own ways.

*Saturday, March 29th, 1777.* News that the English
have left Brunswick, but I believe it to be a lie. Washington, who is Dictator for the present year, has ordered sixteen battalions to be raised (in the States as they call them)
under the appellation of Guards or Washington's Life
Guards. These added to the 88 battalions of Continental
troops, will be a numerous army, but I am persuaded they
will find some difficulty in raising this number of men. If
they, by pressing, drafting, or other means collect this body
of men together it will distress the Country exceedingly
and very probably bring a famine on the country. *Sunday,
March 30th, 1777.* Heard a good sermon by the Revd.
Mr. Griffiths. *Monday, March 31st, 1777.* A great riot
in town betwixt the English prisoners and the Yankees.
Some of the prisoners were ill used by a Scotch tailor now

an Ensign in the Militia, violent, persecuting Scoundrel, one of the followers of Whitefield.

*Saturday, April 5th, 1777.* Employed all this week about the pump, which I have got complete this evening to entire satisfaction of Mr. Kirk. This is the first piece of mechanism of the kind in the Country. The people gape and stare at it with wonder and surprise, coming in crowds to see it work. It gives me pleasure to find it answers so well, as I have never seen one constructed in the same manner.

*Sunday, April 6th, 1777.* Spent the evening with Mr. Mason. Am informed by a Friend that there are two spys to watch all my proceedings, that my Chest is to be broken open and my papers examined before I go. But will take care to disappoint the scoundrels in that particular. *Monday, April 7th, 1777.* Preparing for my journey to Williamsburg. Mr. William Elyey, the Senator, promises to give me a letter to the Governor. This may be of service. *Tuesday, April 8th, 1777.* Left Leesburg. Dined at Mr. Nourse's, whose family is in the Smallpox. Got to Mr. Gibb's in the evening. *Wednesday, April 9th, 1777.* Spent the afternoon at Mr. Reynolds. Spinning wheel and flax-breaks, at every house, they will make more coarse linen in these two Counties than will be used in their families. Some few people makes very fine linen, thirteen or fourteen hundred warp, but don't bleach it well. *Thursday, April 10th, 1777.* Dined and lodged at Mr. Reynold's.

*Friday, April 11th, 1777.* Left Mr. Reynolds. Breakfasted at Mr. Gibb's, whom I parted from with regret, he is a friendly, hospitable, honest man. Dined at Mr. Nourse's, who gave me letters to several of his friends in England, and one directed to Lord Brownlow Berty, Miss

Nourse gave one to my care, which she made me promise to deliver myself, if I go to London. I really felt a sensible concern to bid farewell to this happy family, so much good nature, affability, and harmony seems to subsist amongst them, that I am afraid I shall never see the like again. In short, it is happiness after my own plan, if we may be allowed to judge from appearances. Mr. James Nourse junr. came with me to town, spent the evening and lodged with me. He is very good natured, but not quite so sensible as his sister. It is a pity that this family are *Sleber*.

*Saturday, April 12th, 1777.* Preparing for my departure. Mr. George West profers to lend me his Sulkey, got a small trunk for convenience of carriage. News, that they had hanged a man at Philadelphia who had been employed by Lord Howe to hire Pilots for the Dellawar River.

*Sunday, April 13th, 1777.* Spent part of the day with Mr. Mason, with whom I promised correspondence, if I get home and these differences subside. I am happy and unhappy to leave this Country. This seems a paradox. I am happy in leaving a Country where almost everyone looks upon me with an eye of jealousy and distrust and where I have lived for a long time in a miserable and perpetual state of suspense. Spending money and the most valuable part of my life in indolence, without an object in view, or a probability of one, except I quit the paths of honour, justice and gratitude and commence the parricide, rebel, murderer, plunderer and an open enemy to the country that gave me birth. This my soul abhors. I will sooner starve or beg or steal and be hanged for it, than accept the most lucrative or honorary post that is in their power to bestow upon me. On the other hand, I am unhappy to find frustrated and prove abortive, all my favour concerted schemes " vanish like the baseless fabric of a vision " and leave me a wreck behind. I think I may with propriety compare myself to a wreck, all my ideal views of happiness and opulence are entirely quashed and rendered impracticable. My present situation is next to wretchedness and my prospect of extricating myself exceedingly precarious, entirely dependent on a set of usurping rascals, accountable to none, as they suppose, for their actions. The means of my present support entirely depends on the Whim and caprice of one single person, who I know is actuated by interested principles; therefore I cannot expect his assistance any longer than he supposes it consonant with his interest. All these summed together are not half so grating as the thought of returning to my native country in poverty and rags and then be obliged to beg like a criminal to get my debts paid which I am now contracting, and in course must be obliged to contract before I get home. The bitter reflections, taunts, and sarcasms of my friends will be submitted then upon my conduct. No matter whether it be right or wrong, I have been unfortunate, therefore, everyone thinks they have a right to find fault with my proceedings. I believe their reproofs will be tinctured with a good deal of acrimony, as I took this journey entirely against their consent. I must endeavour to brave all these rubs and frowns of fortune with fortitude and patience, submit myself to them, and follow their councils and advice.

I have been brought up to no trade, therefore have no prospect of recruiting my fortune by merchandizing. Not only that, but I want the means to pursue any sort of trade at present. Indeed, I might turn soldier and get a good living by cutting the throats of my Friends and countrymen. But this my plaguing, squeamish conscience forbids and I must, and will, obey its dictates or I am forever miserable. I have this consolation in the midst of all my troubles and difficulties, to be unfortunate, not guilty, of anything, except it be acting contrary to the advice of my Parents. But I gave them sufficient reasons for the steps I took, tho' I must confess I have more cogent ones, which I did not choose to mention to them or anyone else. And I have the satisfaction to be well assured that my plan was well grounded, admit times had continued as they were when I first came to this country. But this cursed rebellion has ruined all forever.

I am well convinced that I could have lived much better and made more money, as a Farmer in this country, with five hundred pound, than I can in England, with two thousand. Agriculture is in such an infant state and the value of land so low that anyone with the least spark of industry might make what money they please. As a proof of it I will here subjoin a plan I formed to myself in the Spring 1775, as times were then.

An Estimate of the cost and profit of an Estate containing 500 acres supposing it is in Frederick or Berkely County in Virginia.

| Cost. | Vir. Currency. | | |
|---|---|---|---|
| | £. | s. | d. |
| To the purchase of 500 acres of land @ 40s. per | 1000 | | |
| To 30 Breeding Mares £30................. | 900 | | |
| To one Stallion imported.................... | 100 | | |
| To 20 Cows and 10 Oxen @ £4............. | 120 | | |
| To 20 two-year-old Cattle @ 30/—.......... | 30 | | |
| To 30 Ewes and 20 Wethers @ 12/6........ | 30 | | |
| To 5 Men Servants and 2 Women @ £20/- .... | 140 | | |
| To 20 Hogs at 10s/- ..................... | 10 | | |

To Poultry .............................. 2

To Clothing 5 Men & 2 Women @ 50/– ea... 17: 10: 0

To 1 Waggon............................ 20

To 2 Carts.............................. 20

To 4 Ploughs @ 30/–.................... 6

To 2 Harrows @ 40/– ................... 4

To Gear for Waggons, Carts, Ploughs and)
  other necessary implements of husbandry.)

                                     .... 30

Annual quit rent of 500 acres @ 2/6 per 100
  acres. ............................... 12: 6

To 8 tithables @ 10s/– per tithable........... 4

                                      £2434: 2: 6

Profits of an Estate of 500 acres in Frederick or Berkely County, Virginia,

*Profits.*

                                    Vir. Currency.
                                     £.   s.   d.

By 20 year-old Colts at £10................ 200

By the season of 50 Mares exclusive of my
  own @ £4–........................ 200

By 10 Fat Oxen out of my own stock at £10... 100

By 20 Sheep fed on turnips and sold in spring.. 20

By 10 Oxen purchased in the fall, fed on)
  Turnips and sold in the spring supposing)... 30
  each of them to clear £3          )

By produce — of 30 acres of wheat at 12
  bushels to the acre sold @ 2/6.......... 45

By 150 lbs. of wool at 1/6................ 11: 5: 0

                                     £606: 5: 0

Exchange at 25 per cent, the sterling cost is....£1947: 6: 2½

                          Sterling Profit   £485

This calculation is made with ample allowance on the Costs, and a very moderate one on the Profits. On the Costs in particular from Mares of £30 value and the Horse imported, they very often sell at 2 year old for £30, and sometimes more if they are likely for the Course. The Cost of the land is very high. The best land, in such large tracts, seldom averages more than 35s/— per acre, tho' perhaps one third of it is cleared from woods. All taxes are included under the article Tithable, Church, Poor and Road, &c. except the Quit Rents, which are paid to Lord Fairfax as the Proprietor of the Northern Neck of Virginia. The value of manure is not known here. If it is, they are too lazy to make use of it. Their method is to clear a piece of land from the woods, generally put it in wheat the first year, Indian corn the next, and so alternately for six or seven years together. By that time the strength of the Land is gone and they say it is worn out, throw it out to the Woods again, and set about clearing another piece. In a few years it will recover its fertility sufficient to bring Indian corn, which is of great use amongst them, both for their negroes, horses and all sorts of cattle. It makes very indifferent bread and I look upon it as a troublesome and expensive thing to cultivate. It is planted in hills, about 1600 of them in an acre, in the month of April, ploughed or rather hoed every fortnight till the month of August. By that time it is fixed in the ear, they take no further pains with it till November, when they pluck the blades of the stalk for fodder for the cattle in the Winter. The ear remains on the stalk till near Christmas to harden and dry. Indeed, it would keep there all winter without taking the least damage. The plant grows from four feet to 12 feet high and produces from 12 to 30 Bushels to the acre, according to the richness of the land and the attendance. They seldom plant more than two grains in one hill, if any extra ones shoot from the roots of these they are broken off before the ear is formed. Sometimes they sow wheat amongst the corn and get a crop extraordinary. Wheat is sown in the month of September, they are obliged to sow it early or the severe frosts in winter would kill it. Generally a bushel to the acre. Rye, Barley, Oats, Peas, Beans, Hemp and Flax grows very well here, and would produce excellent crops if they would take considerable pains in tilling the land and making it fit to receive the seed. It is really astonishing that it produces any thing but weeds, as they seldom plough more than two inches deep and leave one third of the land undisturbed. I have seen Hemp 14 feet high. I am not a judge in this article, but I have been told by people that are, it is equal in goodness to the Riga Hemp. It is a pity the cultivation of this useful plant is not more encouraged in this part of the world. It would be a means of saving large sums we pay to Russians annually for this article, among ourselves.

In short, the land will produce anything if only they will be at the pains to cultivate. I do not know any reason why crops of wheat might not be produced here, equal in quantity and quality to the general crops in England if the people would take the same method. I have seen Wheat weighed 60 and 63 pounds per bushel very frequently. The cultivation of this article is not altogether profitable, because the market is precarious. When Russia, Poland and Germany are at Peace, Grain can be purchased cheaper there than in America. Consequently they must undersell the Americans at the Spanish, Portugal and Mediterranean markets. The West Indies are the only certain markets they have and in a Country where almost all are Farmers, the price must be low and very little demand, if there was no exportation. But Beef, Pork and Horses will always bear a good price while we have a trade with the West India Islands and the raising of these things are not attended with any great expense. In the back parts of the country there is no bounds to their outlet. When there is a plentiful Mast (what they call Mast are acorns, Walnuts, Chestnuts, and all wild fruits) the Hogs will get fat in the woods with little, or no corn. Great quantities are killed as soon as they are taken out of the woods, salted, barrelled and sent to the West Indies. Sells from 12 to 27 shillings Currency per hundred.

The bacon cured here is not to be equalled in any part of the world, their hams in particular. They first rub them over with brown sugar and let them lie all night. This extracts the watery particles. They let them lie in salt for 10 days or a fortnight. Some rub them with hickory ashes instead of saltpetre, it makes them red as the saltpetre and gives them a pleasant taste. Then they are hung up in the smoke-house and a slow smoky fire kept under them for three or four weeks, nothing but hickory wood is burnt in these smoke-houses. This gives them an agreeable flavour, far preferable to the Westphalia Hams, not only that, but it prevents them going rancid and will preserve them for several years by giving them a fresh smoking now and then. Beef cured in this manner is but very indifferent eating. Indeed the Beef in this country is not equal in goodness to the English, it may be as fat, but not so juicy. I think it is time to go to bed.

*Monday, April 14th, 1777.* Disappointed by the rascal

who was to have gone with me to Williamsburg. There is little dependence to be put in these mercenary lazy scoundrels. Spent the evening with Mr. Mason, who has extorted a promise from me that entirely oversets all my intended schemes and will oblige me to do what is very disagreeable. *Tuesday, April 15th, 1777.* Went to Captn. Douglas and engaged another man but I believe he, like the other, will deceive me. Spent the evening at Leesburg with Mr. Kirk, Mr. Gibbs and Captn. McCabe.

*Wednesday, April 16th, 1777.* This morning I have had my chest searched for treasonable papers, by a certain Mr. Standhope and Ensign McIntire, by order of the Committee, or more properly the Court of Inquisition. These scoundrels have plundered me of a shot pouch and powder horn which Captn. White-eyes an Indian Chief gave me, a Bear's skin Blanket and several other articles of no very great value to me, tho' I am very unwilling to part with them. I believe I might get them again, but the remedy would be worse than disease. I think it the most prudent way to sit down with the loss and say no more about it. I have very fortunately preserved my Journal and the greatest part of my papers, owing to the fidelity of my Boy who suspected something of their business and found means to keep them below, while I hid my papers in my Cardevine case, my diary excepted which had some trifling remarks in it. They seized it with the greatest avidity and bore it off with the rest of their plunder in great triumph to the Committee room, who have been sitting upon it all day. What will be the consequence I can't tell. Confusion light upon them all. *Thursday, April 17th, 1777.* The Committee has puzzled themselves a long time, but can find nothing that amounts to treason against the States of

America in my papers. I am glad of it. If they had, my situation would have been dreadful indeed, an imprisonment of five years, or the fine of twenty thousand pounds would have been the punishment. Neither of these I am willing to submit to, the latter is utterly out of my power, I must in course have submitted to the first. The bare idea of it makes me shudder, the thought of a prison even for debt is horrid. But these infernals for Torys and Traitors, as the rascals call them, make me tremble with fear. I have hitherto escaped them, and may God of his goodness grant, that I may always escape them. If it is my fortune to become an inhabitant of those horrid regions, may I bear my misfortune as becomes the character of an Englishman and a Christian. I am again disappointed of my horses. D——m the pitiful scoundrels altogether. I am determined to go by water to Hampton.

*Friday, April 18th, 1777.* This morning I sent my Chest down to Alexandria and contrary to my expectations it went unmolested, through the influence of my good Friend, Mr. Mason. I invited Mr. Kirk, Mr. Cavan, Mr. Deane, Captn. McCabe and Mr. Henry McCabe to dine with me, as this is the last day I intend to spend in Leesburg. They have all supped and spent the evening with me and got most heartily drunk. And I am now going to bed at *The Crooked Billet,* as drunk as any honest man aught to be. *Saturday, April 19th, 1777.* Settled all my affairs and drew a Bill upon my Father for £69: 10: 2. in favour of Mr. Kirk, payable to Messrs. Broomheads of Sheffield. This is the balance I owe Mr. Kirk. If I escape now I shall not leave the Country one penny in debt, and there is very few Europeans, but what does at this time, except it is those who have had some trade in the Country and those are in general creditors. Left Leesburg but find no reluctance in parting with anyone but my good and worthy friend Mr. Cavan, for whose sincere friendship I have the highest esteem. Lodged at Mosses Ordinary with Mr. Kirk. Drunk again.

# X

## HAMPTON — WILLIAMSBURG — VOYAGE
## TO NEW YORK

*A LEXANDRIA, Fairfax County, Virginia — Sunday,*
*April 20th, 1777.* Got to Alexandria to dinner. All
the townspeople and a Regiment of soldiers that are
quartered here all inocculated for the Smallpox and I believe there is a great number that has the Greatpox along
with them. Such a pock-eyed place I never was in before.
Spent the evening with Mr. Kirk and Mr. T. Crafts, with
whom I lodged till I get a passage to Hampton. *Monday,*
*April 21st, 1777.* Took my passage in a Pilot Boat for
Hampton, for which I am to pay £3, this is three hundred
per cent more than usual fare, so much is the paper currency depreciating in value. Saw a Highlander (a soldier
in the 71st. Regiment, now a prisoner of War here)
whipped by his comrades for enlisting into the Rebel service. He is the only one out of two Hundred and odd who
have been prisoners in this Colony, that has enlisted into
their service. His fellow prisoners held a Court Martial
over him, a Sergeant being the highest officer present, and
condemned the poor wretch to receive 1500 lashes with a
switch upon his bare back, 100 every day till the number
was complete. The man enlisted when drunk and returned
the money as soon as he was sober and absolutely refused to
serve, but this would not satisfy his enraged companions.

*Tuesday, April 22nd, 1777.* This morning my worthy
Friend Mr. Kirk returned to Leesburg. This gentleman's

kindness I hope I shall always remember with respect and gratitude. He has always behaved to me with great friendship, complaisance and hospitality. I have always returned it to the utmost of my power. If my Father honours my bills, I have this satisfaction, that he will be no loser by me, but a very considerable gainer. A certain Collin Keir, a young Scotch gentleman, is to go with me down to Hampton. He is a stranger to me, but appears to be a good hearty joyous companion and a good Christian. News that nine English Men of War are now in Delaware Bay. Saw a seine drawn for herrings and caught upwards of 40,000 with about 300 Shadfish. The Shads they use but the herring are left upon the shore useless for want of salt. Such immense quantities of this fish is left upon the shore to rot. I am surprised it does not bring some epidemic disorder to the inhabitants, by the nauseous stench arising from such a mass of putrefaction. Spent the evening with Mr. Crafts at the Tavern. *Wednesday, April 23rd, 1777.* Waiting for a fair wind. Disagreeable thoughts will intrude themselves in spite of all I can do to avoid them. Spent the evening with Mr. Robert Muir at Mr. Craft's.

*On Board the Pilot Boat "Sally," Potowmeck River—Thursday, April 24th, 1777.* Sailed from Alexandria about noon. Mr. Crafts gave me three venison Hams. Called at Mr. Marsden's to get a litle stock, but he would not let us have so much as one fowl, tho' Mrs. had often requested me to call at her house, if ever I wanted stock for Sea and she would be glad to help me to some for the kindness I shewed her son, Mr. Brooks, in our passage from the West Indies, but Mr. Brooks is dead. Mrs. Marsden drunk and the scoundrel, her husband, in an ill humour, therefore he is determined to keep his fowls and keep them he may for

Nicholas. In the evening ebb tide and wind ahead came to an anchor off Sandy Point. *Friday, April 25th, 1777.* This morning parted our Cable in attempting to weigh our anchor. Obliged to run our vessel aground in Nanjemoy Creek. Went to Nanjemoy to purchase another Anchor but can't meet with one. Dined at Mrs. Leftwich's with my old friend Mr. Bayley. Lodged at Captn. Knox's, with whom and Mr. Wallace, spent an agreeable evening.

*Saturday, April 26th, 1777.* Parted with my good friends, Mr. Bailey, Captn. B. Knox and Mr. Wallace. To these gentlemen I am under infinite obligations for their great care of me in my sickness when I first arrived in this country. These are all Scotchmen, to which nation I had a particular dislike, owing to the prejudice of my education. I was taught to look upon them as a set of men divested of common humanity, ungenerous and unprincipled. I have always found them the reverse of all this, and I most heartily condemn this pernicious system of education by which we are taught to look upon the inhabitants of a different nation, language or complexion, as a set of beings far inferior to our own. This is a most illiberal and confined sentiment, for human nature is invariably the same throughout the whole human species, from the sooty Africans down to the fair European, allowance being made for their different customs, manners and education. Proceeded down the River. Mr. Keir had some business at Cedar Point, but the wind blew so hard he could not get ashore or the vessel lay to till morning. Therefore, we were obliged to bear away for Hampton.

*Hampton, Virginia—Sunday, April 27th, 1777.* Arrived here this evening. Saw several ships in the Bay, but no Men of War. Lodged at *The Sign of the Bunch of*

*Grapes* kept by one Dames, an Irishman. This is a little port town but almost ruined by the soldiers who were quartered here last winter, who made terrible havoc by pulling the wooden houses to pieces for fuel. All the garden palings, fences &c in the neighbourhood are entirely burnt up. *Monday, April 28th, 1777.* Hired a horse to go to Williamsburg to wait upon the Governor and Counsel. This place is rather inconveniently situated for trade, at the head of a small creek, no vessels of any considerable burden can come to the town. Here are 4 of the Gallies here and a great number of row boats for the use of the State. Here is a company of Riflemen stationed here, under the comand of my old friend Captn. John Lee. Tho' we are very friendly, I think he suspects me to be Tory, but he does not know that I am a prisoner and I won't tell him. Here are two Frenchmen at our Inn who have got commissions in this Army, tho' I suspect one of them to be an Irishman who passes here for a Frenchman, for I hear him at this instant cursing the waiter in English or rather Irish English.

*Williamsburg, the Capitol of Virginia — Tuesday, April 29th, 1777.* Set out early this morning. Dined at York-town 24 miles from Hampton. This is a pleasant town situated upon York River which is navigable for the largest ships. Close to the town there are several very good Gentlemen's houses built of brick and some of their gardens laid out with the greatest taste of any I have seen in America, but now almost ruined by the disorderly soldiers, and, what is more extraordinary, their own soldiers, the guardians of the people and the defenders of their rights. Houses burnt down, others pulled to pieces for fuel, most of the Gardens thrown to the street, everything in disorder and confusion and no appearance of trade. This melancholy scene fills the mind of the itinerant traveller with gloomy and horrid ideas. Here is a battery consisting of 12 pieces of heavy cannon to command the River and a company of artillery stationed here, but they make a sorry appearance for so respectable a corps, as the Artillery ought to be. Got here soon after dinner only 12 miles from Yorktown, the road from Hampton is level and sandy through large pine Woods, interspersed with plantations and Gentlemen's houses. The land in general appears barren. The produce is Tobacco and Corn.

This is the finest town I have seen in Virginia. It is situated between two Creeks only navigable for boats, the one falling into James and the other into York River. It consists of one principal street about a mile long, very wide and level with a number of good buildings, the Capitol at one end of the street and the College at the other. Towards endowing this College, King Wm. and Queen Mary gave £2000 and 2000 acres of land and a duty of one penny per pound upon all Tobacco exported to the other Colonies towards the support of it, and there has been several donations to it since, but, like all other public Seminaries, it is much abused. The Capitol is the place where all public business is done, the Colonial Assembly meets, &c. They are both large and elegant brick buildings. In the Capitol is a fine marble statue of the late Governor Batitourt, as large as life, in the attitude of an orator, a roll of parchment in one hand as an emblem of their Charter, and the cap of Liberty in the other. It is mounted on a pedestal and surrounded with iron balustrades. On the front of the pedestal is his Excellency's arms and this inscription:
"The Right Honourable Norbone Berkley, Baron of

ᴸauᴄourt. His Majesty's late Lieutenant and Governor General of the Colony and Dominion of Virginia." On the right of the pedestal is this inscription: "Deeply impressed with the warmest sense of gratitude for his Excellence the Right Honourable Lord Batitourt's prudent and wise administration, and that the remembrance of those many public and social virtues which so eminently adorned his illustrious character might be transmitted to the latest posterity, The general Assembly of Virginia on the 20th. of July Anno Domini 1771, Resolved with one united voice, to erect this Statue to his Lordship's memory."

This underneath: "Let wisdom and justice preside in any Country, The people will rejoice and must be happy." On the left of the pedestal is the following inscription: "America, behold your Friend! who leaving his native Country, declined those additional Honours which she had there in store for him, that he might heal your wounds and restore tranquility to this extensive Continent. With what zeal and anxiety he pursued these glorious objects Virginia thus bears her grateful testimony."

On the back of the pedestal is the figure of Britannia with her spear and shield, America with her bow and quiver, each holding an olive branch over an altar, with this Motto, "Concordia." It is looked upon as a masterly piece of statuary and, what is very remarkable, not in the least defaced tho' exposed to the public, such veneration had the people for this great man. The Governor's Palace is a good brick building, but it does not make a grand appearance. Here is only one Church, none of the grandest, and I suppose there may be about 250 houses in town. Lodged at Anderson's Tavern.

*Yorktown, Virginia — Wednesday, April 30th, 1777.*

This morning I waited upon the Governor at the Palace. Delivered my letters from Mr. Mason and Mr. Elyey and was most politely treated. Had the honour of breakfasting with his Excellency, who ordered me to meet him at the Council Chamber in the Capitol. I did so, and was examined very strictly about my sentiments, some of which I thought proper to deny, and others, tho' very imprudently, to avow. All that I could say would not procure me permission to go on board his Majesty's Ships in the Bay. However, they have given me a permit to go in the *Albion,* a ship that is to come round from N. Carolina to Nansymond River for 133 Scotch Gentlemen who are there waiting for her, but I think she will never arrive there. If she does come and I can't get a passage in her, they in their great clemency will give me leave to go to France in one of their vessels. This is the highest court in the Colony, therefore I can have no other redress. I am determined to risk a passage. Dined at Williamsburg with two Colonels, 5 Majors, 7 Captains, and a number of inferior Officers. The Grace: G—d D—m the King of England, by Colnl. Innis, for the Military dinner. I paid 27s. D—m the Military and the times together. Got to Yorktown in the evening, which I spent with Lieut. Ancram who lodged at *The Sign of the Swan.*

*Hampton, Virginia—Thursday, May 1st, 1777.* Left Yorktown. Got to Hampton in the afternoon. Mr. Keir, who went to Norfolk on some business, is not yet returned. Great numbers of French men in Williamsburg, Yorktown and Hampton, indeed most of the stores are kept by French men. Everything is at a most exorbitant price. At Yorktown I wanted a single sheet of paper, but they refused to sell me one. Unless I would take a quire, I must go without for which they asked 9 shillings. Salt at £3 per bushel, which I have seen sold at 2/– per bushel, since I came into the Country. Linen cloth at 30s/– and 37/– per yard such as they usually sold at 3s/– and 3/6d. per yard. Woollen cloth, if red, green, buff, or blue or any colour fit for uniforms, at £5 and £6 per yard, such as they usually sold at 18s/– and 20/– per yard. Buttons and trimmings if suitable at whatever price they please to ask. Rum at 20 and 30 shillings per gallon, usually sold at 2s/– per gallon. Loaf sugar at 12s/– per lb. usually sold at 1 shilling, in short, everything bears a great price. Their imports in particular, owing to the little value of their paper Currency and the total want of specie. Supped and spent the evening with some Frenchmen. *Friday, May 2nd, 1777.* Mr. Keir arrived in the night, who informs me that the English prisoners have made their escape from Alexandria. About noon my old worthy friend, Mr. Cavan, came to this place on purpose to see me. This is a very great proof of his respect to come almost 300 miles on purpose to bid me farewell. We have spent this evening very happy together, but the probability of it being the last that we may ever spend together conveys a gloomy idea. *Saturday, May 3rd, 1777.* This morning parted with my good and affectionate friend, Mr. Cavan. For this honest and sincere young man I have the warmest friendship I ever yet had for man. May Heaven prosper all his undertakings and guard him in this land of misery. The concern at parting with him, and the thoughts what situation I may shortly be in myself requires all the fortitude I can muster to support it with a tolerable grace. Mr. Keir and I hired a passage boat to carry us to Mapsack Bay to Colonel Lewis's, an acquaintance of Mr. Keir's, providing things necessary for our passage. Spent the evening with Commander Tollever, who has the command of the Gallies here and some French Gentlemen.

*On board the passage boat, "Dorothy," Lynnhaven Bay —Sunday, May 4th, 1777.* Thank God for our good fortune so far. This morning got all our things on board very early, thinking to give them the slip, that is to have got into the Bay before the look-out boats had been stirring. But I believe Commodore Tollever had some suspicion of our design, for he came to our lodgings very early and insisted upon us taking a Julep with him, which we repeated so often that all hands got very merry, my companion excepted, who was too angry with the old Commodore for hindering us. I was well aware of the Commodore's intent, therefore drank plentiful with him, helped him to abuse the King, Lord North and all the British Ministry. This sort of behaviour puzzled the old man a little but made him very friendly and exceedingly complaisant, which complaisance we would very willingly have excused for he would see us on board as he said, to wish us a good passage, but in fact, to send a guard along with us, as it has since proved. No sooner were we got on board, but he called the master of the boat aside, and had a long confab with him. He returned with the boatman and begged that we would give two young men that belonged to his Galley a passage to Gloster Point. To this Mr. Keir in secret objected, but I with seeming cheerfulness consented, tho' in my heart wished them both at the Devil. In a very short time they came with each of them a bayonet at their side, which made my companion curse them very sincerely, but very privately. About 11 o'clock we took our departure from Hampton with our two Galley-men, the Master of the Boat and a

Boy, so that we had four to two, and to add to our misfortune a Boat with a Flag of Truce sailed out of the Harbour this morning for the Men of War and we had two armed look-out boats to escape, which makes our situation very dangerous. However, I felt, and still feel, myself in good spirits, I am determined to effect my escape or perish in the attempt. Before we got out of the Creek, I begun to ply our two Galley-men with Whiskey Grog which they took very freely. My companion in an ill humour, almost despairing of success, imagined the halter already about his neck, and absolutely refused to drink one drop with the men. Before we got out of Hampton Road, by acting the part of the drunken man and behaving in a very free and familiar manner, I had ingratiated myself into the good favour of our two unthinking Galley-men. God forgive me, helped them to curse the King, Lord North &c and, tho' it was Sunday, sung them some Rebel songs. In short, I said or did anything that I thought would please them, or lull them into security.

As soon as we had weathered Point Comfort, the wind came to blow at S.E., the worst wind for us in the compass. This caused a rough Sea and made me most horridly sick. I went to cascade over the bows. Mr. Keir followed me under a pretence to give me some assistance, or rather to make his diversion of me, but in fact to lay a scheme how to secure our guard and the boat's hands, which we happily effected in the following manner. Mr. Keir went into the hold and pulled the spile out of the water cask and came upon deck again. I, as if by chance, saw the water running out and called to the men to go and stop it, or we could have no more Grog. The thought of being deprived of this precious liquor alarmed our two Galley-men. Both, equaly desirous to preserve so valuable an article, jumped into the hold together, but could not find a spile. I picked up a small piece of wood and gave it to the boy, who went down with it. When Mr. Keir and I took the Hatch and shut them below we then had three fools secure. I must ingeniously confess that I did not like the fourth, who by this time had observed what we were about, and said he hoped we were only joking. I desired Mr. Keir to fetch him to the others, which he absolutely refused, alleging that, as he was the heavier man, he could hold down the hatch the better. I then went up to the man, put on the biggest look I could, presented a pistol to his head and desired him to walk forth to his companions. He seemed to hesitate a little. I began to think that I should be under the necessity of giving him his Quietus. But Mr. Keir luckily called out, "Dam his Soul, Blow his brains out," which frightened the poor fellow so that he immediately fell upon his knees and begged his life, which I granted upon condition that he went to his companions without further resistance, which he, I believe with great reluctance consented to. We gave them a Bottle of Whiskey, a Venison Ham and left them to condole their misfortunes together, but we first took care to secure the Hatch.

We had no sooner secured our prisoners then there fell one of the thickest Fogs I ever saw, and the wind continued at S.E. We have been beating about all afternoon in the greatest fear and anxiety. About Sunset the Fog cleared up and we found ourselves at the mouth of this Bay, the wind falling away and flood tide. We stood in shore and have come to an anchor about a quarter of a mile from shore. Mr. Keir and I agreed to keep watch 2 hours at a spell. We have seen no ship, brig or boat since we left

Point Comfort, which is a great comfort to us, without we had seen some of his Majesty's Ships. I write this upon Deck by Moonlight in my watch, our prisoners are all got drunk and cursing each other as the author of their misfortune. I feel a pleasure I have long been a stranger to, in the hopes of once more gaining my liberty. I am happy that we have secured these poor wretches without bloodshed. If we are retaken, hanging will be our certain doom, but I am determined the rascals shall never have the honour of hanging me. Collins is fast asleep.

*On board the " Bell and Mary," Chessapeak Bay — Monday, May 5th, 1777.* Last night or rather this morning, Mr. Keir fell asleep in his watch which is such an instance of carelessness I cannot easily forgive. About 4 o'clock this morning the wind sprung up at N.W. Weighed and stood out of the Bay. Mr. Keir and I near quarrelling about the course we should steer. He was for standing out to Sea, in quest of some of his Majesty's Ships. I opposed this as a very desperate step. We had not provisions on board for more than three days and little or no water, neither quadrant, log, glass or chart, four prisoners on board and a crazy small vessel with a very indifferent compass. If we are blown out to Sea it is almost impossible that we should ever make Land again. Admit that we escape the dangers of the Sea. We must inevitably perish with hunger and fatigue, or, which is worse, perhaps be retaken by some of the Rebels' Ships, without by mere accident we fall in with some of the King's Ships. My opinion was for us to keep in shore, and stand for New York, which is about 100 leagues. We may possibly get there in two or three days, if we have favourable winds, and we have a greater probability of meeting some of his Majesty's Ships that course, especially about Delaware Bay.

We disputed about this matter for some time. Mr. Keir was at the Helm and stood out to Sea till we were about out of sight of land, when he jumped up in an ecstasy of joy, swore he saw the *Phoenix*, Man of War, a little upon our Starboard Bow about 4 miles from us and it really proved to be her in company with a ship, Brig, Sloop and schooner all prizes. We bore down upon her, and in a little time her cutter came alongside of us and ordered us to go under the *Phoenix* stern. As soon as we got on board the *Phoenix* we told our situation to Captn. Parker, who behaved very civilly to us, and understanding that we wished to go to New York, he ordered us to go on Board this Ship who is bound there, as soon as we can get a convoy. Captn. Parker invited us to dinner with him and treated us very kindly and genteelly, and gave me the epithet of the Englishman from the answer I gave to the Officer in the Cutter when he first hailed us. As soon as we made the Ship, our prisoners begged that we would get them at liberty if possible. We immediately threw their bayonets into the Sea and reported the Galley-men as innocent Country lads, and Captn. Parker was kind enough to give them their liberty, all but the boatman, who is an excellent pilot and he is put upon the Ship's Books as Pilot at 9s/ per day.

*On board the "Bell and Mary," off Cape Henry — Tuesday, May 6th, 1777.* This Ship is the first that the Rebels took last Summer then called the *Lady Julian*, loaded with Rum and Sugar from Jamaica for London, Captn. Stephens, and retaken on Saturday last bound to Bourdeaux laden with 468 Hhds. of Tobacco and some Flour. Dined and Supped on board the *Phoenix*, Captn. Hyde Parke junr., of 44 Guns and 280 men. I have had the pleasure of seeing them take one Sloop loaded with Salt and Rice from Carolina to Boston and drive two Schooners on shore this day. The second Lieutenant of the *Phoenix* is Master of the *Bell and Mary*. This gentleman went round the world with Captn. Wallace and is a sensible, well-behaved friendly man. A Mr. Wm. Furnival, a Cheshire man, Midshipman belonging to the *Phoenix* acts as his mate, appears to be a good-natured man, but quite a Sailor. In the evening his Majesty's Ship *Thames* of 32 Guns commanded by Captn. Tyrringham Howe arrived from a chase with a prize Sloop. This ship is to be our convoy to New York. I am a little Seasick, but my mind is much at ease. I have not the fear of a halter before my eyes. Wind southerly.

*On board the " Bell and Mary " towards New York— Wednesday, May 7th, 1777.* Sailed for New York with his Majesty's Ship *Thames* for convoy, in company with a prize Sloop and two Schooners. In the afternoon took a French Brig supposed to be bound for Chesapeake Bay, but said she was bound for St. Peter's in Newfoundland. Thick foggy weather, obliged to fire guns and ring bells for fear of losing convoy. Wind light and southerly. *Thursday, May 8th, 1777.* Find Lieutenant Robinson a very cheerful companion, part of a Virtuosi, but of the sensible sort. He has offered me a passage in this vessel gratis if he goes in her to England. My companion and brother Scape begin to make a poor mouth; indeed we are both poor enough, but it does no good talking about it. Foggy weather and light easterly winds. Our French prize gave us the slip last night and got clear off. *Friday, May 9th, 1777.* Pleasant weather but light winds. I understand provisions are very dear at New York. If I am obliged to stay there any time,

I shall be distressed in my finances. *Saturday, May 10th, 1777.* Light breezes and pleasant weather. We pass our time very happily with Lieut. Robinson and Mr. Furnival whose drollery makes us all merry.

*Sunday, May 11th, 1777.* My thoughts much confused and a very great struggle in my mind. Honour on one side, Revenge, Interest, Inclination and Necessity on the other — which will get the better. I cannot yet tell. Made the Jersey shore in the evening, the land appears very low. Came to an anchor close in with the land, the fleet in company. *Monday, May 12th, 1777.* Weighed and came to sail early this morning. About noon made the Highland of Never Sink upon the Jersey shore. At 3 a.m. passed the Lighthouse at Sandy Hook. It is about 100 feet high built upon the Jersey shore. Here we found his Majesty's Ships, *Syreen, Emerald* and the *Preston* of 50 Guns, Commodore Hotham. Got a Pilot on board. In the evening came to an anchor. Long Island bearing East, Staten Island West. *Tuesday, May 13th, 1777.* Still at anchor in sight of Sandy Hook and the Narrows. Wind at North blowing fresh, the land appears to be hilly and stony. Some very pretty houses along shore, but everything about them seems to be going to ruin and destruction in consequence of this Rebellion.

# XI

## TWO MONTHS IN NEW YORK HARBOUR

*O*N Board the "Bell and Mary," New York Harbour —*Wednesday, May 14th, 1777.* This morning the wind came round to South, weighed and got up to the town about noon. Moored our Ship opposite the Navy Brewhouse which is on Long Island. Mr. Robinson went ashore, but won't permit Mr. Keir and me to go until he has seen the Admiral. I must now determine what to do, whether to enter into the Army or return home. If I was at liberty to follow my own inclination I would enter into the Army, but the solemn promise I made Mr. Mason on the 14th of April utterly forbids it, which was not to enter into any Army for 12 months from that day. To this Gentleman I am under very great and many obligations. Had it not been for his kind interposition on the 20th. of October, 1775, and his offering to be bound in a very large sum, that I should not depart the Colony of six months from that time, I must have been dragged to prison or have entered into their Army. What stamps the greater value upon the obligation, he did it unsolicited and unknown to me. He also gave me letters of recommendation to the Members of Congress and the Governor Council of Virginia. Nay, I believe he extorted this promise from me out of a principle of humanity extended to my parents, who, he understood from my accounts, are much averse to me entering into the Army. I am certain Mr. Mason can have no view of interest in what he did for me, it is impossible that he should have any, only that arising from a generous mind, helping a stranger in distress. Should I let my inclination or my necessity get the better of my honour, I shall forever detest myself, as a mean, dirty rascal. No, forbid it Honour, forbid it Heaven, be the consequence what it will, I will not enter into the Army till the expiration of my promised time. But the thought of returning home a Beggar is worse than death. I can bear to write upon this subject no longer.

*Thursday, May 15th, 1777.* Went ashore with Lieut. Robinson to the Secretary's Office, and had orders to wait upon the General Howe, tomorrow morning at nine o'clock. Dined at the *King's Head Tavern.* Mr. Keir and I took lodgings at a little dirty pothouse, the only one we can get at present. Everything here is very dear, provisions in particular. I believe Mr. Keir intends entering into the Army. I heartily wish I was at liberty to go with him. Slept on Board this night.

*Friday, May 16th, 1777.* This morning waited upon General Howe, and was introduced to him by Major Cuzler. His Excellency asked me about the affairs in Virginia and whether I thought there was a great many friends to Government there. To both questions I answered him with truth to the best of my knowledge. But I think his information has been bad and his expectations too sanguine. I told him my own situation very candidly, gave him my real reasons why I could not enter into the Army. He behaved to me with the greatest politeness, seemed to approve of my honourable resolution as he was pleased to call it, and promised to do anything for me that lay in his power in respect to my getting home. That is, if I meet with a ship to my mind that is bound home he will give me a permit to go in her. I believe Mr. Keir will enter into the Army and have some prospect of getting a Lieutenancy in Major Holland's Guides. He is referred to Sir Wm. Erskine, his Countryman, therefore he needs not fear, for the Scotch will hang together. Lodged at one Captn. Millar's, a Scotch refugee from Norfolk in Virginia. It is a mean dirty nasty hole I am determined to leave it to-morrow.

*Saturday, May 17th, 1777.* Took lodgings at one John Titer's, a Quaker in the Queen Street near the Navy Wharf at 28 Shillings per week and only to have two fresh dinners in the week. This is very high, but the cheapest I can get, I must get from New York as soon as possible. Mr. Keir stays at the old place. It is such a nasty stinking blackguard place, I cannot bear it. *Sunday, May 18th, 1777.* In the forenoon went to St. Paul's Church and heard a Military Sermon by the Revd. Mr. O'Brien. This is a very neat Church and some of the handsomest and best dressed ladies I have ever seen in America. I believe most of them are W—s. In the afternoon went to Church, but don't like the parson. Saw two boys killed by the bursting of a cannon. Drank Tea at Mr. Gresswolds, Distiller. *Tuesday, May 20th, 1777.* I have spent these two days in enquiring about the ships, but I find there is no Fleet to sail for England very soon. Exceedingly uneasy. I see want and poverty coming upon me very fast, and no means of avoiding them.

*Wednesday, May 21st, 1777.* Saw three regiments of Hessians reviewed by Generals De Heister and Heyphausen, Regiment De Donop, Regiment De Losberg, Regiment De Knyphausen. They are fine troops, but very slow in their motions when compared with the English.

They fired several rounds with the greatest exactness. One of their Corporals ran the Gauntlet eight times through the Regiment, he had upwards of 2000 lashes which he bore with the greatest resolution and firmness, not a single muscle of his face discomposed all the time. They appear to be a set of cruel, unfeeling people. They had a train of Artillery consisting of ten fine brass Field pieces which they fired several rounds. Their Artillery men seem to be the only active men they have. When they have a piece of Artillery to draw they move very quick, at other times they seem to be half dead or quite stupid. I live as cheap as I possibly can and I find it will cost me 40 Shillings per week, York Currency, and there is no prospect of getting home soon, or to do anything here to get a living. Patience, Patience.

*Thursday, May 22nd, 1777.* This morning met with Mr. Joseph Brewer, who has just made his escape from Philadelphia. This Gentleman has been obliged to leave his wife behind him to the mercy of the Rebels. The persecution against the friends of Government was too violent for a man of his warm temper to stay any longer amongst them with safety either of person or property. In the afternoon, very unexpectedly but very agreeably met with two old cronies, Captn. Scott and Captn. Buddicombe. I have been at the play with Lieutnt. Robinson to whom I gave a Ticket. My present circumstances will badly afford extravagances of this kind, but this Gentleman has offered me a passage home, if he goes Master of the *Bell and Mary.* I think it only gratitude to oblige him if I can, I know him to be fond of plays and at the same time fond of his money. We had the honour of sitting in the same box with General Piggot. Before the General came to the house, a sentinel came and offered to turn us out, but the old Veteran swore he would not be turned adrift by anyone. This play was "The Liar, Polly Hunneycombe," the entertainment, by the Officers of the Army for the benefit of Soldiers' widows. *Friday, May 23rd, 1777.* Captn. Buddecombe informs me that he has had several letters from my friends about me. The thought of returning to them a Beggar I cannot bear with patience, my misfortunes have been unavoidable, and the common lot of thousands besides myself, but that will be no excuse. I wish I could avoid going home.

*Saturday, May 24th, 1777.* Saw 800 of the Hessian Troops reviewed and their train of artillery. They are fine healthy-looking men but seem to be too heavily clothed for this hot country.

*Sunday, May 25th, 1777.* Mr. Brewer and I crossed the East River and took a view of the fortifications made by the Rebels upon Long Island. A fort above the Ferry called Fort Sterling, which commands the city of New York, appears to be a place of strength, but we could not get admittance into it. About a quarter of a mile from Fort Sterling is another Fort called Cable Hill or Mutton Pie Battery by the Sailors. It is a small round Fort but very strong. From its situation it commands the River and Country round as far as the Guns will reach. There are Subterraneous Magazines for their Stores, provisions and water, the Barracks for the men are Bomb proof. It appears to me, (but I don't pretend to be a competent judge in Military affairs) that a small number of resolute men might have made a stand against the whole of the British Army. When the Rebels were defeated on this Island on the 28th of August last, great numbers of them were killed in attempting to cross a tide-mill dam at low water to get to this Fort, but they stuck fast in the mud and were either killed by our people or drowned at High Water, saw the remains of them sticking up their knees and elbows in the mud. There are great numbers of other fortifications of different sorts which the rascals in their panic left as everlasting monuments of their great labour and great cowardice. Dined at Flat Bush where the Rebels got their greatest drubbing. This is a pretty village, a great number of orchards and some very pretty houses about it. The Land is in general light and sandy. Fences, part stone, part wood, several small hills and stony. Got to town at night.

*Monday, May 26th, 1777.* Some more Troops are arriving from Halifax in Nova Scotia. I believe they are much wanted. Spent the day with Mr. Brewer and Doctor Smith, who read us a narrative of his sufferings amongst the Rebels. This is the same Doctor Smith that I saw with Major Connoly at Frederick Town in Maryland, from which place he made his escape, but was retaken, and made his escape a second time by the help of his Blankets from the top of the new Jail in Philadelphia. Mr. Keir has got a Lieutncy in the Guides or rather Pioneers.

*Tuesday, May 27th, 1777.* Last night it was so hot I could not bear a sheet upon me in bed and this morning it is so cold I can bear to wear my great coat. Dined with Captn. Buddicombe on board his ship. There appears to be something mysterious in Buddicombe's behaviour, but I am at a loss to account for it. News that there had been an engagement at —— that the Rebels have lost a great number of men, but I believe there is as many lies in the papers here as amongst the Rebels.

*Wednesday, May 28th, 1777.* This day 14 Sail of

Transports arrived with Troops from England. I have seen Mr. Robinson, but he cannot tell me when the *Bell and Mary* sails for England, he seems to be in some doubt whether she goes or not. I am determined to get a passage in the first vessel that sails for England if I can. I cannot stay here much longer, my money won't hold out more than another week. O! Poverty, poverty, thou plague of my life, when shall I get clear of thy troublesome company, if company is any consolation in poverty. Here are plenty of poor devils to keep me in countenance. I have not yet betrayed any signs of poverty, only in my dress. I will let that be when I spend my last penny. To be poor and seem so is the Devil.

*Thursday, May 29th, 1777.* I have taken my passage on board a brig belonging to Liverpool, but bound for London, called the *Edward*, John Park Master. I have told my real situation to Captn. Park, who very kindly and humanely offers to supply me with what money I want till our arrival in London. He expects to sail on Wednesday next with a Convoy. *Friday, May 30th, 1777.* Exceedingly tired of my inactive situation. The house where I lodge is kept by a Quaker, he and his wife are two of the greatest Jews I ever knew and two of the greatest hypocrites. These religious hypocrites are of a deeper dye than the irreligious ones, because they make what they call their Sacred Religion, a cloak to cover the vilest of crimes. Some droll cookery here. Molasses in everything, even to Salt pork. They are right Yankees. *Saturday, May 31st, 1777.* Troops arriving. Others embarking. A great fuss and I believe there is very little done. Forty-two Rebels came in today to be whitewashed. Most heartily tired of this place — nothing to do and live at a great expense. Supped and spent the evening with Captn. Scot on board the Brig *Harriet* in company with Captains Buddicombe, Johnston, Powers and Grundy. Buddicombe is a man of great low cunning, Powers low wit, Johnston a satirist and Grundy a Sot, but the best behaved man of the whole. Buddicombe's behaviour is still a mystery that I cannot unriddle. He cannot bear to hear anything said in favour of Mr. Kirk, he has not yet forgot his quarrel. (Mem. be Cautious.)

*Sunday, June 1st, 1777.* My present situation is far from being agreeable, tho' much better than it was a month ago. I now breathe the air of liberty and freedom, which I have been a stranger to since October 20th, 1775. For very substantial reasons, I have never mentioned this in my Journal before, as I have always carried it about with me, and have always had a notion that I should be obliged to make my escape, something in the manner I at last effected it. If my own handwriting had been produced as a witness against me (supposing I had been taken in attempting to make my escape by the people who did not personally know me) I might have had some small chance of regaining my liberty, but had I always carried such a capital witness against me, in my pocket, and have been taken before I had time to destroy it, my life must undoubtedly have paid the forfeiture of my folly and imprudence.

Instead of going to Church I will rectify that mysterious part of my Journal, while it is fresh in my memory. Probably at some future period, when I have less time (for I have absolutely too much at present to do anything as it ought to be done), but more inclination and my mind more at ease than it is at the present, I may revise and correct the many errors that frequently occur in it. I think

I shall defer it till I am an old man, for at present I have no thoughts of turning author.

In the month of March, 1775, I wrote to all my friends in England and freely declared my sentiments upon the present Rebellion. Indeed, I then called it by no other name to my Friends. My letters I sent by a friend bound to Leghorn, but the Council of Safety's Boat boarded him in the Bay and he was obliged to give up all the letters he had on board, mine amongst the rest, which were read before the Council of Safety and sent express to the Committee at Alexandria, with orders to secure my person as one inimical to the rights and liberties of America. But I was gone into the Back Country before the express arrived at Alexandria. However, the letters were lodged with the Chairman of the Committee till my return in October, 1775, when a meeting of the Committee were immediately called and they thought proper in their great wisdom and prudence to make a resolve that the body of Nicholas Cresswell should be committed to the care of the Jail Keeper until he, the said Nicholas Cresswell, was fully convinced of his political errors.

In short, I was arraigned, tried, condemned, and the sentence nearly put in execution before I knew anything about it, but by the kind interposition of Mr. Thomson Mason immediately reprieved, by his offering to be bound in any sum they chose to mention that I should not depart the Colony of Six months without their consent. I was utterly unacquainted with the whole proceeding till the day after the Committee had agreed to send me to Jail. When Mr. Mason in a very polite letter let me know what he had done for me, hoping that I would make myself as easy as possible in the Colony during the limited time, as he did not doubt but matters would be accommodated before the expiration of six months, as he trusted implicitly to my honour, the fulfilling the contract he had made in my favour, at the same time made me an offer of his house and assistance in anything that lay in his power. I then removed to Leesburg and before the expiration of the six months was taken sick and continued so till the latter end of July 1776. In this time I was not disturbed by the Committee. I thought it a proper time to get away. Accordingly, I got letters of recommendation to some members of the Congress from my friend Mr. Mason, by which means I got a pass from the Congress, dated August 29th, 1776.

By virtue of this pass I was permitted to go to New York, from which place I intended to make my escape to our Army then on Long Island. I got to New York on the 7th. of September, 1776, and had laid the plan for my escape to our Fleet or Long Island whichever I could get to, by means of a floating stage that was moored in the old Ship. No other thing, either Boat or Canoe, was to be found. Just as I had found this out I unfortunately met with Mr. Thomson, a Presbyterian Parson and Chaplain to one of the Virginia Regiments then at New York. With this gentleman I had quarrelled about politics in November, 1774. I believe he remembered it and suspected my design, but for that evening behaved with the greatest politeness, only took care to put a guard over me. On the next morning he told me he knew my sentiments and if I did not choose to return to Virginia with Lieutenant Noland I would be put in the provo immediately. I assured him curiosity was my only motive for coming there. I had no intention of going to the Enemy. This would not satisfy the Revd. Sir, I must either return to Virginia or go to the provo. I had no other alternative, and to convince him that I had no intention of making my escape I would cheerfully return with Mr. Noland, but hoped he would not send me in the character of a prisoner. He assured me Mr. Noland would go with me in the character of a companion. I was under the necessity of submitting to this puritanic Priest for fear of worse consequences. Mr. Noland behaved very well to me all the way, always willing to do as I did and had it not been for the thoughts of him being as a guard over me, would have been an excellent companion.

Mr. Thomson had wrote to the Committee of Leesburg concerning me by Mr. Noland, who accordingly met and was for committing me to prison. But by the interest of Mr. Mason I was a second time reprieved and they agreed to take my own parole for four months from the 20th. of September, 1776, to the 20th. of January, 1777. In that time they used many threats and persuasions to get me into their Army. I had got Muller's Treatise upon Fortification and Gunnery, which some of their Military officers had seen in my lodgings. I had got some of the Technical terms belonging to the profession by heart, which I always took care to use before the most vain part of them, especially if I knew them to be ignorant. Such as those are always the best puffs with the vulgar herd. When I happened into company with those who understood it I always took care to give them evasive and ambiguous answers. By these means I became consequential amongst them, and I believe it was the chief reason why they treated me with so much civility as they were pleased to call it.

My first parole was no sooner expired but I was obliged to give a second for three months from the 5th of February to the 5th of May, which I broke with great reluctance only one day. But if such a breach of honour can be excused I certainly may, in justice, claim some title to it, because I suffered in consequence of a Law made after the offence was committed. When I wrote my letters, which were the original cause of my confinement, there was no act or resolve made by the Colonial Convention or the Congress to imprison anyone merely for his sentiments. The act, resolve, edict or whatever name it has for imprisonment and confiscation of the efforts of friends to Government, was made by the Congress in March, 1776, after I had had a *Ne Exit Colonia* upon me for near six months. I think this is a sufficient and ample excuse for my breaking my parole a single day. I am weary with scribbling therefore will give over.

*Monday, June 2nd, 1777.* I have been here almost three weeks and I am as ignorant of the Motions or designs of our Army as if I had been in Virginia. Only this, the Soldiers, seem very healthy and long to be in action. The Commander in Chief is either inactive, has no orders to act, or thinks that he has not force sufficient to oppose the Rebels, but which of these or whether any of them is the true reason I will not pretend to say, but this I am very certain of, if General Howe does nothing, the Rebels will avail themselves of his inactivity by collecting a very numerous Army to oppose him, whenever he shall think proper to leave Mrs. Lorain and face them. I have seen Captn. Buddicombe to-day and I observe he has a very different behaviour from what he used to profess in Virginia, but for what reason I cannot conceive. Whether Mr. Kirk told him anything to my prejudice in hopes to blow up a quarrel between him and me and in hopes to reap some advantage by it I can't tell. Or whether he may think that I am in want of money and is afraid I may ask him to lend, I can't tell. If it is so, he may ease himself of those fears, I never will borrow money from such a mean-spirited wretch. I have been deceived in this fellow. *On Board the Brig "Edward," New York Harbour—Monday, June 2nd, 1777.* Captn. Park invited me to come and live on board the Brig and mess with him as it will be much cheaper than living on shore. I was very glad of the offer, as I have only two guineas left. Accordingly he sent the boat for my Chest and bed. I left my Jewish Quaker, without regret. I have got two pair of drill trousers made here, the stuff cost me 12/ and the rogue of a tailor has charged me 18/ for making them. I am very confident that I could have had them made in England for half a Crown. Everything is most extravagantly high in this place. Money is here in plenty and there is a set of people who, from the nature of their profession and their uncertainty of life, spend it as fast as they can get it. But here is some who profit greatly by their extravagancy and are making fortunes very fast, by the dissipation of the soldierly. Captn. Park don't expect to sail this week. *Tuesday, June 3rd, 1777.* Slinging my cot, and preparing for the voyage. I flatter myself with the prospect of an agreeable passage along with Captn. Park. Fourteen sail of transports are arriving with Hessian Soldiers on board, from England. No news.

*Wednesday, June 4th, 1777.* This being the anniversary of his Majesty's Birthday, at one o'clock Fort George, the Men of War and Ships in the Harbour fired a Royal salute. In the evening Lord Howe gave a Ball to the Officers of the Navy and Army and their ladies. At night the city was illuminated. I observed it was not generally illuminated. A number of Hessian Chasseurs or Yaugers arrived in green uniforms and boots, all armed with rifles. I am told they are as expert with them as the Virginians, but they appear to me to be too clumsy for the Woods and too heavily clothed. I can't conceive why they wear boots, they must be inconvenient and troublesome in this hot and woody country. Spent the evening with Mr. Furneval.

*Thursday, June 5th, 1777.* This morning Captn. Scott and I hired a single horse-chaise and took a tour upon Long Island to Salisbury Plains through a little town called Jamaica, but returned in the evening after a very pleasant and agreeable ride. Our noses were now and then regaled with the stink of dead Rebels, some of them have lain unburied since last August. This Island is about 150 Miles in length and where it is broadest about 22 in width. The land is in most parts rich with small hills and the west part of the Island stony, produces Wheat and grain of all kinds and immense quantities of Apples. Their farms, which are cultivated in the best manner of any I have seen in America, formerly abounded with stock of all kinds. They are famous for breeding Horses and used to have annual Races upon Salisbury Plains, which are well calculated for that diversion. Agriculture has been at some degree of perfection upon this Island. The inhabitants are chiefly Dutch, or the descendants of the Swedes who first settled here.

*Friday, June 6th, 1777.* The Soldiers are very busy in shipping military stores and provisions as if some mighty expedition was on foot, but where this storm is to burst, is a profound secret. Saw the 16th. or Queen's Light Dragoons reviewed to-day, they make a fine appearance, the

Horses all seem in good condition. Commanded by Lieutenant Harcourt, he that took Genl. Lee prisoner. The Regiment is to go on board to-morrow for I don't know where. *Saturday, June 7th, 1777.* My companion Mr. Keir has this day got a warrant for a Lieut. Commission in Major Holland's Guides. I most heartily wish him success. He is to embark for Brunswick to-morrow. The Military is all in motion, certainly something will be done. We can hear them skirmishing with the Rebels every day but nothing of consequence. Sometimes they send in a few prisoners and a number of our men wounded, in short the Hospitals are full of the wounded and the prisons full of the Rebels.

*Sunday, June 8th, 1777.* On board all day. This evening a certain Colonel Cotton came on board, who is going passenger in this vessel for London. He was a Colonel in the North Carolina Militia, but born at Boston in New England and is now a refugee, having been obliged to leave his wife and family in Carolina. I am surprised that he should be a friend to Government for he appears to be a rigid Presbyterian and, if I mistake not, like most of that order has a large share of hypocrisy about him. He talks so much about religion and in such a puritanic style tagging most of his sentences with some scrap of Scripture, which gives me cause to think that he has no religion at all in reality. I don't like your holy Cants, they are seldom what they would be thought to be. *Monday, June 9th, 1777.* No news in the papers to-day. We heard so much firing last week expected something of consequence. Mr. Furneval came and spent the evening with us on board. *Tuesday, June 10th, 1777.* On Board all day. Nothing remarkable, I am quite tired of this inactive lazy life.

*Wednesday, June 11th, 1777.* Captn. Banks, a Master of one of the Transport Ships, dined on board our vessel. A very sensible, well-behaved man. After dinner we took a walk upon Long Island. The fertility of this spot is worth observation. Asparagus grows in the open fields with very little cultivation. I suppose it has been planted some time or other, but does not appear to have had any manure about it for many years. It is now in a flourishing state, and what is more remarkable the land is gravelly and does not appear to be rich.

*Thursday, June 12th, 1777.* A boy belonging to the ship is broken out in the Smallpox. I am afraid this will be of bad consequence, as three of our hands have not had this disorder. I pity the poor boy, am afraid he will want necessaries and attendance. Indeed, all the Crew seems to be afraid of coming near him. *Friday, June 13th, 1777.* Dined in town. Nothing in the papers to-day. This evening a Doctor Blamire, who intends going passenger in this vessel, came on board, and stayed all night. He appears to be a good-humoured man and has seen a great deal of the World.

*Saturday, June 14th, 1777.* After dinner Captn. Park and I went upon Governor's Island where the Rebels have made a great many fortifications, they have taken great pains to let the world see that they can make Ditches and dessert them. In the evening I went with Captn. Park to the Butcher's, where he had a quarrel with some Gentleman about a quarter of Mutton. I don't think Park behaved well. I did expect he would have got a good drubbing, but he escaped it wonderfully. *Sunday, June 15th, 1777.* Captn. Scott came and dined with us. He offers me any money that I want and wishes me to go with him to Newfoundland and Venice, and has made me some offers but as I am circumstanced cannot accept them. *Monday, June 16th, 1777.* On Board all day. There is now the greatest number of Ships in this Harbour I ever saw together before or perhaps may ever see again. It is supposed that there are 600 square-rigged Vessels, exclusive of small craft and four Sail of the Line.

*Tuesday, June 17th, 1777.* Dined with Mr. Furneval on Board the *Bell and Mary.* Furneval and I went ashore and spent the evening at the Hull Tavern. In our return to the Boat, coming by some houses that were burnt down we heard the cries of a Woman. We searched about and soon, to our great surprise, found a poor Woman in labour, and all alone. She told us she was a soldier's widow and begged we would help her to some assistance. We immediately carried her to the house of a Sadler in the Broadway, whom we raised from his pillow and told him the poor woman's situation. But he absolutely refused to let her stay in his house, declaring that he would not keep a lying-in Hospital for our W—s. However with threats, promises, and the poor Woman declaring that it was impossible for her to be removed, he at length consented that she might lay in a back shop he had. We immediately removed her thither and made her a very poor bed of a Bearskin, a Packsheet, and an old Blanket. Furneval went with a negro boy to see for a Midwife, while I stayed with the woman, for fear of the sadler turning her out of doors. The poor woman cried out lustily and I was confoundedly afraid of the young one coming before the midwife arrived. The Irish rogue of a sadler nor the unfeeling jade his wife would not come near us, or offer the poor creature the least assistance, tho' she begged for help in the most pitiful tone I ever heard. I was much afraid that I must have been under the disagreeable necessity of trying my skill in the obstetric way, but in the critical minute Furneval arrived with an old drunken woman he had picked up somewhere or other and she refused to perform the office without we would give her two Dollars. Furneval gave her one and I another. She immediately fell to work, I am sure the pains of labour must be violent for the poor woman roared out most horridly. I think, I hear the sound yet in my ears. However, in about ten minutes she produced a girl which was wrapped in the Mother's apron, with the addition of Furneval's handkerchief and mine, for she had not one single rag prepared for the occasion. We then got some wine, rum, Nutmeg Bread &c. to the amount of two Dollars more, and got the good wife a caudle, which she took without much invitation. In about half an hour she was able to sit up in her miserable bed and returned us her thanks for saving her life, as she said, in the most sincere and moving manner. The D—d unnatural B—h of a Sadler's wife never came near us all the time, but lay in bed cursing the poor woman with the most horrid imprecations. About 12 o'clock we left her in good spirits considering her situation. When we came away I gave her one Dollar and a quarter which is the last and all I have in the world.

The poor woman is heartily welcome to it and I am happy that I had it in my power to relieve such real distress. Furneval gave her two Dollars and swears he will stand Godfather to the child. I have no intention of doing myself that honour, am in hopes it will be dead before morning. We promised to go and see her in the morning, and make her case known to some of the Officers. I hope the drunken jade of a midwife don't rob her before morning, I don't like her looks. Captn. Park is very merry at our adventure and declares he will be at the christening, he says we must keep the child between us, which part of the ceremony I don't like. This is the first birth I have ever been concerned with, and I hope it will be the last time I shall meet with such a complication of distress. She told us a long story about her virtue and sufferings, but she is an Irish woman and I don't believe half of it. I am confoundedly tired with scribbling about the Girl in the Straw, therefore will give over.

*Wednesday, June 18th, 1777.* The Agent Victualer has informed Captn. Park that we are not to sail for England this fortnight. As this time will be very tedious to us, Coln. Cotton, Coln. Reid (another Refugee from North Carolina) and I intend to take a trip to Brunswick to see the Army. Agree to set out to-morrow. Furneval and I won't visit the Girl in the Straw this two or three days. *Thursday, June 19th, 1777.* Went ashore this morning to take our passage for Brunswick in one of the Suttling Sloops, but none goes till to-morrow.

This afternoon I met with John Dodd, one of the people that escaped out of Alexandria Jail, by the assistance of Mr. Keir. He informs me that they all got off safe, but Davis their guide, and a Scotch Sergeant who was so much dispirited at not finding us at Cedar Point agreeable to our promise that they immediately returned, and delivered themselves to the mercy of the Rebels. The rest of the company seized a Sloop in the River which they left for a Pilot Boat, but for fear of meeting with some of the Rebel look-out Boats, they quitted her and took to the Land. By travelling in the night and through the Woods they got to the Delaware Bay, where they seized a Boat and got aboard the *Roebuck,* Man of War. They all arrived here last night except Mr. Rogers, who belongs to the *Roebuck.*

Captn. Parker, one of the company, has got a Virginia paper of the second inst., which informs that Davis has impeached Mr. Wales, that is Mr. Keir's Uncle, Mr. George Muir, Mr. Chisum, Mr. Kilpatrick, Mr. Hepburn and Mr. Murdo, that they were all sent to Williamsburg Jail and had their trials on the 30th. of May. Wales, Chisum, Davis and Murdo were condemned to be hanged on the Friday following, Muir, Kilpatrick and Hepburn to be imprisoned for five years and all their property to be appropriated to the use of the State of Virginia. They likewise offered a reward of 200 Dollars for taking Collin Keir, and Nicholas Cresswell, as the two Villains that contrived, aided and assisted the Tory Sailors and Soldiers that were confined in Alexandria Jails to make their escape. They gave us every scandalous epithet that scurrility, malice and revenge can invent, but what surprises me (tho very agreeable) they never mention one word about me breaking my parole. I hope they think it was fulfilled. I petitioned Captn. Parker to give me the paper but he refused, indeed none of them (Goodrich excepted) have had the good manners to thank us for the risk we ran in assisting them to arms and ammunitions in Alexandria, not to mention the expense we were at in procuring them, and provisions for them, when they should have come on board the pilot boat in the Potowmeck River. They are a set of ungrateful scoundrels. Such is the folly of risking life, character or fortune in doing friendly acts for strangers. I am determined never to be guilty of it again. They are too often repaid with ungratitude.

*Brunswick, New Jersey — Friday, June 20th, 1777.* This morning left New York in company with Colonel Cotton and Colnl. Reid, on board a suttling sloop for this place. When we got through the Narrows we were entertained with one of the most pleasing and delightful scenes I ever saw before. Four hundred sail of ships, brigs, schooners and sloops with five sail of the Line all under-way and upon a Wind at once, in the compass of two miles. A gentle breeze and fine clear day added greatly to the beauty of this delightful view. They are all bound to Perth Amboy, it is said, to take the Troops on board. About noon we got to the mouth of the Rareaton River with flood tide. This River is very crooked and very narrow. We often saw scouting parties of the Rebels and just as we passed a Row Galley that lay in the River, some of the Rebel Rifle men fired upon her from amongst the Weeds, who returned it with two or three great Guns which soon drove the Rascals out of their lurking places and made them seek for safety in their heels.

A little before we got up to the Town we met several sloops loaded with provisions, household furniture, and camp equipage which informed us that the Royal Army was defeated by the Rebels and most part of them cut to pieces. We had heard a heavy cannonade all day and at that instant heard them very busy with small arms, which served to put us in a very great panic. The two Colonels and two of the Boat's hands were for returning immediately, but the Master of the Boat and myself absolutely refused to return till we had been at Brunswick, which we saw then in sight. I don't know whether we should have been able to have prevailed with the two Warlike Colonels to have come up to town, had it not happened that, while we were disputing about it, a party of the Rebels and a party of our Army begun to fire upon each other across the River about two miles below us. This was a weighty reason for us to get these two heroic Colonels up to town, where we arrived about 8 o'clock and to our great joy found the report we had heard to be false. The man we heard it from was a Sutler and had a sloop coming up the River with Calves and Sheep. The one we were in was loaded with those articles and was the only one that was expected to arrive for some time with fresh stock. Could he have frightened us back again, he would have engrossed the whole Market to himself. This I believe was his only motive for telling us the abominable lie. Colonel Cotton soon found some of his old acquaintance, a Captn. Beaumont Waggon, Master General, at whose Tent we were very kindly entertained and lodged. This gentleman informs us that the Army intends to evacuate this place to-morrow and march to Amboy. He does not know what is the meaning of the Cannonade to-day or where it has been. I am convinced both my Colonels are rank cowards from the great trepidation so visible when we heard the false report, but now they have got a glass of wine in their heads, and are as bold and courageous as Mars himself.

*Bonum Town, New Jersey* — *Saturday, June 21st, 1777.*
Spent the forenoon with my old Friend Lieut. Keir in viewing the different encampments which is certainly one of the finest sights in the world, everything is conducted with so much order and regularity. I wish much to be a soldier, more particularly at this time, that I might have an opportunity of revenging myself upon these ungrateful Scoun-

drels. Mr. Keir resents the ungrateful and dishonest behaviour of Parker and his companion, they refuse to pay him for the arms he purchased for their use. About 4 o'clock this afternoon the advance Guard of the Army with about 500 Waggons loaded with ammunition and baggage, marched from Brunswick and camped at this place. Colnls. Reid and Cotton and me rode in a Baggage Waggon and made ourselves very merry with the different scenes that we saw amongst the soldiery and their ladies. Our Camp is within a quarter of a mile of the enemy's Picket guard. We have a good force with us. I don't care if they pay us a visit.

*Staten Island — Sunday, June 22nd, 1777.* Last night I had most uncomfortable lodgings along with Colonel Reid upon a Tent only spread upon the ground in which we wrapped ourselves. Almost bit to death with Mosquitoes and poisoned with the stink of some Rebels, who have been buried about three weeks in such a slight manner that waggons have cut up parts of the half corrupted carcases and made them stink most horribly. By 5 o'clock this morning all the Tents were struck and the Army ready to march.

About 8 the main body of the Army came up. At that instant some of the Rebels' Scouting parties fired upon our Sentinels, which brought on a smart skirmish. I happened to see them in the bushes before they fired, but mistook them for some of our rangers. They were about 300 yards from me. When the engagement began I got upon a little hillock to see the better, but an honest Highlander advised me to retire into a small breastwork just by, without I had a mind to stick up myself as a mark for the Rebels to shoot at. I thought proper to take his advice and retired to the place he directed me to, where I had a very good view of their proceedings. I observed a party of our men going through a rye field, I suppose with an intent to get into the rear of the Rebels and by that means surround them, but they were met as soon as they got out of the field by about the same number of the Rebels. When they were about 100 yards from each other both parties fired, but I did not observe any fall. They still advanced to the distance of 40 yards or less, and fired again, I then saw a good number fall on both sides. Our people then rushed upon them with their bayonets and the others took to their heels, I heard one of them call out murder lustily. This is laughable if the consequence was not serious. A fresh party immediately fired upon our people, but were dispersed and pursued into the Woods by a company of the 15th. Regmt. A brisk fire then began from six field pieces the Rebels had secreted in the Woods, which did some mischief to our men, the engagement lasted about thirty-five minutes. Our people took the Field pieces about 40 prisoners and killed about 150 of the Scoundrels with the loss of 39 killed and 27 wounded.

I went to the place where I saw the two parties fire upon each other first before the wounded were removed but I never before saw such a shocking scene, some dead others dying, death in different shapes some of the wounded making the most pitiful lamentations, others that were of different parties cursing each other as the author of their misfortunes. One old Veteran I observed (that was shot through both legs and not able to walk) very coolly and deliberately loading his piece and cleaning it from blood. I was surprised at the sight and asked him his reasons for it. He, with a look of contempt, said, "To be ready in case any of the Yankees come that way again." About 10 o'clock the whole Army was in motion. It is said our Army burnt Brunswick when they left, others contradict the report and say it was left without damage, but all the County houses were in flames as far as we could see. The Soldiers are so much enraged they will set them on fire, in spite of all the Officers can do to prevent it. They seem to leave the Jerseys with reluctance, the train of Artillery and Waggons extends about nine miles and is upwards of 1000 in number. Some people say there are 20,000 men, but I am afraid there is not so many, the real numbers are for very good reasons kept secret. About 2 o'clock the Van arrived at the City of Perth Amboy 14 miles from Brunswick, the road is through plantations, but pretty good. The Rebels kept skirmishing with our rear all the way, but little loss on either side.

This City (for it is called a City), tho' it does not contain more than 200 Houses mostly built of wood, is the capital of East New Jersey and was called Perth Amboy from its first founder, the Earl of Perth, who was once proprietor of East New Jersey, but surrendered his right to the Crown in 1737. I believe it never was a place of any trade, tho' very conveniently situated for it. There is a fine safe and commodious harbour and within sight of the Sea, but very few Rivers of any consequence empty themselves into it, which perhaps may be the reason why they have no trade here. The City is very handsomely laid out in Hundred acres of land and contains 150 Lots or squares for building upon. There is one Church, a Meeting House. The Courthouse is a good brick building and the Governor's house is an elegant stone building, said to have cost £4000.

Here we found some of the Hessian Light-horse who have just arrived, that is the Men and Horses, but the wise conductors of these matters sent the saddles in another Ship which has not arrived, so that they are of no use at present. These troops are clothed in Green and armed with most enormous long crooked swords. There are good barracks in this town for about 2000 men. We crossed the sound to Staten Island and dined at a public house with Colonel Rodgers, the famous Major Rodgers last War. He is a New Englander by birth, but a mere savage from his education. Then we walked about 4 miles and lodged at a farm house, an acquaintance of Colonel Cotton's. Everyone is surprised at our Army quitting the Jerseys, where they are bound to is a profound secret. The people on this Island begin to be very uneasy, they apprehend a visit from the Rebels very soon. I am confoundedly tired with scribbling.

*On Board the Brig "Edward," New York Harbour—Monday, June 23rd, 1777.* This morning we hired a waggon to carry us to the Ferry with some pigs we had bought for our sea store, at the unreasonable price of 8d. per lb. Staten Island is about 12 miles long and about 9 broad, the produce chiefly live stock, of which in times of peace they raise immense quantities. It abounds with salt Marsh or Salt Meadows which breeds vasts swarms of Mosquetoes, very troublesome insects. Arrived at New York in the evening, found Captn. Park making ready for Sea as fast as possible. Furneval informs me that our child died before morning and that some of the Officers had taken the woman away, which I am very glad of. There are various conjectures concerning the late proceedings of our Army, some say that they are going to Philadelphia by Sea, others say it is only a feint to get Washington out of his stronghold. What is the meaning I cannot guess.

*Tuesday, June 24th, 1777.* On board all day. When I

see this once flourishing, opulent and happy City, one third part of it now in ruins, it brings a sadness and melancholy upon my mind, to think that a set of people, who three years ago, were doing everything they could for the mutual assistance of each other, and both parties equally gainers, should now be cutting the throats of each other and destroying their property whenever they have an opportunity and all this mischief done by a set of designing villains. The reflection is too severe to bear with patience. This City is an unhappy instance of the strange madness and folly that reigns amongst them. When the Rebels were driven out of it in September last by the Royal Army, they formed a hellish design, burnt it down to the ground and then laid the blame upon our troops, they so far succeeded as to burn about one third, the most beautiful and valuable part of the City. If one was to judge from appearances, they would suppose the Rebels had intended to dispute every inch of ground with our troops. In every street they have made ditches and barricades, every little eminence about the town is fortified, but they basely and cowardly deserted them all as soon as ever our people got ashore. Now all these Ditches and fortified places are full of stagnate water, damaged sour Crout and filth of every kind. Noisome vapours arise from the mud left in the docks and slips at low water, and unwholesome smells are occasioned by such a number of people being crowded together in so small a compass almost like herrings in a barrel, most of them very dirty and not a small number sick of some disease, the Itch, Pox, Fever, or Flux, so that altogether there is a complication of stinks enough to drive a person whose sense of smelling was very delicate and his lungs of the finest contexture, into a consumption in the space of twenty-four hours. If any author had an inclination to write a treatise upon stinks and ill smells, he never could meet with more subject matter than in New York, or anyone who had abilities and inclinations to expose the vicious and unfeeling part of human nature or the various arts, ways and means, that are used to pick up a living in this world, I recommend New York as a proper place to collect his characters. Most of the former inhabitants that possessed this once happy spot are utterly ruined and from opulence reduced to the greatest indigence, some in the Rebels' Jails by force, others by inclination in their Armies.

*Wednesday, June 25th, 1777.* Went ashore in the morning and saw Mr. Goodrich, who gave me a kind invitation to dine with him, but I declined his invitation. I won't dine with such a set of ungrateful scoundrels. All the City in a political ferment concerning the motions of our Army. Colnl. Cotton has taken a ride upon Long Island, with a pretence to buy stock, but I rather suppose he is gone for a very different purpose, I know him to be a hypocrite.

*Thursday, June 26th, 1777.* This morning the Agent Victualler came on board and told us to prepare for Sea, to be ready at a moment's warning. I immediately got a horse and chair and went in quest of Coln. Cotton, found him at a Farm house about 6 miles beyond Jamaica upon Long Island, where we lodged. There has been a heavy cannonade since one o'clock this morning without intermission and still continues. *Friday, June 27th, 1777.* Got on Board to breakfast, but we did not need to have been in such a violent hurry. The fleet is not to leave New York this three days. Went ashore in the afternoon. News that our Army had entirely routed the Rebels, killed 2000 and taken 4700 prisoners, with the loss of 800. I am afraid this is too good news to be true. This affair should have happened at Amboy. *Saturday, June 28th, 1777.* Yesterday's news is contradicted to-day, it is said that there are only 50 killed and 70 taken prisoners, with the loss of 8 killed on our side. There are as many lies in circulation here, as there is in Virginia. The lie of the day is, that Washington is taken prisoner.

*Monday, June 30th, 1777.* On board, where I intend to stay, as much as possible. I have no money but what I borrow and I can't go ashore but it will be some extra expense to me. O! poverty, poverty thou worst of curses, tho' an old companion, I hate thee. *Tuesday, July 1st, 1777.* On board all day—a very good reason for it, want of money. Captn. Park suspects my reason for being low-spirited and very kindly offers to assist me to what money I want while we stay here. I am determined to accept it, let the want come at the last.

*Wednesday, July 2nd, 1777.* Went on Board his Majesty's Ship *Centurion* of fifty guns commanded by Robert Brathwait Esq., with Coln. Cotton, Colnl. Reid and an Irish Captain. Saw General Lee who is prisoner on board this ship, who, understanding that I came from Virginia, invited me to drink tea with him and had a good deal of chat with me about his plantation in Berkley County, Virginia. He is a tall, thin, ill-looking man and appears to be about 50 years of age. He has been particularly active in this Rebellion, he is very sensible, but rash and violent in his sentiments as well as actions. News that our troops had left Amboy and have camped upon Staten Island. Colnl. Cotton informs me we are to have a Young Lady passenger. I think she is an ammunition wife of his.

*Thursday, July 3rd, 1777.* On board all day. No news

from the Army, we hear them exchange a few shots now and then. *Friday, July 4th, 1777.* Mr. Furneval, Captn. Jolly of the *Ellis* and Captn. Nailor of the *Valliant* (two letters of Marque) dined with us on board to-day, all hands very merry. I even forgot my poverty in a cheerful glass and good company. Colnl. Cotton is a little disappointed about his little girl. O! the religious old hypocrite.

*Saturday, July 5th, 1777.* This day arrived three Men of War with General Clinton on board, likewise a fleet with provisions from Cork. I hope they have brought something better than sour Crout. Our Army still inactive.

*Sunday, July 6th, 1777.* Dined on board the *Valliant,* Captn. Nailor, a letter of Marque belonging to Liverpool, carries 14 guns besides swivels. Very merry.

*Monday, July 7th, 1777.* This morning we had orders to get our water on board with everything ready for sea and proceed to Hell-Gate to-morrow, the place appointed for the fleet rendezvous. About 4 o'clock Furneval came on board and insisted upon me going with him to spend the evening along with some gentlemen of the Navy and Army, at the Hull Tavern, where we stayed till about 12 o'clock. I thought it too late to go on board. Went to my old lodgings in Queen Street. As I went down St. John's Street I heard something floundering in the Ditch. I stopped and by the light of the moon could perceive something like a human being stirred the mud a little. I plunged in and found it to be a man, whom I hauled to the shore quite insensible. I pulled the dirt out of his mouth with my fingers and in a little time I could perceive him make a noise. I then went to the next sentry, who happened to be a Hessian. I told him the situation of the man below in the Street, but he did not understand English.

After we had sputtered at one another for some time, the Sergeant of the Guard came who could speak English. He very civilly called a light and went with me to the man who by this time could speak, and told us that he had been insulted by a Girl of the Town and had been imprudent enough to treat her rather indelicately. One of her bullies had cut him in several places in the head, knocked him down and dragged him into the ditch. He desired that we would help him to his lodgings in Queen Street, which the Hessian Sergeant and I did. The bruises he had received and the muddy stinking water he had swallowed made him very ill. I went as soon as we had got him to bed and called Doctor Smith to him who immediately let him blood. He appears to be a genteel, well-behaved man, returned me thanks in the most polite terms for saving his life. I am happy that I have been an instrument of preserving it.

*On Board the Brig, "Edward," Hellgate — Tuesday, July 8th, 1777.* This morning I called to see the man I found in the ditch last night, but found him asleep and did not choose to wake him. I understand his name is Leydum an English gentleman who has lately made his escape from Philadelphia jail where he had been confined several months for his attachment to Government. I have heard of this Gentleman in Maryland. Breakfasted and dined with Furneval on board the *Bell and Mary*. In the afternoon got underway with the first of the Flood tide at 5 in the evening at Hellgate 6 miles from New York. Here the River or Sound passes amongst some rocks, the East River and New England tides meet and cause the water to whirl round the rocks with amazing velocity. The violent commotion occasioned by the meeting of the tides causes the water to rise to a great height and flow over the rocks. In some places it seems to fall perpendicularly down, which makes the navigation very dangerous. The channel is about 20 yds wide; if you miss it you are certainly lost, which has been the case with many vessels attempting to pass it at improper times.

*Wednesday, July 9th, 1777.* Went to New York in the boat with Colnl. Cotton to purchase stores for the voyage. Dined with Captn. Scott on board the Brig *Harriet.* Drunk tea at Mrs. Bennett's with Major L's Lady and several other ladies. After Tea I waited upon Mrs. L to her lodgings. She insisted upon me staying to sup and spend the evening with her and I did not need much solicitation to spend an evening with a handsome and polite young lady. After supper and a cheerful glass of good wine we entered into a very agreeable *tête-à-tête* and then O! Matrimony, matrimony, thou coverest more female frailties than charity does sins! Nicholas, if ever thou sinned religiously in thy life, it has been this time. This kind, affable, and most obliging lady in public was most rigidly religious. At Mrs. Bennett's she had treated the character of a poor lady in the neighbourhood, who had made a slip and unfortunately been caught in the fact, in a most barbarous and cruel manner. She ran over the Scriptures from Genesis to Revelations. In that strain she continued till after supper and then I soon found she was made of warm flesh and blood. Recommend me to the Girl who has compassion upon those who in an unguarded moment may have given way to the weakness of human nature, with honesty enough in her composition to confess that she has all her natural feelings, but philosophy enough to deny improper requests with good humour and with little levity or wantonness in her disposition (Perfection I do not expect to find in a human being). Such a one I think would make me very happy, but rather than I would marry one who overacts the part of religion, pretends to so much chastity and is in appearances a stiff, prudish, formal lump of mortality, I would go into Lapland and be dry nurse to a bear. *On Board the Brig, Thursday, July 10th, 1777.* This morning returned to the Ship. Ruminating upon my last night's adventure most of this day, it will not bear reflection. Understand we are to have the *Niger* Frigate for our Convoy. Went ashore with Colnls. Reid and Cotton, but returned on board in the evening. This has been one of the hottest days we have had this Summer. *Friday, July 11th, 1777.* A note, or rather billet-doux from Mrs. L. I am determined to go. It would be ungrateful to refuse so kind an offer. My Shipmates begin to smell a Rat, I am rated by them confoundedly, but let them go on. While I fare well at no expense to myself I care not. Should like her better if she were not so religious.

# XII

## GENERAL WASHINGTON

*SATURDAY, July 12th, 1777.* I think I have taken my farewell of New York, tho' I promised to pay one visit more, but never intend to perform. Cannot bear the abominable hypocrite. I wish to be at Sea but hear nothing of our sailing this week. I wish to be at home and yet dread the thought of returning to my native Country a Beggar. The word sounds disagreeable in my ears, but yet it is more pleasing and creditable than the epithet of Rascal and Villain, even if a large and opulent fortune was annexed to them, though one of the latter sort is in general better received, than an indigent honest man. I am poor as Job, but not quite so patient. Will hope for better days. If I am at present plagued with poverty, my conscience does not accuse me of any extravagance or neglect of sufficient magnitude to bring me into such indigent circumstances. However, I have credit, Health, Friends and good Spirits, which is some consolation in the midst of all my distresses. Better days may come.

*Sunday, July 13th, 1777.* News that our Army has surprised Washington and taken him prisoner. Afraid it is too good to be authentic. His great caution will always prevent him being made a prisoner to our inactive General. Washington is certainly a most surprising man, one of Nature's geniuses, a Heaven-born General, if there is any of that sort. That a Negro-driver should, with a ragged Banditti of undisciplined people, the scum and refuse of all nations on earth, so long keep a British General at bay, nay, even, oblige him, with as fine an army of Veteran Soldiers as ever England had on the American Continent, to retreat — it is astonishing. It is too much. By Heavens, there must be double-dealing somewhere. General Howe, a man brought up to War from his youth, to be puzzled and plagued for two years together, with a Virginia Tobacco planter. O! Britain, how thy Laurels tarnish in the hands of such a Lubber! The life of General Washington will be a most copious subject for some able Biographer to exercise his pen upon. Nature did not make me one of the Biographic order. However, I will make some remarks concerning this great and wonderful man.

George Washington, the American Hero, was second son of a creditable Virginia Tobacco Planter (which I suppose may, in point of rank, be equal to the better sort of Yeomanry in England). I believe his Mother is still living and two of his Brothers. One of them lives in Berkley County in Virginia, the other in Faquire County in Virginia. Both able Planters and men of good character. In the early part of his life he was surveyor of Fairfax County in Virginia. It was then a Frontier County and his office was attended with much trouble but not any considerable profit. This business accustomed him to the Woods and gained him the character of the best Woodsman in the Colony. His older brother, Mr. Augustine Washington, was a Captain in the American Troops raised for the expedition against Carthagena, but afterwards incorporated with the regulars. He died in the service, and our Hero George came to the patrimonial Estate.

In the Year 1755 he was chosen by the Assembly of Virginia to go to the French Forts on the Ohio to know the reason why they made encroachments on the Back parts of Virginia, which office he performed to the entire satisfaction of his employers. On his return he published his Journal which did him great credit and first made him popular amongst his countrymen. In the Year 1754, the Governor of Virginia gave him the command of about 1000 troops (all Virginians), with orders to drive the French from their encroachments in the Back settlements. In this expedition he proved unsuccessful. On the 3rd. of July 1754 he suffered himself to be surrounded by the French and Indians at the Big Meadows in the Alliganey Mountain and was obliged to capitulate, but upon what terms I do not recollect. He by some means or other got from the French very soon and had the command of a Regiment of Virginians, and was with the unfortunate General Braddock when he was defeated by the French and Indians on the Banks of the Moningahaley River July 9th. 1755, prior to which he, with a part of his Regiment, fell in with a scouting party of his own in the woods, an engagement began, and a number of men were killed before the mistake was discovered. He continued in the Army most of the War, but never performed any action to render himself conspicuous.

Before the expiration of the War he married a Mrs. Custis, a widow lady, with whom he had a very good fortune. By her entreaties he left the Army, in which he never gained any great esteem by his own country Officers or men. By all accounts it was his frugality that lost him the goodwill of his Officers, and the strict discipline he always observed, the love of his men. Indeed, any kind of order or subordination illy agrees wtih his countrymen, in general. After he quitted the Army, he was made a member of the Virginia House of Burgesses, in which he was much respected for his good private character, but always looked upon as too bashful and timid for an orator. He lived as a Country Gentleman, much noted for his hospitality, great knowledge in agriculture, and industry in carrying his various manufactories of Linen and Woollen to greater perfection than any man in the Colony.

On the breaking out of these troubles he was chosen, in company with Messrs. Peyton, Randolph, Richard Henry Lee, Patrick Henry, Richard Bland, Benjamin Harrison, and Edmund Pendleton Esqs., to act as Deputies or Delegates for the Colony of Virginia in the First Congress or Sanhedrim held at Philadelphia September 5th. 1774 and appointed General and Commander in Chief of all the Rebel forces (by Congress) June 17th, 1775. I believe he accepted this post with reluctance but the great and almost unexpected success he has had may now soothe and become agreeable to his natural ambitious temper. He undoubtedly pants for military fame and, considering the little military knowledge and experience he had before he was made a General, he has performed wonders. He was generally unfortunate (indeed I may with propriety say always) in every action where he was immediately concerned until the affair at Trenton in the Jerseys. Since that unlucky period (for us) he has only been too successful. His education is not very great nor his parts shining, his disposition is rather heavy than volatile, much given to silence. In short, he is but a poor speaker and but shines in the epistolary way. His person is tall and genteel, age betwixt forty and fifty, his behaviour and deportment is easy, genteel, and obliging, with a certain something about him which pleases everyone who has anything to do with

On Board the Brig Edward, Hell-Gate, July 13th – 1777

Cond.

——— those Foolish, Giddy, and Expensive, frolicks, natural
to a Virginian. He keeps an excellent Table and a
stranger, let him be of what Country or Nation he will,
allways met with a most Hospitable reception at
His entertainments were allways conducted with the
most regularity, and in the genteelest manner, of any
I ever was at on the Continent (and I have been at
several of them, that is, before he was made a General)
temperance he allways observed ——— He was allways
cool-headed and exceeding cautious himself. But took
great pleasure in seeing his friends entertained in
the way most agreeable to themselves — His Lady
is of a Hospitable disposition, allways good-humoured
and chearfull, and seems to be actuated by the same
motives with himself, but she is rather of a more lively
disposition, they are, to all appearance, a happy pair — &c

FACSIMILE OF PAGE FROM DIARY OF NICHOLAS CRESSWELL

him. There cannot be a greater proof of his particular address and good conduct than his keeping such a number of refractory, headstrong people together in any tolerable degree of decorum.

His House is at a place called Mount Vernon about 12 miles below Alexandria on the Banks of the Potowmeck River in Virginia, where he has a very fine Plantation and Farm, but by the best accounts I could get, his Estate, altogether, before these troubles did not amount to more than £300 per an. Vir. Currency. But Estates in this Country are seldom valued by the year, it is some difficulty to know exactly what they are worth where they keep great numbers of negroes and make large crops of Tobacco. His friends and acquaintances reckon him a just man, exceedingly honest, but not very generous. Perhaps they may give him this character, because he manages his Estate with industry and economy, very seldom enters into those foolish, giddy and expensive frolics natural to a Virginian.

He keeps an excellent table and a stranger, let him be of what Country or nation, he will always meet with a most hospitable reception at it. His entertainments were always conducted with the most regularity and in the genteelest manner of any I ever was at on the Continent (and I have been at several of them, that is, before he was made a General). Temperance he always observed, was always cool-headed and exceedingly cautious himself, but took great pleasure in seeing his friends entertained in the way most agreeable to themselves. His lady is of a hospitable disposition, always good-humoured and cheerful, and seems to be actuated by the same motives with himself, but she is rather of a more lively disposition. They are to all appearances a happy pair.

He has no children by his wife, but she had two by her first Husband, a son and daughter. The Daughter died unmarried, the son, Mr. John Custis, a very worthy young Gentleman, is lately married and lives with his Mother at Mount Vernon. He lives entirely as a Country Gentleman, has no post civil or military.

The General seems by nature calculated for the post he is in, he has a manner and behaviour peculiar to himself and particularly adapted to his present station and rank in life. It is said (and I believe with great truth) that he never had an intimate, particular bosom friend, or an open professed enemy in his life. By this method of behaviour he in a great measure prevents all parties and factions, and raises a spirit of emulation amongst his Officers and men. As there is no favourite to pay their court to and pave their way to preferment, and the General, I believe, is proof against Bribery, they have no way to advance themselves but by merit alone. His private character is amiable, he is much beloved and respected by all his acquaintances.

From my personal acquaintance with him, and from everything that I have been able to learn of him, I believe him to be a worthy honest man, guilty of no bad vice, except we reckon ambition amongst the number, and here we ought to judge charitably. The temptation was very great to a mind naturally ambitious. Nature made him too weak to resist it.

As an Officer, he is quite popular, almost idolized by the Southern Provinces, but I think he is not so great a favourite with the Northern ones. The ignorant and deluded part of the people look up to him as the Saviour and Protector of their Country, and have implicit confidence in everything he does. The artful and designing part of the people, that is, the Congress and those at the head of affairs, look upon him as a necessary tool to compass their diabolical purposes.

He certainly deserves some merit as a General, that he with his Banditti, can keep General Howe dancing from one town to another for two years together, with such an Army as he has. Confound the great Chucclehead, he will not unmuzzle the mastiffs, or they would eat him and his ragged crew in a little time were they properly conducted with a man of resolution and spirit. Washington, my Enemy as he is, I should be sorry if he should be brought to an ignominious death.

The Devil is certainly got on Board the *Newmarket*. They are fighting like furies.

*Monday, July 14th, 1777.* Went ashore on Long Island, drank Tea with some very agreeable young ladies. These people before these unhappy disputes lived in ease and affluence, but are now obliged to wash and sew for bread. The manner in which these unfortunate people bear this great reverse of circumstances is worthy imitation. Got on board late in the evening.

*Tuesday, July 15th, 1777.* This afternoon Captn. Park and I went in the Boat to Fort Knyphausen, it is about 12 miles above New York, was built by the Rebels and taken from them by Lieut. General De Knyphausen and all the Rebel Garrison made prisoners of War, about 8 months ago. Situated on an advantageous eminence, it is a regular fortification, surrounded with a deep and broad dry ditch and strong abbatis. The Magazine is said to be bomb proof, with embrasures for 35 guns, but at present they have not so many Guns mounted. There is a small battery of some heavy Guns to the West of the Fort, close to the North

River, likewise another small battery to the Northward about a Musket shot from the Fort, which cut off a great number of the Hessians when they made their attack. It seems to be a place of great strength, both by nature and art, capable of making a vigourous defence. If it had been garrisoned with veteran troops, I think it would scarcely have been possible to have taken it by storm. It is an ugly disagreeable Country, full of large rocks and woods, and seems entirely calculated for the Rebels to exercise their skulking cowardly manner of fighting to the greatest advantage. The North River is almost straight as a line for several miles here, but wide and good navigation, great rocks on both sides, some almost perpendicular and a prodigious height, something like Matlock in Derbyshire. Hessian Garrison at the Fort.

*On Board the Brig "Edward," Flushing Bay, Long Island — Wednesday, July 16th, 1777.* This morning had orders to weigh, proceeded to this place. General De Heister came on board the *Niger*, understand he is going passenger for England. News that General Prescott is taken prisoner at Rhode Island and that Ticonderoga is taken from the Rebels.

*Thursday, July 17th, 1777.* This morning General Pigot came on Board the *Niger*. He is bound to Rhode Island to succeed General Prescott who was taken by the Rebels, in bed with a Farmer's Daughter near Newport. This is the second time the General has been prisoner with the Rebels. A.M. A light wind. Got up to the City Island. The *Lady Gage*, an armed Ship belonging to Lord and General Howe is appointed our Rear Guard. *Friday, July 18th, 1777.* At noon weighed light breeze and pleasant weather. The sound is now about 6 Leagues over. Marks of ruin and devastation on both shores. Calm in the evening at Anchor.

*On Board the Brig, "Edward," Long Island Sound—Saturday, July 19th, 1777.* Most part of this forenoon at Anchor, quite calm. At M. a light breeze got under way. All this afternoon we have kept close in with the Connecticut shore. The Country seems as if it had been populous, but this cursed Rebellion has totally ruined this part of it, almost every house seems to be deserted and the Major part of them in ashes. Strange that the artifices of a few designing Villains should have it in their power to ruin such a number of honest, well-meaning people, that they should so far infatuate them by their horrid lies and mean pitiful arts, to give up the invaluable blessings of peace, the sweet enjoyment of real and happy liberty in exchange for all the dreadful horrors of War, poverty and wretchedness. All this is done (as the poor deluded wretches are taught to believe) with a view to secure to themselves, and posterity, what they have long been in possession of, in the greatest latitude of any people on earth, but unfortunately never yet knew the intrinsic value of it. In short, they are like the Dog in the Fable, quit the substance for an empty shadow.

If we have good luck, we shall not be long before we leave sight of this unhappy Country, this Country, turned Topsy Turvy, changed from an earthly paradise to a Hell upon terra firma. I have seen this a happy Country and I have seen it miserable in the short space of three years. The Villainous arts of a few and the obstinacy of many on this side the Water, added to the complicated blunders, cowardice and knavery of some of our blind *guides* in England, have totally ruined the Country. I wish the Devil had them. These unhappy wretches have substituted tyranny, oppression and slavery for liberty and freedom. The whims, cruelty and caprice of a vile Congress give them Laws, and a set of puritanic Rascals retails the Scriptures and gives them the little religion they have, but for the good it does them, they might as well be without.

These unhappy wretches are as much divided as it is possible to be without actually drawing the sword against one another (I mean in political opinion), but the strict and tyrannical laws, made by the Congress and executed with the utmost rigour by their Committees, deter the more sensible part of the people from declaring their real sentiments. The Congress under the fallacious pretence of nursing the tender plant, liberty, which was said to thrive so well in American soil, have actually torn it up by the very root. In short, these people's pride, obstinacy and folly, have brought more calamities on their own heads than ever Pharaoh did by his obstinacy bring upon the Egyptians.

A man suspected of loyalty (which in this place is a more heinous crime than sinning against the Holy Ghost) is in more danger, by far, than an Old Woman and her Tabby Cat was formerly in England and Scotland, if she was suspected of witchcraft. To cheat him is lawful, to steal from him is serving the cause and Country. If he is imprudent enough openly to avow his sentiments, Tarring and Feathering was the punishment they at first underwent, but now they are proscribed in the public papers by order of that diabolical infernal set of miscreants, the Congress. Confiscation of their whole property, imprisoning and hanging, nay, even firing their houses or poisoning them, is thought a sweet smelling savour before the Most High. As the Rascally Presbyterian Clergy have all along been the chief instigators and supporters of this unnatural Rebellion, they commonly honour the loyalists with the title of Tory, atheist, Deist or the most opprobrious name that the most inveterate malice can invent, aided by that cursed enthusiastic, uncharitable, bloody-minded and cruel persecuting spirit which in general constitutes a considerable part of the character of these *fanatic* brawlers, or rather *Bellows* of Sedition and Rebellion. Divine teachers, or Godly teachers, I cannot call them without a vile prostitution of that sacred function.

These religious scoundrels have a wonderful knack of reconciling the greatest opposites and uniting the most jarring differences when they have an opportunity to turn those things to their advantage. For instance, a Papist, that a few years ago was a more reproachful name than a murderer (amongst the New Englanders) is now become a friendly appellation when applied to any of their friends. At the same time they execrate his Majesty for allowing the Canadians liberty of conscience or a free use of their religious ceremonies. They endeavour to persuade the people that he is actually turned Papist, that his subjects are all going to revolt and cut off his head. Everything is done to make the ignorant multitude believe that the Kings of France and Spain, the Pope, Pretender, King of Prussia and the Grand Turk will invade England with innumerable hosts, in support of their glorious cause. The Empress of Russia, Prince of Hesse and others who have given any assistance to Great Britain are all to be deposed, and their dominions divided amongst the other European powers who are friendly disposed towards the virtuous Americans. The happy United and blessed Independent

States, as a reward for their glorious struggle are to be put in possession of the Brazils.

Not withstanding these ridiculous assertions and extravagant bravadoes, vast numbers of the people awake from their delirium, yet are unwillingly compelled to submit to the arbitary proceeding of Congress. With seeming patience and with apparent reverence they kiss the rod that so tyrannically strikes them, but secretly curse the hand that unjustly enslaves them under the specious mark of Guardians of their liberties. France is freedom's self, compared with America. Freedom of speech is what they formerly enjoyed but it is now a stranger in the Land. The boasted liberty of the press is as a tale that was told.

Many people have been confined in jails for several months without coming to a trial, or even knowing the crimes of which they are accused, and at last discharged without a word, but if they can prove that they are well wishers to his Majesty's Arms, dreadful is their situation indeed. If they are fortunate enough to escape with life, all their property is confiscated and their persons forced into their army. To render their misery complete, their Magistrates are chosen from the most violent part of the people, in general very fond of using their usurped authority without mercy, whose notions of political law, justice, and equity are such as make them truly contemptible, but of this no one dare complain. Their military officers are, in general, people of desperate fortune and violent dispositions who wish to establish their beloved Independence, that they may avoid paying the debts they owe to their Mother Country.

Before I bid farewell to this once Happy Country, I will mention the remarks and observations I have made of the Country and people while I have been amongst them. New England I know little about, except it be the trade and people. They have more Naval craft than all the Continent beside, great numbers of which are employed in the Fisheries. Their exports are Fish, Salt Provisions, Horses, Cattle and Lumber. Imported are Rum, Sugar, Molasses, Corn and European goods. They import large quantities of Molasses from the West Indies, which they distill and sell to Africa and the other Colonies, which goes by the name of Yankee Rum or Stink-e-buss. They generally exchange this article with the Southern Colonies for Corn and Flour as they do not grow Corn sufficient to serve themselves. They are very industrious people and in general very sober, but naturally addicted to all kinds of meanness that will any way serve their interest and the greatest Hypocrites on earth. As to their religion, Hudibras describes it to a title:

> " Tis Presbyterian true Blue,
>    For they are of that stubborn crew
> Of errant Saints, whom all men grant
>    To be the true Church militant,
> Such as do build their Faith upon
>    The holy Text of Pike and Gun;
> Decide all Controversy by
>    Infallible artillery;
> And prove their doctrine orthodox
>    By apostolic blows and knocks;
> Call Fire and Sword and desolation
>    A Godly thorough-Reformation."

Their cruelty to the innocent Quakers that settled amongst them about seventy years ago will always be remembered, not only by the Quakers, but by every human person, with the utmost detestation. Their present behaviour sufficiently shews, that they are willing to act over again those tragic scenes in which their Oliverian ancestors took so much delight, but enough of these scoundrels.

The province of New York was pretty much the same as New England, that is, the exports and transports nearly alike, but the nature and disposition of the people more hospitable, honest and generous. The face of the Country, as far as I have seen of it, is hilly and rocky but well cultivated. They have large Orchards of Apple trees from which they make excellent Cider and export large quantities of Apples to the other Colonies. A great deal of Peltry, Pot-Ashes and Naval stores was annually sent to England from New York before the Rebellion, most of which came down the North River from Albany. There are a great number of genteel houses in the neighbourhood of New York, chiefly built by officers who served in America the last War, and like the Country too well to return to England at the Peace. Great numbers of Dutch settled in the Back parts of the Colony.

The Jerseys are Hilly in most parts but very small hills, with a good deal of stony land. The general part of the Land that I have seen in the Jerseys, is light and Sandy, but well cultivated, much after the English method. They grow great quantities of grain of all kinds and export a great deal of wheat and flour to the Eastern Markets. They are famous for Hams, which go under the name of Burlington Hams and are esteemed the best in the world. The greatest part of their exports are Salt-pork, live cattle and grain, with some lumber. Few large Towns in the Jerseys, it is chiefly in large Farms and small Villages. Here are a great many stone houses, Barns, Granaries, Mills and likewise stone fences. The Country is well cleared of wood, the roads and fields tolerably regularly laid out with a great number of public-houses for the accommodation of travellers at a very small expense.

Pennsylvania is one of the most flourishing provinces on the American Continent. Philadelphia is the Capital, but I have before described it. Tis a proprietary province belonging to the Family of the Penns. The face of the Country is much the same as the Jerseys and likewise the produce. Great numbers of beautiful ships have been built at Philadelphia, it was a considerable branch of their trade. The back parts of the province amply supply them with timber for that purpose, with Iron in plenty and hemp for rigging. The inhabitants of this province are a strange mixture of English, Scotch, Irish, Dutch and Germans with a considerable number of Jews. Their religion is as various as their country, but the Quakers are the most numerous. It was a piece of sound policy in the Proprietor, to tolerate all kinds of religion, no matter what Sect or profession they are of. If they acknowledge one supreme God it is enough. They had the free liberty to pay their devotions in whatever manner they pleased. Before this unhappy Rebellion these people, so very different in respect to Country, Language and Religious tenets lived together in the greatest peace and harmony. Each profession maintains their own teachers, no established religion amongst them.

The inhabitants in general are remarkably industrious and have established some manufactories amongst them, one at Germantown about six miles from Philadelphia for Woollen stockings, another at Lancaster sixty miles west of Philadelphia for Guns, Axes, Hoes and various kinds of hardware of that sort. These are the only manufacturing

Towns of any note that I know on the Continent. There are several Snuff mills and paper mills in Philadelphia and its neighbourhood. In the Town there are some very large distilleries for Rum, and a large Brewhouse for Ale and Port. I have drunk Ale and Port brewed here from malt made in the Country, as good as we generally meet with in England.

Maryland is (or with greater propriety) I may say (was) a Proprietary Government or Province, belonging to Lord Baltimore. The face of the Country is delightfully pleasing, but not so full of inhabitants, or so well cultivated as the Northern provinces. The principal part of their exports is Tobacco, likewise Wheat, Flour, provisions, Lumber, and great quantities of Iron. The land is in general level, and in some places very rich, and might have been purchased upon very moderate terms. Their taxes are paid in Tobacco, likewise their Church benefices are collected in Tobacco, but there are always some Glebe Lands annexed to the living. There are a great number of Roman Catholics in this province, but not such a spirit of trade as there is in the northern provinces. They can procure a good livelihood with very little industry, and have such numbers of Slaves, it makes them quite indolent. Annapolis is the Capital.

Virginia is the finest country I ever was in. It is said by some people to extend from the Atlantic, westward to the Mississippi River. In such an amazing extent of country there is all sorts of land. From the Sea to the Blue Mountain it is pretty level and in general rich, but thinly inhabited and badly cultivated. The chief produce is Tobacco and Indian Corn. The Blue Mountains intercept the colony in S.W. Direction, in North Carolina they are

lost in the Appalachian Mountains. They are a ridge of
barren hills for the most part, though there are some very
fertile and pleasant valleys interspersed amongst them.
From the Blue Mountains, westward, to the Appalachian
Mountain is about 150 miles and one of the pleasantest
countries I ever beheld. The land is rich beyond conception, the face of the country beautiful and the air and
situation healthy, but very thinly peopled. The produce is
Wheat, Hemp and Tobacco. Great numbers of Hogs and
cattle of all sorts are bred and fed here.

If the Potowmeck River was made navigable to the
mouth of the Shanando River, this would be one of the
most desirable countries, that my ideas are capable of form-
ing. Indeed, they have attempted it and have had a nephew
of the famous Mr. Brindleys to view it, actually begun to
work upon it and got a considerable subscription for defray-
ing the expense. But they have entrusted the management
of the work to such an unsteady, worthless sort of a man
that, with the distraction of the times, I am afraid will
render it abortive. The country westward of the Appalachian Mountains, I think I have before described. The
chief and staple produce of Virginia is Tobacco, of which
they export great quantities, more than all the other Colonies put together, likewise great quantities of Wheat, Flour,
provisions, Lumber and Tar, with some little Hemp and
Indigo, but the last article does not thrive very well here.
There are people of all kinds of religion, but the Prostestant
is the established one. This Colony abounds with large
navigable Rivers, more than any other Colony on the Continent. All discharge themselves into Chesapeake Bay, the
finest bay in the World. But the people, in general, seem
insensible of the great advantages of these fine Rivers.

Very few Virginians apply themselves to trade, but trust wholly to their plantations. The great number of negroes they have, the warmth of the Climate and the very easy manner in which a comfortable subsistence is procured in this plentiful country all conspire to make the inhabitants exceedingly indolent. A very considerable part of this Colony belongs to Lord Fairfax, Chesapeake Bay on the East, Potowmeck River on the North, Rappahannock River on the South and the Appalachian Mountains on the west are his Lordship's boundaries, but any lands that are not taken up or already possessed are easily procured. Any person who finds a piece of land unoccupied applies to the Surveyor of the County, who surveys it and sends a plot of it to the General Office, a grant is immediately made (if no other person claims, by a prior survey) without any other expense than paying for the Survey and a Chiefs or Quit rent of two shillings and sixpence sterling annually for every hundred acres; neither is this Quit rent paid until they have had it in possession three years. Government lands give ten years.

North Carolina I never have been in, only the uninhabited parts of it, but I believe it is much like Virginia, only fewer inhabitants and a greater number of Negroes. They grow more Indigo, some Rice but not so much Tobacco as Virginia, the other produce is much the same as Virginia, wheat excepted. More Tar and Pork is exported from Carolina than Virginia. Very little naval craft belongs to North Carolina.

South Carolina, I have only been in the uninhabited parts of, but I believe it is much the same as North Carolina, only warmer and thinner inhabited, with greater numbers of slaves. Their produce is chiefly Rice and Indigo.

Georgia east and West Florida, I know little about, I believe they are very thinly inhabited and very flat, disagreeable and unhealthy country to live in. Great numbers of cattle are bred on the frontiers of Georgia South and North Carolina which, in the latter end of the year, they drive into the Northern Colonies to sell. The Land is remarkably rich and affords good pasture, in the back parts of those Colonies. Along the coast the inhabitants are in general wealthy, but indolent to an extreme.

The Continent of America, take it all in all, is undoubtedly one of the finest countries in the World. It plentifully abounds with every necessary of life, and almost every luxury that the most voluptuous epicure could desire may be procured with little trouble or expense. Every part of the Continent abounds with large navigable Rivers, all of them plentifully stored with Fish of various sorts. I have seen upwards of 50,000 Herrings caught at one haul in the Seine, with several hundred Shadfish. In the winter incredible numbers of Swans, Geese and Ducks come down from the Lakes and frequent these Rivers. The face of the Country is in general delightfully pleasing, the air good and mostly clear and serene, but subject to very sudden transitions from heat to cold. If the wind comes from the N. or N.W. it is very cold in Summer or Winter. The first of a N.W. Wind in the summer is generally attended with severe gusts, thunder, lightning and rain and in the winter with very severe frosts, much harder than any we have in England. These sudden alterations and the disagreeable vapours that are exhaled by the heat of the Sun from the marshy lands occasion fevers and agues, which with the Flux I believe are the only disorders that predominate in this Country.

The inhabitants, particularly in the southern Colonies (what I mean by the Southern Colonies is all South of New York) are—or rather were, for these unhappy times have positively made a great alteration in their disposition as well as circumstances—the most hospitable people on earth. If a stranger went amongst them, no matter of what country, if he behaved decently, had a good face, a good coat and a tolerable share of good-nature, would dance with the women and drink with the men, with a little necessary adulation—of which, by the way, they are very fond—with these qualifications he would be entertained amongst them with the greatest friendship as long as he pleased to stay. If he is a traveller he is recommended from one Gentleman's house to another to his journey. I believe it possible to travel through both Carolinas, Virginia and Maryland without a single shilling, the Ferryages excepted. In short, there would be no fear of anything, but the constitution, which probably might suffer from the excess of good cheer.

They are rather volatile than otherwise, but in general have very good natural capacities. If they have any genius, it is not cramped in their infancy by being overawed by their parents. There is very little subordination observed in their youth. Implicit obedience to old age is not among their qualifications. Their persons are in general tall and genteel, particularly the women, they are remarkably well shaped. I think I have not seen three crooked women in the country. Few, or none of them wear stays in the summer and there are but few that wear them constantly in the winter, which may be a principal reason why they have such good shapes. But to counterbalance this great perfection they have very bad teeth. Very few of them have a good mouth at twenty-five. It is said that eating so much hot bread (for they in general bake every meal) and fruit, is the reason why their teeth decay so early. They are good natured, familiar, and agreeable upon the whole, but confoundedly indolent. The men are universal Mechanics, Carpenters, Sadlers and Coopers, but very indifferent Husbandmen. Though the inhabitants of this Country are composed of different Nations and different languages, yet it is very remarkable that they in general speak better English than the English do. No County or Colonial dialect is to be distinguished here, except it be the New Englanders, who have a sort of whining cadence that I cannot describe.

The great population of this country is amazing. The emigration from Europe, added to the natural population, is supposed to double their numbers every twenty years, some will say, every sixteen years. It is certain that they increase much faster than they do in England, indeed they marry much sooner. Perhaps one reason may be, in England they cannot maintain a family with so much ease as they do in America which I believe deters many from marrying very early in life. None in England, but those who have not the fear of want and poverty before their eyes, will marry till they have a sufficiency to maintain and provide for a family. But here there are no fears of that sort and with the least spark of industry, they may support a family of small children. When they grow to manhood, they can provide for themselves. That great curiosity, an Old Maid, is seldom seen in this country. They generally marry before they are twenty-two, often before they are sixteen.

In short, this was a paradise on Earth for women, the

epicure's Elysium and the very centre of freedom and hospitality. But in the short space of three years, it has become the theatre of War, the Country of distraction, and the seat of slavery, confusion, and lawless oppression. May the Almighty of his infinite goodness and mercy, reunite and reestablish them on their former happy and flourishing situation. I am almost tired with scribbling, but these hints may be of service if ever I correct my Journal.

Heard several Guns fired, suppose them to be signals made by the Rebels.

# XIII

## RETURN VOYAGE—EDALE ONCE MORE

*SUNDAY, July 20th, 1777.* The first part of these 24 hours light breezes. Evening the Fleet becalmed. The land on the Connecticut Shore appears good. Long Island, sandy and barren. *Monday, July 21st, 1777.* This afternoon a fine breeze from the westward, a rebel privateer dodged us, the Swan Sloop gave chase drove her into New London Harbour. She fired several shots at the Privateer, but at too great a distance to do any execution. At 10 p.m. the east end of Long Island called Montauk point, bore west of two leagues from whence we take our departure Lal$^{td}$. 41°° 18″ N.Lon$^d$. 70°° 20″ W. I now probably may bid a long farewell to America. *Tuesday, July 22nd, 1777.* A heavy gale of wind came on last night, and still continues. The sea a roaring, the ship a rolling, the rigging breaking, the masts a bending, the sails a rattling, the Captain swearing, the Sailors grumbling, the boys crying, the hogs grunting, the dogs barking, the pots and glasses breaking, the Colonel ill of the C—p in bed. All from the Top Gallant truck to the keel, from the jibb boom to the taffrail in the utmost confusion. Few of the Fleet in sight. I am confoundedly sick.

*On Board the Brig, " Edward," at Sea, towards England —Wednesday, July 23rd, 1777.* The gale has continued violent till this morning. Shipped several heavy seas in at the Cabin windows. More moderate this evening. We have four of the fleet missing. Several have been carried away, Top-gallant masts, yards &c. *Thursday, July 24th, 1777.* A high and short Sea, suppose ourselves to be in the Gulph stream. Weather moderate. The missing vessels are the *Lady Gage,* a Tobacco Ship, and two brigs. *Friday, July 25th, 1777.* Contrary, but light winds. Very sick. *Saturday, July 26th, 1777.* Fine wind and pleasant weather. The hypocritical Colonl. Cotton is sick of a certain fashionable disorder that one would scarcely expect to find in so rigid a presbyterian. But I find all men, be their religion what it will, are made of flesh and blood. I do not pity him. *Sunday, July 27th, 1777.* Fine wind and pleasant. At M. saw a sail from the masthead to windward of us. *Monday, July 28th, 1777.* Good wind and pleasant. Caught a Dolphin, the flesh is remarkably white, but very dry. Sick, sick, sick. *Wednesday, July 30th, 1777.* Fine wind and pleasant weather. This day one of the missing vessels joins the Fleet, a Brig with Tobbaco. *Thursday, July 31st, 1777.* Pleasant weather and a good wind. I hope I have got pretty well over this confounded Seasickness. *Friday, August 1st, 1777.* Pleasant weather and a fine wind. The good humour and honest behaviour of Captn. Park are very agreeable. *Saturday, Aug. 2nd, 1777.* Cloudy weather. Wind came round to eastward.

*Sunday, August 3rd, 1777.* Light breezes in the morning from the eastward. Evening calm. Saw a very uncommon sea monster alongside, but cannot pretend to give a particular description of it. Captain Park and I sank an empty bottle well corked into the Sea about 100 fathom deep. We tied a piece of Leather over the cork, but upon our drawing it up again we found the cork forced into the bottle and the bottle filled with water, but could not perceive any difference in the taste of the common sea water from that in the bottle. I suppose the extreme cold at that depth condenses the air in the bottle and the great weight of the water above forces in the cork. *Monday, Aug. 4th, 1777.* Hazy weather and an easterly wind. *Tuesday, Aug. 5th, 1777.* The wind has come round to W.S.W. blows hard. Comodore gave chase to a sail to windward of us but without success. *Wednesday, Aug. 6th, 1777.* Wind westwardly. With rain and hazy cold weather. *Thursday, Aug. 7th, 1777.* Fine clear weather and good wind. *Friday, August 8th, 1777.* Pleasant weather but a heavy rolling sea from the N.W. *Saturday, Aug. 9th, 1777.* Thick foggy blowing weather, wind from the eastward. *Sunday, Aug. 10th, 1777.* Very pleasant weather and a fine wind. Killed one of our pigs. *Wednesday, Aug. 13th, 1777.* Fine weather and good wind for three days. Nothing remarkable. *Thursday, Aug. 14th, 1777.* Pleasant and fair wind. The Commodore spoke a French Brig. *Friday, Aug. 15th, 1777.* Saw three ships standing to the eastward. I cannot write my journal, but I must be overlooked by this Hypocritical Colnl. Cotton, a pimping dog. Yr. Honble. Servant Sir, this has driven him upon deck in a violent passion but he does not own it. Pleasant weather. Fair wind.

*Saturday, August 16th, 1777.* Light airs and pleasant weather. At M. His Majesty's Ship *Resolution*, 64 Guns, commanded by Sir Cholonee Ogle, came into the Fleet. At 4 p.m. hove the lead and got ground in 95 fathom water. Fine white sand and black specks with small shells, Scilly Island Bears N.11°° 39″ E. Dist. 60 leagues. At 7 p.m. the Lieutn. of the *Resolution* came on board and pressed one of our men.

*Sunday, August 17th, 1777.* General De Heister dined

on board the *Resolution*. On his going over the side, was saluted by the *Resolution* with 13 Guns. At M. hove the lead ground in 60 fathom. Fine Brown and Black sand. At 9 p.m. the *Niger* made signal for all masters. Orders to proceed to Portsmouth. *Monday, August 18th, 1777.* Pleasant weather. This evening a strange sloop came into the Fleet and spread an alarm. The Commodore fired at her and brought her to. Can't learn what she is. *Tuesday, Aug. 19th, 1777.* Fair wind and pleasant weather. Caught a small blue shark. *Wednesday, Aug. 20th, 1777.* At 6 p.m. St. Agnew's Light-house, on the Island of Scilly bore N.N.E. Dist. about 6 leagues. Find an error of 4 degrees Longd. in my reckoning, owing to our Log-line being too short. Fine wind and pleasant. *Thursday, Aug. 21st, 1777.* At M. the Start bore N.N.E. distance 4 leagues very pleasant weather.

*Friday, August 22th, 1777.* This morning saw the West end of the Isle of Wight, that gives a universal joy to all on board, myself excepted. The thought of returning to my native Country a Beggar is more than I can support with becoming fortitude. It casts such an unusual damp upon my spirits that I am more dead than alive. At 11 a.m. came to an anchor at Spit-Head, all the Fleet in company. We have had an agreeable passage of 33 days from our departure from the East end of Long Island, and an absence of three years four months and thirteen days from England. Colnl. Cotton and Captn. Park will hurry me on shore. Had rather stay on board.

*On Board the Brig, "Edward," Spithead, Portsmouth—Saturday, August 23rd, 1777.* Last night Colnl. Cotton the Captn. and I went ashore. The wind blew so hard that we were obliged to make the first land we could. Were several times very near oversetting. The *Hector*, Man of War, carried away her main top mast turning up to Spithead, while we were in the boat. Landed near the South Sea Castle on Portsmouth Common, hauled our boat ashore. Supped and lodged at *The Blue Posts*. This morning, by the interest of Mr. Furneval, saw the dockyard. The great quantities of naval stores of all kinds and the very great conveniences for building and refitting Ships of War are very well worth seeing. This afternoon went to Hospital for invalids. A noble building indeed. Very accidentally met with Mr. John Legdum, the person I helped out of the Ditch in New York. This Gentleman has been imprisoned and ruined in America, is now in very great distress, but has too much pride to return to his friends in his present situation, they are people of property near Coventry. His gratitude caused me to spend every penny I had with him. My very imprudent conduct and very narrow escape in this place will not bear reflection. Got on board late in the night.

*On Board the Brig, "Edward," from Portsmouth towards London — Sunday, August 24th, 1777.* My last night's adventure need not be mentioned here. I shall always remember it. This morning had orders to proceed to Deptford. His Majesty's Ship *Kent* is appointed our Convoy to the Nore. At a.m. got underway, at 6 p.m. the Swan Cliff on the Isle of Wight, bore N.E.B.N. Distance 4 leagues. Pleasant weather. *Monday, Aug. 25th, 1777.* At 4 P.M. abreast of Dover. Got a Pilot from there. 6 P.M. came to an anchor off Deal in the Downs. Bought some things here. Borrowed the money from the Captn. *Tuesday, Aug. 26th, 1777.* A fine gentle breeze and pleasant weather. We have kept close in shore all day and had a most delightful view of the country. At anchor in West-coat Bay. *Wednesday, Aug. 27th, 1777.* We have had a very fair wind all day and pleasant weather. If it had shifted as we could have wished, it could not have been better. Came to an anchor at Deptford at 6 p.m. We have a pilot who is upwards of 60 tho' has been in this trade all his life and never had a wind to bring him up the River Thames in one day before. The prospect has been beyond description, pleasing all day. Mr. Abby, the mate, has got a bad wound on his foot with the anchor. Thames a narrow crooked river.

*On Board the Brig, "Edward," Deptford — Thursday, August 28th, 1777.* This morning the Captn. and I went to London by water. Found Mrs. Dixon and Mr. John Ellis, of whom I have borrowed twenty pound upon my own credit. I was in very great want of money. Wrote to my Father and spoke for some new clothes. I have great occasion for them, for I am a ragged, shabby weather-beaten mortal. Got on board at night.

*Friday, August 29th, 1777.* Went up to Town. Dined with Mr. John Ellis. Spent the evening at the Tavern with Tim Dixon and Furneval. I believe half the people in this bustling place are Rebels in their hearts. Lodged at Mrs. Dixon's, where I shall make my home for the time I stay here. *Saturday, Aug. 30th, 1777.* I have been under a necessity of getting ten pounds more from Mr. Ellis. God knows when or how I shall be able to repay him. *Sunday, Aug. 31st, 1777.* Went to St. Dunstan's Church in the forenoon, St. James' Park in the evening.

*London — Monday, September 1st, 1777.* Went to Mrs. Hughes and delivered all Mr. Nourse's letters to her. *Tuesday, Sept. 2nd, 1777.* Dined with Mrs. Hughes.

Spent the evening with Mr. John Green, my old school-fellow. *Wednesday, Sept. 3rd, 1777.* Saw Mr. Robert Needham Junr. he informs me that my Uncle Tym is dead. Some other very disagreeable news concerning the family. Went with him to Drapers' Hall, and to see the Lord Mayor proclaim Bartholomew Fair in Smithfield. *Thursday, Sept. 4th, 1777.* Went with Sam Dixon and some other company to see Vauxhall Gardens. This is the last night that they kept open for the Season. There have been some lamps broken by the Mob, and other riotous proceedings. *Friday, Sept. 5th, 1777.* Went to the theatre in the Haymarket, with Miss Dixon. Henry the Eighth and the Fairy. *Saturday, Sept. 6th, 1777.* Got my Chest ashore. Seeing the humours of the Town in the evening. *Sunday, Sept. 7th, 1777.* Went to St. Dunstan's Church in the forenoon. Spent the evening at *The Dog and Duck* with I. Dixon and Captn. Deacon.

*Monday, September 8th, 1777.* This day I received a very kind letter from my Father. I have returned him an answer. I am utterly at a loss what to do. Stay at home I cannot, without things are altered for the better since I left it. I am determined to wait upon Lord Dunmore when he returns to Town and endeavour to get a Commission in the Marine service. In the evening went with Miss Dixon to Danbury Tea Gardens. *Tuesday, Sept. 9th, 1777.* Very uneasy in mind. I dread the thought of going home. In the evening went to Baggnige Wells with I. Dixon and Furneval. *Wednesday, Sept. 10th, 1777.* This morning settled my account with Captn. Park and Colnl. Cotton. This has reduced me to beggary again, I am still in debt to Captn. Park £2/15s. He has behaved to me with the greatest kindness, honour and good nature.

*Thursday, Sept. 11th, 1777.* Went to visit Miss Astley this morning. Afterwards waited upon Doctor Solander, by Mr. Robinson's introduction and at his request. The Doctor very politely shewed me the British Museum. Such an amazing collection of curiosities I can't describe it. In the evening at a Conversation Club in Bread Street with I. Dixon.

*Friday, September 12th, 1777.* Went with Mrs. Dixon to the Old Bailey to hear the trials but could not get admission under a crown apiece. This is more money than I can at present spare. After dinner Sam Dixon went with me to see Newgate Prison. Such another place I never wish to see. Instead of punishing vice, this is a nursery for it. Those that have been confined here, and afterwards are acquitted, may justly say, that they have studied in the Thieves' Academy. Tis a new, strong and good building.

*Saturday, September 13th, 1777.* This morning went to Westminster Abbey with Mr. Wommersley. This is the largest building I ever saw. The monuments numerous and grand, but I cannot pretend to give any description of them. In the evening went with Sam Dixon to Sadlers Wells, saw the Tumblers, Rope Dancers &c. *Sunday, Sept. 14th, 1777.* Dined at Charles Founce's Esq., at Chelsea. Here is a noble hospital for disabled and superannuated soldiers. I cannot learn that Lord Dunmore will return to town this month.

*Monday, September 15th, 1777.* I want to be at home, yet I am afraid of going, but my money is almost done. What a curse it is to be continually poor. Drank tea at Mr. Brown's. Spent the evening with Furneval, seeing the humours of this overgrown town. Some scenes that I have this night seen are almost incredible. *Tuesday, Sept. 16th,*

*1777.* I am under the disagreeable necessity of borrowing five guineas from Sam Dixon. Confound this poverty, it has been my constant attendant for a long time but I am not yet reconciled to it. Spent the evening with Miss Astley.

*Wednesday, September 17th, 1777.* I am determined to wait no longer upon his Lordship. Have taken my passage for Ashbourne in the coach which is to start on Sunday evening. Saw the town with Mr. Wommersley and some ladies of his acquaintance.

*Thursday, September 18th, 1777.* Wrote to my Father to meet me with horses at Ashbourne. Saw Ellis Barber, who informs me that my brother Richard is married, and that they felt the shock of an earthquake in Edale last Sunday. *Friday, Sept. 19th, 1777.* Went with Mr. Hughes to Levers Museum. An amazing large collection of the rarest curiosities and arranged in the greatest order but too extensive for me to pretend to describe. Dined with Mr. Hughes. Spent the evening with Furneval. *Saturday, Sept. 20th, 1777.* Preparing for my journey home. No news of Lord Dunmore. My spirits are very low, almost as low as my pocket. Got my Chest to the Waggon.

*Sunday, September 21st, 1777.* Dined at Mrs. Dixon's with Sam Dixon and his wife. I am much obliged to this good family. Furneval and Sam Dixon accompanied me to the coach. Sorry to part with the honest and generous Furneval. Six inside passengers in the Coach, outside covered like a pigeon house. Supped and changed horses at St. Alban's. Changed horses again at Dunstable, Woburn and Newport Pagnel. *Monday, Sept. 22nd, 1777.* Breakfasted and changed horses at Northampton, again at Marketharbro'. Dined at Leicester. Changed horses at

Loughbro'. Lodged at *The Bell* in Derby. Very low spirited and very ill. *Tuesday, Sept. 23rd, 1777.* Got to Ashbourne to breakfast. No horse arrived for me, very ill and low spirited. Obliged to go to bed at 3 o'clock in the afternoon.

*Edale — Wednesday, September 24th, 1777.* Hired a horse of the Landlord at *The Blackamore's Head.* Dined at *The Forrest.* Got home in the evening. My parents seem very glad to see me, particularly my poor Mother. She is much aged since I left England. My Father set out for Chesterfield Fair soon after I arrived, but remembered to order me to shear or bind Corn to-morrow. I think this is rather hard. I am so weak with a violent lax that I can scarcely walk a hundred yards without being much fatigued. My Mother is overjoyed at my arrival. My spirits are very low, but I endeavour to keep them up as well as I can. All my Brothers that are at home are much grown. Dick, I understand has been a bad boy.

*Thursday, September 25th, 1777.* This forenoon I have been binding Corn. It is very disagreeable exercise in my present weak condition. In the afternoon, Mr. Champion, my worthy friend, came to see me. The old gentleman looks well. I am happy to see it. He condoles my misfortunes more like a parent than a friend. Mr. Lingard came to see me in the evening, *Friday, Sept. 26th, 1777.* I have been binding Corn all day. So much fatigued that I can scarcely get upstairs to bed. It is very hard, but I am determined to bear it without murmuring, if I possibly can.

*Saturday, September 27th, 1777.* Went to the New Smithy to Robert Kirk's. The old man is very happy to hear from his son. I am confoundedly stark, weary, and low spirited.

*Sunday, September 28th, 1777.* Went to the Chapel, the people stare at me as if they would devour me. I could hear some of them say, "What a poor dun looking Man he is." My old friend, Mr. Bray, came to see me and Mr. Lingard, who is as inquisitive and absent as usual.

*Monday, September 29th, 1777.* Shearing all day, hard labour indeed, but I must bear it with patience if I can. I am much better in health than I was, but low-spirited. *Tuesday, Sept. 30th, 1777.* My excessive fatigue prevents me sleeping but I still go to bed and do the best I can without grumbling. At least, in appearance, O! patience, patience. *Wednesday, October 1st, 1777.* Employed in shearing, but don't like it a bit better than I did. Resolution and Patience, come to my aid. *Friday Oct. 3rd, 1777.* Employed as above, but it is far from being an agreeable exercise. I am under a necessity of submitting to it.

*Saturday, October 4th, 1777.* This evening my Brother Richard and his wife came to see my Father for the first time since his marriage. I understand he has been a very wild obstinate youth. Tis no more than I expected, the marriage has been against the consent of his friends. His wife seems to be a young, innocent girl, but appears good-natured and modest. I am afraid he will make a poor husband, he has the look of a rake. There is no provision made for them either by her friends or his own that I can learn. What strange infatuation can induce people to be so cursed foolish to marry without knowing how they are to subsist afterwards? *Sunday, Oct. 5th, 1777.* This day my Brother Richard and his wife made their appearance at Edale Chapel. Miss Thomson, his wife's Sister (a perfect original by Heavens) and her brother (an awkward Country lad) were with them. Mrs. Charington and Mrs. Lingard and some other company dined with them at my Father's. All appeared to be in high spirits, except myself. However, I have affected a cheerfulness, but in fact am very uneasy. I greatly pity these two unthinking mortals. *Tuesday, October 7th, 1777.* At home, shearing. As my strength increases, this exercise is not so disagreeable. I begin to have an uncommon voracious appetite. *Wednesday, Oct. 8th, 1777.* Went to Hassop. Dined with Mrs. Needham at Rowdale. I am rather surprised to find all his daughters unmarried. I know of no young ladies that are more likely to make good wives. *Thursday, Oct. 9th, 1777.* At home employed in shearing. It is still very disagreeable business, but it will be over shortly.

*Friday, October 10th, 1777.* I acquainted my Father that when I was in London I had borrowed £30 of Mr. John Ellis, which I had promised to pay on the 11th prox. He has kindly given me the cash. Dined at Sheffield, found little alteration here, only the people are in general here & everywhere else prejudiced in favour of the Rebels. Got to Chapeltown in the evening, where I found Mr. John Ellis. *Saturday, Oct. 11th, 1777.* Paid Mr. John Ellis Junr. the money which I borrowed from him in London. Left Chapeltown and got to Middop, where I found all my friends well. *Sunday, Oct. 12th, 1777.* Dined with Mr. Perkin at Ughill, whose family I find just as I left it. Got home in the evening. I am tired with answering very silly questions, they appear such to me, though some of them are asked with great simplicity.

*Monday, October 13th, 1777.* There is such a sameness in my life at present it is not worth while to keep a Journal.

I am afraid it is likely to continue longer than I could wish it, as no proposals have been yet made to me concerning my future way of life. I imagine my Father expects I shall stay at home in my present dependent situation. I cannot bear it. Though at present his behaviour is very kind and in some respects indulgent, but that moroseness he observes to some of the family is very disagreeable to me. I expect something of the same sort as soon as the first gust of paternal affection subsides, but I am determined to stay with seeming patience till April next, and behave in such a manner as not to give any just offence. I call this waiting the Chapter of Accidents, something fortunate may happen. (Mem. Never to have anything to do with my Relations, I know their dispositions only too well. Some of them begin to hint at my poverty already. I must be patient and if possible, Silent.)

On Saturday, April 21st, 1781, Nicholas Cresswell was married at Wirksworth in Derbyshire to Mary Mellor, the youngest Daughter of Mr. Samuel Mellor of Idridgehay, in the parish of Wirksworth, by the Revd. Mr. Bennett. Mr. Robert Poole stood Father, Mr. Samuel Mellor, Junr. and Miss Hannah Dawson, present at the ceremony.

My rambling is now at an end.

# APPENDIX

| Dates in Diary | Dates in American History |
|---|---|
| April 9th, 1774. Sailed in *Molly* from Liverpool. | 1773. Colonists boycotted English tea, as protest against tax. |
| May 17th, 1774. Landed at Urbanna, Rappahannock River, Virginia. Ill, voyage recommended. | May, 1774. Massachusetts appealed to other colonies for united action against Britain. |
| July 29, 1774. Sailed in Schooner *John* for Barbados. Arrived August 31st. | |
| Sept. 17th, 1774. In Schooner *John* returned to Virginia. | Sept. 1st, 1774. Continental Congress met in Philadelphia. |
| Feb. 27th, 1775. Set out from Winchester, Va., for trip down Ohio River to survey land in Illinois. | |
| April 16th, 1775. Visited site of Gen. Braddock's defences in 1755 on banks of Monongahela River. | April 19th, 1775. Battle of Concord and Lexington. June 17th, 1775. Battle of Bunker Hill. |
| July 11th, 1775. Returned to Fort Fincastle. Trip down the Ohio given up. | |
| August 21st, 1775. Started on trip in Indian territory. | |
| October 19th, 1775. Returned to Alexandria. | July 4th, 1776. Declaration of Independence. |
| August 23rd, 1776. Left Leesburg for Philadelphia. | August, 1776. General Howe at New York. |
| Sept. 7th, 1776. Set out for New York, to join English army. Could not get to army. Decided to return. | |
| Sept. 19th, 1776. Back in Virginia. | Dec. 8th, 1776. Washington crossed the Delaware. Congress fled to Baltimore. |
| | Dec. 25th, 1776. Washington took 1400 Hessians at Trenton. |
| | Jan. 3rd, 1777. Washington defeated Cornwallis at Princeton. British withdrew to New York. |

April 21st, 1777. Took passage for Hampton.

April 30th, 1777. Received by Governor at Yorktown. Permission given to leave country, but not on British warship.

May 4th, 1777. On board *Dorothy*.

May 6th, 1777. On board *Bell and Mary.*

May 14th, 1777. New York harbour.

August 21st, 1777. Arrived at Portsmouth, Eng.

September 24th, 1777. Edale once more.

April 21st, 1781. Married Mary Mellor.

October 17th, 1777. Burgoyne surrendered at Saratoga.

September 3rd, 1783. Treaty of peace signed at Paris. American independence acknowledged by England.

CPSIA information can be obtained at www.ICGtesting.com
Printed in the USA
LVOW07s1559181214

419451LV00003B/599/P